Tales of
TWO
FAMILIES

JOHN BURWOOD

authorHOUSE®

AuthorHouse™ UK
1663 Liberty Drive
Bloomington, IN 47403 USA
www.authorhouse.co.uk
Phone: UK TFN: 0800 0148641 (Toll Free inside the UK)
        UK Local: 02036 956322 (+44 20 3695 6322 from outside the UK)

Published by AuthorHouse 02/11/2021

ISBN: 978-1-6655-8518-7 (sc)
ISBN: 978-1-6655-8517-0 (e)

Dedicated to the memory of Richard Warwick Burwood (1949-2020) without whose indefatigable decades of genealogical research this book would not be possible.

On 5th June 1947 Maurice Richard Burwood and Marjorie Ethel Tanner were married at the Church of the Resurrection in Portsmouth.

Marjorie was 27 and Maurice 44. They spent 22 years together - years not without problems but not with their marriage until Maurice died in December 1969 - ending their dreams of enjoying a happy retirement together.

When Marjorie finally rejoined Maurice in February 2012 many papers and letters came into my possession. Long before that my eldest brother Richard had extensively researched the genealogies of both Burwood and Tanner families.

Marjorie's sister Olive died in 2010, at 95, after moving in with Marjorie to be cared for in 2007. During that time Marjorie encouraged Olive to keep her mind active by writing down memories of her life – a substantial if incomplete pile of handwritten memories to which Marjorie added a lesser number of pages before her death two years later at the age of 92. After their death, and my subsequent retirement, I edited and published their handwritten memories in a publication entitled *Memories from Ninety Years: the lives of the Tanner sisters of Portsmouth*. In the process of that, and sorting out family papers and documents, the idea came to write this book – based on letters from or to relatives and friends, surviving family documents and diaries – and the aforementioned memories of my mother and aunt – all anchored by the researches of my brother Richard. I make no claim to this being a systematically structured story – there are gaps and digressions and limits to what I know or surmise, but I think the tales are worth telling.

I hope you will agree.

CHAPTER ONE

Ladysmith

My paternal grandfather William John Burwood died 29 years before I was born, so I only know him from his letters – mostly to his wife Ada, who I only faintly remember as she died when I was 7.

My father died when I was 14 so never got to talk to me about his parents, and I was never interested. Following the death of my mother I discovered old family papers and letters along with other documents concerning my grandfather's participation in the Siege of Ladysmith.

*****

The Background to the Siege of Ladysmith

(N.b. some facts such as dates quoted come from *HMS POWERFUL and the Ladysmith Naval Brigade 1899-1900 - compiled and edited by David Fill)*

The Second Boer War began in October 1899.

I do not plan to detail the convoluted political origins of the conflict, nor its progress and consequences. It is sufficient for my purpose to say that Ladysmith was a town besieged by Boer armies from November 1899 to February 1900.

HMS Powerful was a Royal Navy Cruiser which left Britain for the China Station on 7th October 1897 and arrived at Singapore on December 29th. After 2 years on station, including stops at places like Hong Kong, Nagasaki, and Manila, it was heading home until ordered to South Africa instead. It departed from Singapore on 24th

September 1899, picked up soldiers at Mauritius, and arrived at Durban on October 10th.

As Ladysmith needed artillery, special carriages were improvised to transport naval cannon, and a gun crew of 280 men called the Naval Brigade - under the command of Captain Lambton - was despatched from HMS Powerful to Ladysmith. Naval Brigades were specifically trained to assist land forces in combat when required. Two trains travelled through the night to the nearest station, then the Naval Brigade manhandled their guns across rocky terrain into Ladysmith, arriving just in time to attack Boer positions on 30th October 1899 before Boer forces surrounded the town.

Their arrival helped prevent the immediate fall of Ladysmith, but they became besieged with other British forces. During the siege over three thousand soldiers died defending Ladysmith, and many townspeople died of disease or starvation, but the Naval Brigade helped fight off Boer attacks until a relief column, including a Naval Brigade from HMS Terrible, ended the siege.

G W Steevens, a correspondent who was in the siege and died there of enteric fever, wrote that *"This handful of sailors have been the saving of Ladysmith"*. The Royal Naval Field Gun Competition commemorated the contribution of the Naval Brigades from HMS Powerful and HMS Terrible to the defence and relief of Ladysmith.

HMS Powerful returned to a massive hero's welcome. Its crew pulled their guns through cheering crowds in the streets of Portsmouth. A public appeal raised money to give each member of the Naval Brigade an inscribed silver watch, and they were treated to a formal banquet at Portsmouth Town Hall on 24th April 1900.

Leading Seaman Will Burwood was in the Naval Brigade from HMS Powerful. His diversion to Ladysmith came while he was engaged to Ada Hollingdale of Brighton, where Will lived before joining the Navy on 29th January 1885. He was born on 15th September 1968 in Brighton according to his birth certificate, though his Naval Service Certificate quotes his birthday as 15th December 1869. Ada, born 18th January 1874 also in Brighton, would marry him in 1900. Some of his letters to her during their courtship have survived, and I have tried to transcribe them – though some written from inside Ladysmith were written hastily on scraps of paper. They are faded and folded and over a century old so are difficult or even impossible to decipher.

This chapter is based around those transcriptions.

*****

This first transcription is probably the first ever letter to Ada Hollingdale from Will Burwood, judging from his reference to 'taking the liberty' of writing to her, from Will writing with almost calligraphic neatness, and only calling himself friend and brother, but Ada clearly was known to Will's widowed mother Hannah who died in 1895 at only 50 of stomach cancer, so maybe Hannah was already in poor health - making Ada's kindness towards Hannah especially appreciated.

> *W Burwood*
> *4 Block*
> *Whale Island*

Dear Miss A Hollingdale

Many thanks for the book you so kindly sent me. I have not read it yet so cannot pass an opinion. I have not apologised for taking the liberty of writing to you but I am sure you will forgive me. I managed to get your address from Mother although I did not know you had left it. I was very sorry I did not see you on Monday but I was more so when I found you did not come on Sunday we waited for you but at last gave it up. I think you might be so kind as to drop me a note now and again it would be very kind of you do you know I think a great deal of you and you are so kind to my Mother and those that are kind to her are so to me.

I hope you will enjoy your stay in London and also I hope we shall get a glimpse of you in Brighton before I go away there are 36 of us going away from here and I fancy I am one of the number if you do write you must do so before Sunday and until such time as you see or hear from me believe that I remain.

> *Your most sincere*
> *Friend & Brother*
> *W.J.Burwood*

PS
If there is such a thing as hope I beg you have patience and wait. WB
Please excuse this beastly scented note paper. I have had it in a scented
wooden box and it had got tainted and I am run out of other paper
WB

Whale Island has since 1891 been the home of HMS Excellent – a Royal Naval Shore Establishment. From 1891 to 1985 it hosted the Royal Naval Gunnery School. Will's Naval Service Certificate records him as at HMS Excellent from October 1893 to May 1894 and again between January and April 1897. These periods would have supplied the gunnery and land warfare training which led to him joining the Naval Brigade to Ladysmith. As his mother was still alive, Will must have sent this letter during his first period at HMS Excellent when Ada was 19 or 20 years old.

Among family papers I found the front cover of an envelope with Will's same calligraphic neatness of address to Miss A Hollingdale, No 3 Salisbury Rd, West Brighton, Brighton, Sussex – sent from Portsea in Portsmouth according to the postmark. It must have some special significance for Ada to so scrupulously preserve just the addressed front cover.

Possibly it contained his first ever letter to her?

*****

This second letter seems to be the first letter Will sent to Ada under an "understanding" – the word engagement is not used - and it was sent years before he was assigned to HMS Powerful. It was sent from HMS Assistance, which his naval certificate of service dates as being between May and September 1894, and I think was a stores ship. Will and Ada did not marry until 1900, so it was a long courtship – probably because he was away so much on Naval Service and they could not afford to marry earlier.

With this letter, as with many of Will's letters, much was written on limited amounts of paper so was crammed small, leaving me uncertain where sentences or paragraphs were meant to begin or end. To facilitate reading them I have chosen to insert some full stops and paragraph breaks where they seemed appropriate from the context of the words.

I do not guarantee to have deciphered every word correctly as I had to guess at some, and some lines I could not decipher enough to even guess at – and some simply do not understand, such as the very first line of this letter. I have no idea what is meant by an ear turning a deep black!

HMS Assistance
Portsmouth

My own Dear Ada

(If my left ear is turning a deep black) For such may I address you now to begin my letter, I really don't know. I hope you arrived quite safe last night as I did but very tired and was very glad to turn in.

We had our turn out today which was hardly a success as we all got on board wet through about half past two, but still I feel pretty happy as this is my first letter to you under the footing we now stand, and I can tell you the reason it is because I have found a young woman that has a feeling for me when I go away even if it only for a week or two. All young women that has seen me off have treated it as a matter of fact not one pang of remorse <u>that</u> has caused me to flirt. I thought all women were the same until I met your own dear self. In your hands I give myself to make me what I want to be an honest man in word, thought and deed instead of trying to shun church which I am sorry to say I have often done. You must teach me to be otherwise.

All women except my own family and yourself I give up and consider them well lost. I am afraid I shall not be down again for a fortnight but you may be secure that I shall be down as often as circumstances permit. Another thing Ada you will have to go through a long separation from me but you will not mind that as time soon flies and the sooner I leave England the sooner I shall return. You know my reasons for wishing to go away. I don't know that there is much more to say concerning myself. I miss your photo from my box perhaps you noticed how I had it in the envelope. You must let me have one as soon as possible, you can always see mine at home whereas I have nowhere to look for yourself.

I hope you did not catch cold last night when you got out of the train. I realised it was very cold when I got out but I am all right and another time, Ada we must say goodbye where there are not eyes to see, we can never be fortunate enough to get a carriage to ourselves. How did mother get on with Warwick on Sunday and did you say goodbye to Edith for me. I am so sorry I missed her. I don't know what made me miss her very careless of me. I must close now as my mess mates are on the move. Will you kindly give my love to mother & Frank and any of my family accepting the same from

Your Affectionate
Will

PS

I shall expect a long letter from you in spite of my short one. I should like to hear from you every day but I could not answer please.

Will

I do not send X in my letter but you know they are meant even if not put

Will

The 'Warwick' Will mentions was his youngest brother who lived until 1959 after a career as a colliery blacksmith, and earned an O.B.E. – no idea why or when.

Frank was another brother of Will's – see the next letter for more about him. Both Will and Ada had sisters named Edith, so I am unsure which Edith Will meant.

Ada's sister named Edith was married in 1903, to an Alfred Tyler, and died in 1956. Jumping ahead of the timeline brings me to their son Victor or Vic who became a regular correspondent to Maurice and Marjorie even after Vic emigrated for Australia with his wife Maureen. Their eldest son Alf or Alfie died in 1964. Their oldest child was called Pearl Edith, born on 29th June 1903 after a marriage in March 1903 – maybe causing problems between Pearl and her mother.

On the other hand the problem might just have been Edie Tyler herself. On 23rd January 1951 her husband Alf Tyler would commit suicide – probably because of serious health issues - but a letter written to Maurice by his mother just after the funeral included this quotation *"Alfie is at his wits end to know what to do, no-one on Earth could ever put up with Edie, you understand, but Alfie wonders if I had their front room on my own if I could come here rent free, he says that would be the ideal thing if I could manage it, but dear me, at my age I surely must have a more peaceful life."* A letter written by Alfie contains this line *"We don't see a lot of Aunt Ada though she is quite near which is perhaps just as well for her, as Mum's company is bearable by most people in small doses only."*

Returning to family origins, I found a note by Ada saying that her father and grandfather came from Poynings – an old village of Saxon origin just north of Brighton. Poynings Parish Church War Memorial records a Private Ernest Charles Hollingdale of the Royal Sussex Regiment dying in 1916 – son of Charles and Amelia Jane Hollingdale of Poynings Street, Poynings - according to www.roll-of-honour.com. I have no idea if they are relatives of Ada, but my brother believed that there were two Hollingdale families in the two villages and ours came from Ditchling. However Ditchling and Poynings are two neighbouring villages just to the north of Brighton so two families with the name of Hollingdale so close together were probably related.

*****

This third letter is written from Hong Kong on Thursday 27th but does not specify which year. It states that Will's brother had just died – seemingly after a long illness, and Will's brother Frank died in 1897 at only 23 years old.

However he also refers to Dec 3rd and, according to David Fill, HMS Powerful was in Hong Kong from Jan 3rd to Mar 7th 1898 and according to *timeanddate.com* 27th Jan 1898 was a Thursday. It would have taken weeks to receive letters from home so that would fit Frank dying in late 1897.

Frank apparently suffered from fits – possibly epilepsy - which matches Will saying *"He at least is at peace. His poor tired brain is at rest."* Far from the last tale of suffering in this family history.

Among papers I found the front of an envelope with Hong Kong stamps dated Ju 3 98 to Miss A Hollingdale, Feldheim, Wimbledon Common, London, England. I can match no letter to it so presumably it has not survived.

An internet search has revealed references to 'Feldheim' being the sort of residence where Ada could only have been a servant. I cannot be one hundred per cent certain who Ada's employers were, and whether they were aware that their servant's fiancée was in Ladysmith, but I suspect that the family name was Delcomyn – as will be explained in chapter five when I mention the 1st East Putney Scout Group.

But I digress – this is Will's letter.

HMS Powerful
Hong Kong
China
Thursday 27th

Sweetheart.

The news has come at last. I cannot say I am sorry. He at least is at peace. His poor tired brain is at rest. Would that some of ours were equally so. How dark things seem overhead. I knew this must come. They were right when they said troubles never come singly. I don't seem to get clear of them and Heaven alone knows how I try. I see nothing in front of me but sheer darkness.

The mail that brings this news also brings news of debts. I have enclosed it – do not tell my sister. I will tell them about it after I have paid it and sent it back. I even owe you money that I am unable to pay yet ah dot how I feel these things. I am telling you of these troubles because it is alone your hand that leads me on – were it not for you I should have gone down, down I don't know where - when I have thought of you and all that might be.

I have struck out again only by this mail to be drawn back again. I have had visions of a home for myself and you but now how far it seems away. I am not weak enough now to say I will give up. I was brought up to think the darkest hour is the one before the dawn. Is this the darkest hour or am I to hear the boy has no home and has lost his situation is that the next news that I am to hear. How I wish the dawn was close at hand. Sometimes I think Heaven is against one but that is wrong. Never mind dot it hurts me to think of all these things but I will rise again with God's assistance alone for once there is no failure.

You will do what I ask won't you. Don't tell my sisters and above all don't offer assistance. I know before you read my letter your thoughts. I will help & I will pay some and tell him afterwards. Your heart is good but do be kind to me give me your hand your sympathy but not your money. My letter is full of despair forgive me and it. I will write before the mail leaves again it does on Thursday but you will see the difference in the two letters one where I am in the mire the other where I am struggling out. Au revoir my love

> *From yours*
> *For ever*
> *Will*

PS Please send the letter back

> *Will*

Do not think I am in debt though not sending money home I was in debt to that amount on Dec third & how awful what must it be now.

Do not think I do not feel the loss of my Brother. I feel it but yet I thank God he has taken him. It is one lost to us but one Angel more in heaven. You will see I have put some hard words in my letter have scratched them out they did not read with the meaning I intended them for you.

On Friday week I have to sing at a concert that is something like Dakin's night *is it not I am singing the Wicket Gate would that you could hear the echo.*

In his postscript Will Burwood refers to singing at a concert. The reference to 'Wicket Gate' probably means a romantic ballad "At the Wicket Gate" published in 1880 by Lee & Walker of Philadelphia. I found a handwritten copy of a lyric of 'the Wicket Gate' among old family papers, which is transcribed below:

The Wicket Gate

Verse 1

It was in the autumn time when the twilight shadows fell
Beside a wicket gate he bade his last farewell
As far across the sea his fortune went to try
He lingered with a village lass and this his last good bye

Chorus

Remember me dearest when far from thee I'm roaming
Think of me sometimes when I am far from thee
Recall back the time love when in the autumn gloaming
Our farewells were spoken O think still of me.

Verse 2

The maiden waited on and the autumn came and passed
Yet still her heart would whisper he will return at last
And one bright summer's day at the dear old wicket gate
Both sailor true and maiden fair did meet their happy fate

Chorus

Welcome me dearest to her he whispered fondly
Home I've returned love to claim you for my bride
Sad was our parting but happiness awaited us
As floating together down life's tranquil stream.

The lyrics are so appropriate to Will and Ada's situation that it is obvious why he would want to sing it and wish that she could 'hear the echo'.

*****

This fourth letter is dated 12 August and describes them as anchoring outside Hong Kong for the night after just arriving and being due to head south shortly. David Fill's dates quote HMS Powerful as arriving in Hong Kong on 13 August 1898 and departing for Manila in the Philippines on 7th Sept which confirms it as 1898.

I am unsure which port I could not decipher - David Fill quotes Powerful as leaving Wei Hai Wei on 27th July and Yokohama on 7th Aug. Yokohama is Japan's largest port city and Weihaiwei was a territory in the north-east of China around Port Edmund. I have underlined and left blank the indecipherable name.

HMS POWERFUL
HONG KONG
August 12ᵗʰ

3.30p.m.
My darling Sweetheart

I have kept you waiting for a letter for about 9 days but it could not be helped. I am sorry indeed in fact it seemed a month for not writing we left _____ about 9 or 10 days ago and we have just arrived outside of Hong Kong where we anchor for the night – the mail is leaving H.K. to-morrow morning so they are sending them by boat into port to catch it as we shall not arrive until after the mail had left.

No doubt you are all full of excitement with your sister's wedding coming off, in fact by the time you get this it will be all over. I have their present but could not send it on account being north but will try to while I am here. There is not a day not even an hour that I do not think of you. Just to-day I was shown the English time. My first thoughts flew to you and you were asleep darling at the time. Here the time was ¼10 of a.m. but the English time was 5 mins to 12 o'clock midnight. Oh would that I could have just slipped into your room and quickly on my toes and kissed your forehead. That would have been enough to know that you were well and at peace, and then have left as quietly as I came.

I am afraid I should not have left so quietly. I know I should have picked you up in my arms and saved out <u>no</u> I will not go and I know when you awoke so suddenly you would not let me leave. How my feelings are carrying me away into fields of imagination still it is nice to lose oneself in a letter to the sweetheart if it is missing a lot.

What about our day, darling, my love. I long for it to come. I can see you coming down the aisle of the church on my arm, mine and just how beautiful. I shall be too proud to speak – it feels even now to be well and what is the good of my trying to describe I cannot do it a shadow of justice and won't I take care of the sweetheart that God has given me. I wish I could dream something of you not that my memory of you dear is getting dim but that I should like to see you again if only in a dream. My memory grows dim but never.

I shall always know you as a good little girl, because it makes me fancy you require my hand to help you along and that you look to me for protection and yet it is the other way round actually. I look to you for love to inspire me all day long for strength to guide my soul and you can never know how dear you have become to me. I cannot help it we are sweethearts and what we say to one another is for our eyes and ears only.

I cannot say much about Christmas. I am not going to send any more money home unless it is applied for, and I shall save now in dead earnest for our home. I sent you the size of my neck in the last letter. I am pleased to say I am blessed with good health and I hope you are having the same, dear. The heat is scandalous but I don't mind we are continually bathed in perspiration and are going still further south shortly and now darling I must close now in order to catch the mail with ever devoted love to you and best respects to all especially to Mr & Mrs Brown. I conclude

Believe me to be your affect sweetheart

Will

There are references to Ada's sister getting married and to a Mr & Mrs Brown. Ada's elder sister Clara married Joseph Brown 13th August 1898. A letter from Clara to Ada. marked by Ada as written 12 days before Clara's death, confirmed that Ada had been staying with Clara for Christmas, so clearly they remained close until the end – closer than Ada and her other sister Edie.

36 Freshfield St
Brighton
Jan 16th 48

Dear Ada

We were very glad you arrived home & found a loving welcome, you deserve it. People do not miss you as a rule until you are not there, and glad they had something for you. I always make it a rule when anybody arrives after travelling to give them a nice meal, as you know. We done very well over the Xmas days didn't we, we gathered up all the little pieces of cake especially the plain & crumble it up & put it in a jelly, was very good.

Miss Strutt enjoyed talking to you, we were very glad it fitted in all around. Hope to see you again, perhaps some time we might be able to sit out of doors in the sunshine, we have had a lot of rain here to-day it looks like snow. Alf pops in now & again since he gave up work, very glad to see somebody sometimes especially this dull weather. He comes up to look at the chicken for a change he says. Edie says tell you that three are laying now & it looks as though the other one will be starting this week.

The graves are returfed last week, turfed all over so they just be kept tidy by just clipping the grass. Edie asked the man that done them, he said at any time if you wanted any done, if you gave him the number. He would do yours for you anyway you may be down again before long 15/6 I paid him for mine Edie paid the same for hers. Well there is surely no need for you to work so hard "what for".

I cannot get about too early & get the nice hot weather it helps the aches & pains, as it is we are more fortunate than a lot, we can have plenty of fires etc. Do not keep us too long without a few lines, when the days lengthen & sun shines I may yet be tripping up to you. "Who knows".

Here's all the best for the year that has begun take care of yourself & cheers. XXXX is the sincere wish of I

> *Your loving*
> *Sister Clara*

The Edie mentioned in this letter is Clara's daughter Edith Ada May who was born in 1901. She regularly visited my parents and we all visited her after my father's death. She married twice but never had children of her own, only a stepdaughter from her second husband - a James Colyer – known as Jim - who died in 1957. The graves mentioned would be of their three husbands, as Will died in 1926. Clara's husband Joe died in 1939, and Edie's first husband Fred Mclees died in 1943.

For many years Edie was a landlady running a bed and breakfast at 36 Freshfield Street in Brighton, but in later life settled on just one long standing permanent lodger – a Mr Alfrey - until shortly before he died. 'Auntie Edie', as we all called her, was a great character and a great favourite with all us children.

She died in Brighton shortly after her 90th birthday in 1991.

*****

This fifth letter is clearly dated from 1899 when HMS Powerful was preparing to head home but before it was redirected to South Africa, although I am not sure exactly when in 1899 as it is not dated and I have Ada's birthday recorded as 18th January.

David Fill quotes HMS Powerful as being in Hong Kong between Sept 7th and Sept 17th 1899, so probably Will is just referring to Ada's birthday as being the 18th rather than January. Clearly Will was anticipating leaving the Navy on his return and getting married as he mentions having 'just on' finished his time - meaning the time for which he had signed on to serve in the Navy.

This expectation of expected discharge being delayed – with the real possibility of Will's death – must have made his deployment all the more heartbreaking for Ada and his family back home, especially for Ada when she was eagerly anticipating finally getting married.

Will inserts the word 'dot' in several letters. Based on future family letters I believe it is an acronym for 'Dear Old Thing'.

HMS Powerful
Hong Kong
China

My own darling Sweetheart Dot

I am to tell you the news that your heart longed to hear and me as well we are to proceed to England to pay off we leave here on the 18th (your birthday) I am glad to bring my ship home, for several reasons of course it will alter all our meeting plans. You will certainly have to come to meet me now if it is only for a day and we are to come home as far as present arrangements via the Suez Canal so it will take us 6 to 8 weeks after we leave Hong Kong.

Oh darling how glad I am I cannot tell you and I could not believe the news until it was confirmed by the notice on the board. Family in England week, homeward friends, my first thought was (Oh! Dot) does it not seem funny that things should so arrange themselves, well darling it is because I have prayed that God's will be done, that he would take me to England just when he thought proper, of course this is one of the shortest commissions that there has been. O how I long to see you. I like to think of you standing on the Quay with Annie. She will be there and I shall have to ask her to kiss my cheek because my lips were last touched by yours and they shall be the first that touch them again I promise you.

I have your white silk slip for the dress. I got it about last Thursday. Of course I don't know if it is good or bad according to a lady's idea but I send you just a small puttee let me know if it is all right there are 24 yds and the width is 22 in. I must tell you the wife of a missionary was with me when I bought it. Perhaps you would like to know the price but you won't so don't ask me when you write but to proceed with my letter it is a fortnight ago since I heard from you so I cannot answer any of yours. You ought to see the fellows about getting their things really fancy. Some of them here have years more to do yet and I am just on finished my time.

We arrive in England in December so I shall have time to look out for a situation won't I and then as soon as I get it well we will go home together for good. I have thought so much about our home since we have had the orders and I wonder will I be able to make it good enough for you. I don't know about things darling but I do know this that whatever we have it shall be brightened with love or where-ever we are if it cannot be so good as we hoped well we must get it afterwards and be a help to one another in order to do it.

One thing we have got to be particular in and that is if Jesus was to come upon Earth he would be able to find peace and comfort in our home and that we will always try and keep it so for where there is love born of him who has been so kind & merciful to us. In our lives there is sure to be happiness.

I had a letter from Annie the same time as I had your last and she tells me she is about to get married well I do hope so it is nearly time. I should be ashamed to keep you so long although our courtship had no alternative when taking everything together we have not been with one another long have we sweetheart and yes our love has grown most wonderfully and there is room for it to grow more. I have been thinking how you will look dot as you stand on the Quay. I hope I am nice and black would you mind much if I were. I don't think so I know I should not mind if you were black I should kiss you just the same. I really don't know what to say. I feel so pleased and no doubt you do so as well now.

Don't rush into the kitchen and shout out he's coming home or they will think I must be something extraordinarily wonderful or else you are mad and when I telegraph or write to you you must come down just for the day. If Annie is married you must have about 3 days holiday while we are paying off and get her to put you up.

I cannot tell you if I should get any leave or get my discharge before I leave the ship or if I shall have to come back to the Depot to get it. I can tell you that if there is time between the time we pay off and the 15th Dec I shall have 1 months leave. Any way I am shine to have a week or so. That will give me time to look out for a place. You must not give notice to leave your situation there until I tell you this at present may seem hard to you darling (but it would not do to have two of us out of a situation) but you know I have your welfare at heart and let me in this judge what is best won't you dear.

The reason of all this is because any life after I leave the service to me seems a blank. I cannot make future plans. This is where I feel so helpless dot, why just go to our dear Saviour in prayer and he wants me always to be helpless. I have faith to believe that the Lord will provide and we must not stop praying because we know he will provide or we shall soon doubt it and my sweetheart I am just about to go about some duty that will keep me an hour so I must conclude now with the fondest and best of love. I remain

Your Affec sweetheart
Will
Till it should please Jesus to call one or the other.

The Annie referred to was Will's eldest sibling (born in 1865) who was married 9th December 1899 to Charles Williams – 34 when she married. As was not unusual for that century Will had nine siblings of whom five had died young. I know of a Mabel (1879-1880) and Alfred (1881-1885), a Maud (1870-1888) who was blind, an Edward (Ted) (1872-1889) who died during or following an operation, and the aforementioned Frank who lived from 1874 to 1897.

Will had three other surviving siblings as well as Annie – all younger - Nellie (born 1876), Edith (1878), and Warwick (1883). Annie died in 1944 and the other three died in the 1950s. I presume the white silk slip for Ada was for the wedding – about to be delayed indefinitely.

*****

This sixth letter is written very hurriedly when Will was sent to Ladysmith with the Naval Brigade, and shows Will turning to his faith in Jesus at this time of trial. I read that the 21st Psalm is a psalm of praise for deliverance from the enemy – so very appropriate.

Psalm 21st 1st verse is answer to prayer
The king shall joy in thy strength, O lord
HMS POWERFUL

My own darling sweetheart

You must know by now that the Naval Brigade has gone to the front and it has pleased the dear Saviour that I should go, and I do rejoice in so much that I go in his strength and under his care and protection.

Now my sweetheart for myself I do not mind but I want you just now go alone in your bedroom and kneel and tell Jesus all about it and tell him from your heart that you will trust him and while on your knees tell him that you are willing and that his will will be done.

It maybe that I will not get the chance to write to you again so do them won't you dot. It may seem hard and cruel to you but He knows best and actually all things work together for good to him that love the Lord. Suppose Darling I did not know Jesus as I do now that is worse to think of than anything else – now, my own little girl you must know that I have loved you and do love you with all my heart and if it should please the dear master to take one – live sweetheart so that you may meet me amongst those we read about in Revelations 7th chapt 9,10,13,14,15,16,17 Verses for me – belong to that multitude.

I cannot only tell you once again that I love you like I have loved no one else and if needs be I would give my life for yours darling, but God knows best now sweetheart we come down to business. I am leaving word that all the things I have shall be sent to you so you must have them.

There are three boxes. One with a set of china and one pure Vases and a camphor Wood box full up with things and infills & 9 white shirts and a pajama suite for Warwick. I large China bowl and 4 walking sticks of course. You can do with things as you like they are in the possession of a young man. Here is his address A. Timms, Stoker 18 Mess, HMS Powerful. Of course you won't get them unless something happens to me and Nell will hear of it first on account of it being one of the family.

You may find one or two things amongst the letters or a photo of a young person but believe me sweetheart that I did never dishonour you by word or deed or thought. The young lady is a Capt in the Salvation Army and one card I had from Mary a little woman in Scotland. I really kept it to tease you with as you will know now darling that I loved you with a love made pure by a Christ like life do not notice what you see in papers.

I will write to you as often as I can but keep on trusting Jesus now darling. I must close I must write to all of them and I have not much time – address Powerful as usual, forever sweetheart

> *I remain God Willing*
> *Yours for ever*
> *Will*

PS Your locket and photo was with me along with my bible they will come to you then you will know there has something happened.

My address HMS Powerful
Cape of Good Hope
Africa southern

Warwick and Nell were his brother and sister. I presume Nell would have been notified of Will's death as the oldest sibling still at home after Annie's marriage – with both parents dead and Will still unmarried.

The letter included an impression of Will's lips in ink kissing the paper. He carried that bible throughout the siege of Ladysmith and it still exists as does a locket with pictures of both Will and Ada.

*****

This seventh letter is the first written in Ladysmith itself. The Naval Brigade arrived and got straight into combat. Will refers to the first 24 hours being 'very warm indeed'. The Naval Brigade made a critical contribution to preventing the Boers from capturing the town that day - firing on and disabling a Boer artillery piece. The town was completely surrounded within hours of the Brigade's arrival. If they had not arrived Ladysmith might well have fallen.

Powerful's Naval Camp
Ladysmith
Natal

My own darling sweetheart

My letter now are very dear to you but I cannot spare more than half a sheet and only a short note. I am more than glad to say I am quite well and happily trusting in Jesus. We are having pretty peaceful period the last 48 hours. Our first 24 hours was very warm indeed. It please God to let us all come out of the engagement without death and he had promised to take care of one and he will. What a blessed thing it is to trust him on sweetheart now what should we do without him to go on. I don't know when I am likely to get letters from you still I am just hoping for them. I am not going to tell you anything about war at all when I write to you it must be peace and love poor.

Yet it must worry you dear but don't fear it will draw us still closer on to another for these trials. You think you would not mind if it was you in this war and not me and I think I am glad it is me and not you. For myself I do not fear but I can imagine your feelings how pleased you must be to read this. It quite livens you up don't it now sweetheart. Think you must your letters must be with me I have your photo with me in my bible and it is nice to look at Both of them. Now darling just write and tell them all I am well and I will write to you as often as possible.

Another thing will you send 10/- to the Secretary, Hearts of Oak Benefit Society Fitzroy Square by the 21st Dec and put on the back W.Burwood 18091 for me. I get money while here now. Darling that is all I have to say with thanks to the Christ both for his loving mercy and asking his blessing for both of us I remain your affect sweetheart

Will

The Hearts of Oak Benefit Society was a Friendly Society founded in 1842 to protect its members from sickness – a sickness insurance scheme subsequently including maternity and death benefit schemes for members like Will Burwood.

*****

This eighth letter is dated 29 Dec 1999 – nearly two months into the siege, so Will probably means 3rd November rather than 3rd October.

> *Naval Brigade*
> *Ladysmith*
> *Natal*

Dec 29th

<u>Am quite well</u> that is the Best news for as you know since the 3rd of Oct we have been cut off from the world but it has pleased the Lord to keep us safe. Not all are here but those that are left are thankful at least I hope so my dear it is not much good one going into detail because I have not the paper we are glad to get hold of even this that I use but as we are at – war – dot – you will understand no ink dirty paper and scribble of course you I understand that I have had no letters or any news from anyone now there is a notice up to the effect that the post office is taking letters pending the communication being again established so we are not relieved up to this date – no doubt by the time you get this Ladysmith will be relieved and God willing other letters will be under weigh.

I have concluded you have been in a poor state or a worried state and I have thought perhaps poor girl she has not been able to do her work on account of it or has left or has made herself ill and left so I send this to 9 Rich Hill. I do hope though nothing of the kind has happened, and that you have been trusting in the Lord to keep one safe. My prayers have been for my safety and you bearing up under the trial that you have been through my dear. You know letters are not safe now so one cannot say what they would like to still dot it is good to have any news isn't it.

I don't know about when I shall be home I am time expire and they may send us home before the ship comes but I hardly think so Christmas day was extremely hot out here we thought a great deal about home and loved ones and Christmas puddings and our hearts whispered a merry

Xmas to all we think the same for a happy new year and to you and me a
very very happy new year no dot I must done with fondest love

Yours
Will

PS tell all my brothers and sisters of this

Will and Ada and their families lived in and around Brighton and '9 Rich Hill' means 9 Richmond Hill in Brighton - home of Ada's carpenter father Richard Hollingdale. Will's reference to being 'time expire' means that his time in the Navy would have been over had he not been diverted to Ladysmith.

That must have made it even worse for Ada.

*****

The most faded of the letters from Ladysmith – written in pencil on paper scraps and not sent until the end of the siege - was written on 25th January 1900. The first line written separately is a later addition. It seems that they were hoping for the siege to end at the beginning of February, but it was another month before the siege finally ended because the Battle of Spion Kop on 23-24 January was a failed attempt to relieve Ladysmith.

In this letter several lines were indecipherable – mostly at the creases. I have underlined the gaps.

I put this in as I had it with writing – Date of posting 2 March

Naval Brigade
Ladysmith
Natal
S. Africa

My own little girl

Once again by the Grace of God I am able for to send you news of myself. I am more than glad to say that I am enjoying a good health and my one thought and hope is that you are doing the same this 3 months life has been a very trying time. _____ all know of these _____ do not know if the names _____ and _____ those who have died of fever have been published _____ perhaps it was good some of the homes did not know at Christmas time about them.

One could write so much of one's thoughts about Xmas time and I have thought so much about you this month and I could not even send you a line but there. We hope & trust that all will come right in the end in God's own good way we can say we are living on the fat of the land but that don't matter much.

16 days we heard the soldiers outside fighting the Boer in face we can see the shells bursting so it gives us hope. I take it that we shall be relieved by the 3rd or 4th of Feb but we have been here since the 29th of October last.

Tell me up to what time you received my last letter before Christmas and when you got the last one after and the date of my last letter not this one there is a great talk about the Naval Brigade going back from here to our ship but I don't know what we really shall do and you know more about the war than I do of course I know a good bit about Ladysmith but outside of it I am done. I only hope that you and all at home are well both your and my family.

You must not mind if this letter has been opened dot we are in troublesome times and they want to keep the enemy in darkness concerning our movements so they read all letters and you then can understand why I write just as I do but never mind my dear little girl I often picture you coming to meet me and the good things to come.

Hereafter would you like to know what we are living on now well (yes) well so should I & one _____ per day. Thank God we have that yet. Breakfast a 4.30 a.m. neat gin

Dinner 12 o'clock 1st course soup De clear

– 2 course ¾lb beef de Gough

On trees

Nothing

Tea 4p.m. _____ of tea and a biscuit

of this bill of fare is weak men but dear we are not unhappy through it all because we have one above who looks after us and he keeps our spirits up – Praise him. Now I have wrote this on 25 Jan and I will date it for posting as soon as the mail goes out that is when communication is re-established. Tell all I am well ever yours

Will

The fever which killed many during the Siege of Ladysmith was enteric fever – aka typhoid fever. Dysentery was a major problem. The cause of both was the Boers cutting the water supply forcing the besieged to rely on polluted water from the river that ran through Ladysmith.

I surmise that 'soup de clear' was very watery, and that beef de Gough was not beef – possibly horseflesh. As to why the word 'Gough' – it may have been coincidence but a Captain John Gough of the Rifle Brigade distinguished himself among the defenders of the town.

*****

The last letter from Ladysmith.

Ladysmith
2nd March

My own Darling Dot

Thanks be to the Lord we are relieved at last after 4 months we have had a very trying time living on horse flesh and a biscuit and a quarter a day. I have a bad finger so you will excuse bad writing – now – sweetheart does it not seem good if only to be able to write to one another again and know that your letter will reach oh how I have thought of you especially during Christmas and your birthday.

I feel so weak but oh so glad of our relief to be in communication with the outside world we have not had any mails in yet. I am only just dashing you off this letter so that you might rest assured the Lord has answered your prayers in keeping me safe. I will write a long letter as soon as possible to you.

I have prayed often that you might be safe and well and I don't know what your letters will say. Oh darling the time is drawing near when there will be no more earthly partings and I am longing for it we shall soon be

*leaving here I believe for the ship. The one great thing now is hunger –
hunger for food hunger for mails and hunger for kisses and a sight of
your dear face. I don't know what may have happened at home so cannot
answer anything but in conclusion I must say my love is all your own from*
    Your ever and ever affec

                                 Will

    P.S. mail closing
Tell all hands
Letter to address ship
This is first opportunity of mails

                                 Will

              *****

I could not read the date on this next letter but Will says he left
Ladysmith on 7th March and travelled about 4 days so it was about
12th March 1900.

                        HMS POWERFUL

                        ————

                        Capes

My own Darling girl

*Here at last we arrived on board yesterday at 1.20 after travelling
about four days from Ladysmith and I must tell you that I sent a letter
almost as soon as I possibly could but am afraid I shall be <u>home</u> before
it because I sent on to the ship at the same time and I arrived here before
it came we are leaving almost at once and the mail leaves at 10 o'clock
tomorrow. One's heart is almost too full to put what stuff would like to. I
don't know how to start it seems that I must write something else, but my
darling praise God over and over again.*

*I am well but indigestion is turfing me out on account of having
change food and none of us are strong in fact but that don't matter we
are coming home to those we love and as soon. If you write back write to
Portsmouth. This is my last letter to you before I arrive and I am just too full
to propose what to do & can only leave it in the Lord's hands if he allows*

you to come down you will come down he knows what is best we need not be afraid of others sending me letters now what if others would know of our love, they can only know it is sure and true.

But darling I would like to write so much but cannot it seems all so wonderful, the free air, the sea, the white bread, the love of my sweetheart all combined all here who gave it all. You prayed that I might not go to the war, but the Lord willed it otherwise and said I will take him in the greatest of dangers and then bring him out whole. He did not say I will take him to the edge of dangers and then bring him out whole. Oh how we see his all-powerful arm shielded round about us surely goodness & mercy have followed us all the days of our life.

I have no time to write to others, now my girl, but tell them all I am well and hope soon to see them all in years to come not by pen, but by deed, this is the first time I have written a proper letter for over 4 months. We got into Ladysmith on 30 Sep and came out of Ladysmith on the 7 of March, so we have been out from the world but not from the Lord. He knew all about us and I had some long talks with him about us both. I don't know what I would have done without him and now I bring him (and yet he is there in England with you) oh so very soon behind this letter. Let us both thank him now together and we will again when we meet – now my only sweetheart I leave you yet in his hands, and mind the duty proper. My hands are dirty but my heart is clean and it is just jumping with prayer and thanksgiving because he has kept us safe through all.

Good night darling, its late. God bless you in the prayer of

> *Yours for ever*
> *Will*

Don't forget. Write to Portsmouth.

> *Will*

I do not know if this letter reached Ada before HMS Powerful reached Portsmouth on 11th April 1900 – or if any letters from Ladysmith reached her before Will. The letter shows how sincerely religious Will had become – in comparison to his earlier confession that he was prone to 'shun church' - so his experience of war clearly increased his faith in Jesus.

On a less happy note he mentions coming away with what he called 'indigestion' – no surprise after months of poor food and contaminated water with widespread disease. He was clearly luckier than some, but that does not mean that he avoided long-term physical consequences - but back to happier points.

Firstly, there was an address of thanks from the Mayor of Simonstown in March 1900. Simonstown is near to Cape Town on the Cape Peninsula in South Africa and has been a Naval Base for two centuries – currently for the South African Navy but then for the Royal Navy, so it was where HMS Powerful had waited for its Naval Brigade.

The address reads:

PER MARE AD TERRAM
THE HONORABLE HEDWORTH LAMBTON, C.B.
OFFICERS AND MEN

We the <u>inhabitants of Simons Town the Naval Station</u> rejoice that this opportunity is afforded us on behalf of all loyal <u>South Africans</u> of welcoming You back from the seat of war, and to record our admiration of the very conspicuous part You have performed in so gallantly and worthily upholding the best traditions of the British Navy and in maintaining the supremacy of our Queen and Empire.

We are proud to recognize that <u>the Naval Brigade</u> has so materially contributed to the brilliant successes which have attended our arms in <u>South Africa.</u>

We are not unmindful of the bravery of Your colleagues who have sacrificed life to duty in the cause of justice and freedom to our countrymen in this land and that many among You are still suffering the effects of dangers and privations through which You have passed. We however trust the voyage home and the welcome awaiting You there will in vigorate and strengthen You and that You may be long spared to see the fruit of Your gallant actions in the development of this country as a united <u>South Africa</u> under the glorious old Union Jack.

On behalf of the inhabitants of Simons Town.

Simons Town March 1900.

The document was signed by the Mayor of Simons Town, but his signature is indecipherable.

Then there was a Civic Banquet put on by the Town of Portsmouth on 24th April 1900 to honour the returned Naval Brigade, and at some point there was the presentation of the watch. The inscription on the watch reads:

SIEGE OF LADYSMITH
118 DAYS
1899-1900
W. BURWOOD
L.S.
H.M.S.POWERFUL

The banquet invitation is equally formally inscribed. On the back is a drawn depiction of HMS Powerful at sea, and the front cover reads:

BANQUET
To
THE OFFICERS and MEN of
THE NAVAL BRIGADE
By the Mayor, Corporation, and Inhabitants of
PORTSMOUTH
In appreciation of Services rendered by them to their
COUNTRY, in SOUTH AFRICA
At the Town Hall, Portsmouth
Tuesday, April 24th, 1900
H.R.PINK, Mayor

Then comes the MENU page, and Portsmouth did not stint on the menu.

MENU
FISH
Boiled Cod (Oyster Sauce)
REMOVES

Roast Turkey. Ox Tongue.
Roast Chicken. Ham. Fillet of Veal.
Boiled Leg of Mutton, (Caper Sauce).
Roast Beef.
Roast & Boiled Potatoes, Broccoli and other
Spring Vegetables.

———

SWEETS
Plum Pudding (Brandy Sauce).
Wine Jellies. Fruit Jellies.
Strawberry Blanc-Mange. Vanilla Blanc-Mange.
Fruit Tarts

———

Cheese & Salad.

———

DESSERT
Bananas, Apples, Oranges.

Particularly impressive for men who, less than two months earlier, had been surviving and fighting on such meagre rations.

The last other page of the invite covers the toasts, but the list of toasts is preceded and tailpieced by two verses of poetry.

"Now joy, Old England, raise!
For the tidings of thy might,
By the festal cities' blaze,
While the wine cup shines in light."
TOASTS
THE QUEEN

———

The British Empire

———

Capt. the Hon. Hedworth Lambton, R.N.C.B.
& the Naval Brigade.

———

General Sir George White, V.C., G.C.B., &c.
The Defender of Ladysmith.

"The meteor flag of England,
Shall yet terrific burn,
Till danger's troubled night depart,
And the star of peace return."

From some unknown source Will also obtained a small brown purse embroidered with a Union Jack and the words NAVAL BRIGADE 1900. In it I found a small anchor, a very small pipe bowl, a small embroidery of a crown, and a small nail with an attached note *dad dived in China a piece of the ship Chusan* (Chusan is a Chinese island).

One more award was due, as proven by a letter from the Admiralty dated 12th April 1901 – almost exactly a year since Will's return to England.

One thing different is the address given for Will. Green Meadow Cottage is not 7 Emlyn Terrace which is the only Talywain address I otherwise have for Will and Ada.

Admiralty, S.W.
12th April 1901

Mr W. J. Burwood

I beg to acknowledge the receipt of your letter of the 1st Inst, respecting a Medal and Gratuity, for the operations in South Africa, and to acquaint you that when the same are ready for distribution due notice will be given by advertisement.

Your Parchment Certificates returned herewith.

I am
Your Obedient Servant
R.D.AWDRY
Accountant-General of the Navy

Green Meadow Cottage,
Church Street,

Talywain,
Near Pontypool,
Mon

Medals and gratuities might take their bureaucratic time coming, but I am sure that Will was thinking about neither when he first arrived home. He had literally made it home through the horrors of battle to marry his sweetheart – and give her a real kiss instead of just the picture of his inky lips which he sent to his beloved in a letter.

Will Burwood's lips kissing the paper of the letter he sent home to his beloved Ada as he was setting off to fight for Ladysmith

Young Will Burwood

I believe this to be Will's father, William Burwood at Agra in India while apprenticed to the East India Company from 1857 to 1865. Family legend says that he later taught Winston Churchill to swim in Brighton

Ada Hollingdale aged 16

Richard Hollingdale & his children. Jim & Edie
behind him, Clara on his right & Ada on his left

CHAPTER TWO

Tanners & Combes

My mother's family history includes no Ladysmith, but that does not mean it was uneventful.

Marjorie Ethel Tanner was born on 11th December 1919. She had an elder sister born on 11th April 1915 called Olive Zena, whose memories – written down in her last year of life – provide significant linking information for the next two chapters. Marjorie's and Olive's parents were both born in 1887 as Walter Richard Tanner and Sarah Ethel Hale, although Sarah Ethel was generally called Ethel. Ethel lived until 1974. Her birthday of 4th August was shared with the late Queen Mother and the first Duchess of Sussex – and with Britain entering the First World War in 1914.

Walter Richard Tanner's parents were born William Richard Tanner in 1864 and Emma Jane Combes in 1866, while Sarah Ethel Hale's parents were born in 1852 as Athwell Matthew Hale and Sarah Ann Cripps. Both ancestries experienced struggles with early bereavements and poverty. Both histories were characterised by large families and infant mortality. Both had involvements with the Navy – as had the Burwoods with whom there are many parallels, including mysteries as to dates and relationships. I will deal with the Hales and the Cripps in the next chapter, and focus on the Tanners and the Combes in this chapter.

I have fewer letters and papers about my mother's side of my family – but my brother Richard researched and provided extensive family trees and other supportive research including the following paragraphs on the early history of the Tanner family.

Our Tanner family lived in Boldre, between Beaulieu and Lymington in the New Forest. John, son of Thomas, became an apprentice blacksmith in 1764 (for 7 years). The apprentice document exists – although rather tatty. Josiah, son of Hannah, also became an apprentice blacksmith in 1803 (for 9 years), now at Beaulieu. This apprentice document exists too.

According to family tradition, this Tanner family owned a plot of land in the Boldre area, but when the neighbouring landowner wanted to expand and claimed the plot, the Tanners were unable to prove ownership as the relevant page had been torn out of the official land registry book.

William was apprenticed to his father Josiah, a blacksmith, of Whippingham on the Isle of Wight in 1831 (for 7 years). The family had moved to the Island. Later they moved via Portsmouth to St Mary, Portsea, and later still to Portsmouth, Milton, and Farlington.

Richard also identified several marriages of Tanners in the Boldre area during the 18th and early 19th centuries, and there are Tanners still living there.

*****

Most of this chapter and the next one will be based around memories – notably from *Memories from Ninety Years: the lives of the Tanner sisters of Portsmouth*, in which I only edited and annotated memories written down by my mother and her sister, Olive, in the final years of their lives. This chapter will paraphrase or quote passages from that publication.

One thing both families have in common, not only with each other but also with the Burwoods, is involvement with the Royal Navy or the Royal Naval Dockyard at Portsmouth. In those days the Navy and its Dockyard were the major employers in Portsmouth and the surrounding areas.

*****

The following paragraphs include extracts from Olive's memories. .The first paragraphs concern her father's family, the Tanners.

"My Great Grandpa had been in the Navy, & I think had 'been in the Egyptian War' - to quote Grandpa."

This Great Grandpa Tanner was William Clark Tanner, born 1840, who I will continue to call William Clark to distinguish him from his eldest son William Richard Tanner who was Olive and Marjorie's Grandfather.

The Tanners, as coincidentally so did the Burwoods, had a habit of carrying the name William down through the generations, because William Clark Tanner's father, who was born in 1815, was also called William – the William apprenticed to his blacksmith father Josiah in 1831. William Richard Tanner then named his eldest son William Herbert Tanner. I make that four successive generations of William Tanner, but the tradition stopped with William Herbert Tanner when he only had one daughter while his only brother Walter Richard Tanner only had two daughters – so neither carried on the William name.

The Tanner name continued because William Clark Tanner married at least twice more – and the name William was not the only Tanner family tradition to continue – there was also the matter of employment because, as Olive remembers.

"The great grandfather I remember was also a blacksmith. He worked in the Dockyard, & was also in the Navy - a bosun's mate. I don't know when he was in the Navy, but remember Grandpa showing my father the medals, & heard him say "that one must be for the Egyptian War." Somewhen about the time of Gordon, & Khartoum, I suppose. Troops went by sea, not air, then, transported, or guarded by the Navy."

The siege of Khartoum was 1884-1885 and part of the Mahdist War between the forces of the Sudanese leader called the Mahdi, Egyptian forces and British forces, but the Anglo-Egyptian War of 1882 began with a British Naval bombardment of Alexandria and a naval blockade so is probably when the medal mentioned was earned.

The family holds two Egypt Campaign Medals – one of them a five-pronged star - presumably both won by William Clark Tanner. Supportive evidence for this comes from the 1881 census which shows a William Tanner of the right age being an Engine Room Artificer aboard HMS Iris, and – bizarrely – an antique print advertised on *Amazon.co.uk* of HMS Iris together with gunboats Beacon and Decoy blockading Damietta in the war in Egypt of 1882.

Damietta is a port in the Nile Delta so it is probably a print of a ship on which William Clark Tanner was serving.

My aunt had a little more to say about my great, great grandfather Tanner.

"Great Grandpa Tanner died in 1930 or 1931, at the age of 91. Then Grandpa had some papers & medals given to him. They were to do with apprenticeships of ancestors. They dated back to 1817 when a Tanner was apprenticed to his father, a blacksmith, & they lived in the New Forest. The father's name was Josiah Taner. Another was for a Tanner, at the Isle of Wight, at Whippingham. From what we have gathered from my nephew's searching the records, Josiah had several children - & they had quite big families, so we must have quite a lot of relations, somewhere."

Big families were normal for the nineteenth century. Unfortunately so were high rates of infant mortality.

My aunt had more to say about William Richard Tanner and an accident that changed the family's fortunes dramatically – but ultimately for the better – but before that my aunt had some memories of the extended Tanner family.

"Grandpa was the son of William Clarke Tanner (Great Grandpa) whose first marriage was to Helen, or Ellen, Hooper. She died, I think at Grandpa's birth, & he was brought up at Portchester - by his Aunt Kate, but she died - I don't know when."

William Clark Tanner married Ellen Mary Hooper (born 1841) in 1863 but she died in 1864 when William Richard Tanner was born. She died of puerperal fever – commonly called childbed fever – a major killer of the time.

I found among family papers an old Book of Common Prayer which had a section on *the Thanksgiving of Women after* Childbirth, which starts with the words *"Forasmuch as it has pleased Almighty God of his goodness to give you safe deliverance and hath preserved you in the great danger of childbirth"*. The words *"great danger"* are there for good reason, and the lack of anaesthetics brings to mind Kipling's line of poetry *"She who faces death by torture for each life beneath her breast"*.

As William Clark Tanner was in the navy it would have been normal for him to be away for long periods – and he must have continued working when Ellen died, so it was natural that his motherless baby son was looked after by another member of his extended family – at least until he remarried. Marry and provide a stepmother is exactly what William Clark Tanner did, remarrying in 1865 and not, as far as I know, having another child until 1867.

William Clark Tanner's second wife was called Rebecca Elizabeth Brown. She was born in 1849 and so would only have been 16 (although the record of marriage claimed that she was 18) when she married William Clark Tanner in 1865 – when he was still a blacksmith by profession, probably in the Dockyard. They had a daughter called Lydia Emma in 1867, yet did not apparently bring up William Richard. The census of 1871 records William Clark Tanner as an Engine Room Artificer in the Navy. ERAs were in charge of maintaining and operating machinery such as the engines on Royal Naval warships at the time. The same census also records him as living with both Rebecca and Lydia but not William Richard.

I do not know why William Richard was not with them – maybe Rebecca did not welcome a stepson. My brother discovered that William Clark Tanner divorced Rebecca in 1879 for 'misconduct' with the father granted custody of the daughter. Lydia married a Samuel Reeves in 1889 and had children Bessie (in 1890), Leonard (1893), Lydia (1895), Samuel (1896), Florence (1899), Ada (1902) and Alfred (1904).

At some point, certainly 1870 if not before, William Clark Tanner joined the Navy, and remained in the Navy until at least 1886. Inevitably he was away for long periods, maybe explaining Rebecca's 'misconduct' – said 'misconduct' producing a son named Albert Jackman.

Following the divorce, William Clark Tanner in 1880 married a widow called Anne Gilderdale Bolitho (née Roberts), who brought into the family a son Arthur - who was not the only son brought into the family home because the census of 1881 records William Richard Tanner aged 17 living with new stepmother Anne Tanner and Arthur Bolitho – William Clark Tanner is not recorded at that address due to being on HMS Iris.

It seems that only after William married Anne did William Richard finally start living in his father's household, but that still leaves open the problem of identifying the 'Aunt Kate' who brought him up earlier.

The first candidate for 'Aunt Kate' is William Clarke Tanner's sister Catherine Anne – born 1843 so three years younger than him, who in

1862 married a John Parkes and had daughter Mary Catherine in 1862 followed by Ada Elizabeth in 1865, though John Parkes died in 1864. In 1866 she married a Peter Fitzer and had a daughter named Alice while acquiring two Fitzer stepchildren named William and Adelina – although there is a mystery about the family tree as there are records of two births for Alice, in 1866 and 1867.

It seems bizarre that there could be 2 Alices born to the same mother, but when we get to the Hales we will find that infant death could be involved, and in the 1871 census there is no Ada so maybe Ada was another early death.

There is also no William Richard Tanner mentioned as living with Catherine Anne in 1871, and Peter Fitzer had died in 1870. In 1871 she was in the Essex town of Waltham Abbey with two Fitzer stepchildren (William H, born 1860 in Malta, and Adelina, born 1862 in Portsmouth). In 1881, only Catherine and Alice were with Matilda Welch in Crockham Grange. In 1891, Alice was a Domestic Cook in service at Liss, sharing a cottage with a housemaid, Harriet Mills.

Crockham Grange is a listed building near Westerham in Kent. Liss is a large Hampshire village by the main road from Portsmouth to London. Catherine Anne married Henry Knight in 1884, and had a daughter Olive Maud in 1885, so was still alive in 1881 and not at Portchester for either census. It is unlikely that she was 'Aunt Kate' - nor William Richard's other aunt to whom Olive refers next.

"An aunt, I suppose a sister of his mother, was in Durban, & Grandpa went out to her. He must have been quite young. He did not like it & returned. According to Grandma, he was 21 when they married, & she was 19. He was then a carpenter in the Dockyard."

Unless Olive has misremembered 'Aunt Kate' dying, I can rule out Catherine Anne as 'Aunt Kate', so an alternative candidate must be considered – a sister of William Clarke and Catherine Anne's mother Abigail. That sister was also Catherine (surname Clarke) and born in 1826 so nearly 40 when William Richard Tanner was born. I have no idea whether Catherine Clarke ever married or when she died or where she lived so nothing to support her candidature other than her name. Maybe she never married so was happy to bring up her great-nephew, and being so much older would increase the statistical probability of her dying while bringing him up. In that case 'Aunt Kate' should strictly have been 'Great-Aunt Kate', but maybe it was not her either.

The 1881 census described William Richard Tanner as a 'joiner' which would fit the 'carpenter' description. I have no idea when or for how long William Richard was in South Africa – nor do I know the identity of the aunt in South Africa.

His mother was born in 1841 as Ellen Mary Hooper and had three sisters that I know about – Harriett (born 1845), Matilda Catherine (1850), and Sarah Ann (1853) - plus a brother, Samuel, born in 1849. Depending on how long he was with 'Aunt Kate' I suppose that any of them could have been the Aunt in South Africa, but Olive was not even definite that it was a maternal aunt.

He did have two more paternal aunts in the forms of two younger sisters of William Clarke - namely Elizabeth (born in 1848) who married a William Oliver in 1870, and Matilda (1855), who married a George Welch in 1873. Of these two Elizabeth is the likelier prospect as Matilda was only nine years older than the baby, and George and Elizabeth Welch had several children whom my brother has identified in this country, so Elizabeth Oliver is a likelier candidate for the aunt in South Africa if it was not one of Abigail's sisters.

But I could be completely wrong. It highlights both how extensive families could be, and needed to be for the sake of the children. Otherwise children would end up in orphanages or the workhouse – or as homeless children on the streets.

Digressing slightly, though not from the subject of extensive families, my brother supplied the following paragraph from his census research about the George Welch who married William Clark Tanner's youngest sister Matilda.

George WELCH was a coachman at Crookham Grange (1881) or a Groom living in Little Hambrook Street off King's Road, Southsea (1891) with Matilda and eight children. Two others born at Westerham (Matilda and Alfred) had died by then. In 1881, daughter Ada was with grandparents William and Abigail in Leigh-on-Sea.

I know of George and Matilda Welch having another ten children - George, Harriett, Ada, Elizabeth, Annie, Edward, Frederick, Ernest, Herbert, and Ethel – plus Matilda and Alfred who died young.

Large families are a global historical norm when early deaths are common for both mothers and children. The extended family did their best for William Richard Tanner, but he cannot have spent much time with his father. William Clark Tanner was cared for in old age by other family – as Olive remembers.

"I remember that we were coming back from North End, when I was about 6 or 7, I think it must have been, or perhaps a bit younger, not sure - & we were going though one of the roads off Chichester Road, I think it was Beresford, or a name like that - & someone came out of one of the houses & called to my father. It seems it was Roly Tanner, my grandfather's half-brother. Then an old lady came out. I was tired, & thirsty, & she brought me out a drink of milk."

Roly was Rowland Edward Tanner. William Richard Tanner was the only child of William Clark Tanner's first wife Ellen, and Roly the son of William Clark Tanner and his third wife Anne whom he married in 1880 – also acquiring a stepson named Arthur but known as Arky or Archy.

"Somewhen we went to tea one Sunday. There was Roly & his wife, & Great Grandpa - no-one else. I had heard that Great Grandpa had a glass eye, & tried to make out which eye that was, but didn't see any difference. I have some vague memory of them saying that they had a daughter who was, or had been on the stage, but I may be getting muddled with some other memory - I can't think what!"

Rowland Edward Tanner and his wife Annie had at least four daughters (Gladys, Beryl, Mabel, and Phyllis – plus a son, another William). My brother thought that it was Phyllis who chose a career on the stage.

Clearly Olive's great grandfather William Clark Tanner was being looked after in old age by youngest son Roly and wife – Roly being the son of William Clark Tanner's third wife. The 1991 census recorded William Clark as a publican at a pub called The British Queen in Queens Road, Portsmouth. He was living then with third wife Annie, stepson Arthur, son Rowland – and his own parents William and Abigail – born respectively in 1816 at Ryde and 1820 at West Cowes - both on the Isle of Wight.

It was normal for elderly relatives to live with their children's family, and maybe Annie was more welcoming of William Clark's family than Rebecca. William Richard married in 1884 and moved out with wife Emma and two sons leaving Rowland at home with their father, and apparently father William Clark and son Rowland continued living together to the end.

"I did hear from Father, many years later, that Roly had a son who had been in trouble (forged my grandfather's name on a cheque), & later he "jumped ship". I know no more than that."

Olive knowing *no more than that* implies that William Richard Tanner was not close enough to his father and half-siblings for his granddaughters to meet them regularly or know too much about them. Maybe William Clark not raising William Richard contributed to that.

"We did see Roly once or twice when we met him in North End & he had a lovely Alsatian dog. That would have been before the War.

"The next time I met him was after my father had died. I came home from teaching at Paulsgrove, & he had come to visit Mother. He was so like Grandpa. I never heard anything more about the family, or met anyone again, until about ten or twelve years ago. I did know that Roly had a half-brother known as Archy - who lived over the hill, & had, in early days of buses, run a small bus "The Denmead Queen" between Waterlooville & Denmead. Great Grandpa's third wife was a widow with one son, known as Archy, who took the name of Tanner."

The Denmead Queen was an omnibus service that ran between Hambledon and Portsmouth Guildhall, via Denmead, Waterlooville, and Cosham, before the Second World War. The buses were built in Waterlooville & were run by Frederick Tanner, who stored the fleet at Denmead, & whose five sons drove the 15 buses. The bus service was taken over by Southdown in the 1930s.

According to my brother, Frederick Tanner ran the service with his 5 sons Evelyn, George, Edward, William, and Ernest. Arky Tanner married a Louise Roberts, and then had five or six children including a Frederick who was born in 1907 so not old enough to run the Denmead Queen.

There is a Tanners Lane in the village of Denmead, and my brother Richard believed that Crabbick Farm in Denmead was the site from which the Denmead Queen was run. Sadly, according to www.roll-of-honour.com, Private Gordon Seymour Tanner - son of Frederick George and Edith Tanner of Crabbick Farm, Denmead - was killed in action on 22 March 1918 while only 19 years old, and is commemorated on the war memorial at All Saints Church in Denmead.

Olive has one last relevant memory here.

"We had arranged a coach trip & one of the people brought two friends, from Horndean or Waterlooville or somewhere over the hill. One was a Miss Tanner, & it transpired that Archy Tanner was her grandfather. She knew about Archy's bus, but did not know he was not a Tanner family member. She was sure she came from an old farming family."

This memory presents a real mystery. We have got more than one person remembering Archy's bus, but other records credit it to Frederick Tanner and his sons. Confused? I am.

Time to shift from Olive's Grandpa William Richard Tanner to his wife – born Emma Jane Combes.

"On my Father's side of the family, my grandmother was, I think, brought up by her grandmother. My grandmother was born in 1865, I think, and went to school at Fratton. There were several in the family. I have heard of Walter, Bert, Will, Flo, Jack, Fanny, & Flo - I think, not sure - & Nellie."

My mother's and aunt's grandmother was born Emma Jane Combes in 1866 – first born of the 1864 marriage of bricklayer William Combes (born 1843) and Jane Jennings (born 1845 and daughter of a Dockyard millwright). According to the 1881 census William was born in Fareham but living in Portsea.

The *'brought up by her grandmother'* puzzles, as Emma was living with William and Jane Combes at age 15, while William and Jane had at least another nine children over the next twenty years and Jane lived until 1908.

Maybe Olive's memories are confused here. My brother traced a family tree for the children of William and Jane showing that Olive did not remember all the names of Emma Jane Combes' siblings.

The tree shows Emma as the eldest (born 1866 not 1865), then Amelia (1867), Edith Annie (1869 and possibly misremembered by Olive as Fanny), William (1871), Felix (1873), Walter Richard (1875 and named just like Emma's second son so maybe a favourite), Florence Louise (1878), and Albert Edward (1880). The tree shows three others born after the 1881 census: Maria Alice (1881), Ernest (1883), and Nellie Kate (1886). Felix and Amelia may have died before Olive was born but Maria lived until 1945 so I do not know why Olive does not remember her – maybe she and her husband moved away. The 'Jack' she remembers was actually Ernest but known as Jack.

Mysterious, you might think, unless you remember that Oscar Wilde's classic play *The Importance of Being Earnest* was first performed in 1895, and that in it a Jack Worthing is portrayed as using the name Ernest. Easy to imagine the family coming away from watching a performance and lumbering him with the name 'Jack' – or maybe he preferred Jack. Or maybe it was pure coincidence – but that is less fun than blaming Oscar Wilde.

Olive had some additional memories about the children on that list – starting with poor Nellie – not the last Nell to know tragedy in this history.

"Nellie had two boys, younger than I, & I can remember them when we were little. Nellie had married Percy Spenser, who was a tailor's cutter in London. Sadly, Nellie became ill, & was advised to live in a better climate. The boys must have been somewhere about 7, 8, or 9. They came to see us before they went to Australia. Next, we heard Nellie had died on the voyage. I've got, or had, relatives somewhere in Australia."

According to the family tree, Nellie was the youngest – born 1886, married 1910, and died in 1925. Her two boys would be Bernard and Raymond Spencer, born 1916 and 1917. Maybe their descendants still live in Australia.

"Walter - my great uncle, I suppose - I saw once. We - my mother, father, & sister, went to see our grandparents at Drayton on Sunday night, & one night Walter & his wife made a very surprise call on Grandma. He had gone to St Alfred's at Winchester, & was teaching in Southampton."

This great uncle – remember – shared his forenames with Olive's father, his nephew.

"Jack was in the Navy, & an instructor at Osborne House. I saw him & Winnie, his wife, when they came to see us as they returned from Greece where he was stationed after the War. Joyce, his daughter, was three years

ahead of me at secondary school, & went to Bishop Otter College (B.O.C.) before I did. I last saw her at a London B.O.C. Guild meeting at St Georges College, Stockwell in 1958 or 59, I think it was."

Osborne House on the Isle of Wight was built as a summer residence for Queen Victoria and Prince Albert and remained a royal residence for half a century until Queen Victoria died there in 1901. It was then given to the nation and became the Royal Naval College, Osborne from 1903 to 1921. Young naval cadets were trained there before going on to the Royal Naval College at Dartmouth.

Terence Rattigan's famous play *The Winslow Boy* was inspired by the real life case of a boy expelled from Osborne College after being falsely accused of stealing a postal order – a *cause célèbre* which reached the High Court before he was exonerated.

Bishop Otter College at Chichester was where Olive did her teacher training, but I will return to Olive's memories of William Richard Tanner and his family – and to an accident that nearly ruined his life.

"My grandfather suffered the misfortune of his mother dying at his birth, & then his aunt died, so he went to join an aunt in South Africa. About 1930, an elderly lady came to us, to look for my grandfather - it was this aunt, now very elderly. Grandpa had not liked South Africa, & had returned.

"Grandpa, it seems, after returning from South Africa, worked as a carpenter in the Dockyard. The family were quite comfortably off when Grandpa had a fall from his bike, & injured his arm. The ball & socket joint were injured, & it seemed that they could not be repaired. He could no longer work in the Yard, & times were hard.

"For a while they worked in a tobacconist's shop, & Grandma took on dressmaking again. I remember Father, one day, saying that if his father had a bit of fish, he was given the bone to suck.

"Somehow, I don't know how, after two years he got to St Thomas Hospital in London, & though, as I remember, too, he could not lift that arm above shoulder height, their work on the joint meant that he could work again."

St Thomas's Hospital was originally founded in Southwark in the 12th century by a mixed order of monks and nuns to provide shelter and treatment for the poor, sick, and homeless, but since 1871 moved to Lambeth directly across the River Thames from the Palace of Westminster. It must have been quite an event for William Richard Tanner to go there for treatment, and no doubt he went because of its charitable tradition of providing healthcare freely to the poor.

"At that time there was much building going on in the Eastern half of Portsmouth, & he became a carpenter for a Mr Bowler.

"Grandma continued with dressmaking, & they managed to save £20 - a good sum in those days, Mr Bowler retired, Grandpa bought the business, & went on building in Milton."

William Richard Tanner went on to build quite a few houses in the years before the First World War put an end to his business. There are plaques over terraces of houses in Alverstone Road naming them as built by W.R.Tanner.

Back then it was common practice to buy one house to live in and another house to rent out with the rent substituting for a retirement pension. Even better to build them yourself. Not all of the houses William Richard Tanner built were sold immediately, some remained as rentals in possession of members of the family until the 1970's before being sold off – but mostly sold before the massive surge in house prices of recent decades – sold with relief because the last decades of rentals were restricted by so-called 'Fair Rent' laws which made the rental business far from profitable.

Aunt Olive had the following memory related to this: *"When selling a house in Bramshott Rd, Milton, I saw on the deeds that the land on which he bought a plot for a few houses had been previously bought from the Goldsmith family - who had owned a lot of Milton, & had lived in a big house opposite the park in Milton Road. My Grandma Hale told me that she could remember the house, & seeing peacocks behind the big gates.*

"Grandpa later built some houses in Alverstone Road, Vernon Ave, Catisfield Road, and Hollam Road. Building, of course, stopped when World War I came. I remember seeing a spare plot of land at the end of Hollam or Catisfield Rd, with a shed on it, & where, I suppose, he would have built.

"They moved from Powerscourt Road, or Queen's Road - I am not sure which - to Bramshott Road, and then to a corner house he built in Carisbrooke Road. During the war, they moved to Bedhampton."

Jumping ahead to finish the story of William Richard Tanner in his daughter Olive's words.

"Grandpa had a stroke in 1933, & I don't think he went out again, or at least rarely. There were two dogs, a brown Pomeranian, & a very tiny black one. The little one was the constant companion, spending much time just sitting on his knee, & looking quite ferocious if one got too near - she was just guarding him!! Grandpa died just after Xmas, 1936. The little dog sat under the coffin, & stayed there."

The residue of William Richard Tanner's successful building career was duly reflected in his will. His will was dated Sep 7th 1927 and gave his address as "Westmorland", Havant Road, Drayton. It appointed his wife Emma Jane Tanner and son Walter Richard Tanner as executors.

He died on 28th December 1936.

His wife was left his house named "Westmorland" along the main Havant Road in Drayton.

His daughter-in-law Mrs Caroline Edith Tanner, widow of his late son William Herbert Tanner, got two houses - one in Carisbrooke Road, Portsmouth, and the other in Vernon Avenue, Portsmouth.

One house in Hollam Road and three in Vernon Avenue went to trustees.

Yet another house in Vernon Avenue went on trust for granddaughter Ena Edith Tanner when she became 21.

The residue of the estate went to Walter Richard Tanner.

When probate was granted in 1937 his estate was valued at a gross figure of £6156:17s:2d and estate duty was paid of £224:8s:5d.

Not bad for a man who lost his mother at birth, nearly lost his ability to work due to an injury, and started as only an employee of a builder before taking over the business for himself.

*****

William Richard Tanner married Emma Jane Combes in 1884, and had three children. The eldest was William Herbert Tanner, known as Bert, while my grandfather was the second son Walter Richard Tanner, known as Wally.

Aunt Olive remembered that *"Bert was born in 1886, & Father in 1887. Father went to Stamshaw School, & later to the Boys' Secondary (in those days it was called the 'Higher Grade') & from its special Dockyard class passed the exam for the Dockyard, & was apprenticed as a shipwright. Uncle Bert also went to work in the Dockyard."*

Uncle Bert – William Herbert Tanner – was actually born in 1885, and in 1914 married a Caroline Edith Berry (born 1886). Unfortunately he died in 1917 leaving a single daughter Ena Edith – known as Neen (or Nene or Nean) – born in 1915. Neen would marry Clive Sansom in 1940 and have 2 children (John and Gillian) and grandchildren and great-grandchildren.

However William Herbert and Walter Richard were not the only siblings in the family – as Olive sadly remembers.

"Not long before the war my Father showed us a tiny grave in a corner of Kingston Cemetery. He said that it was his little sister's grave. I did once ask Grandma about it. She said "They told me it was a girl, but I was too ill to know anything," so this babe died at, or soon after birth. After the war, these children's graves were no longer marked. All that corner had altered. I wonder if a bomb fell there!!"

My brother Richard thought that Olive might have meant that the baby girl was buried at Milton Cemetery, which is where other family members were buried, and he records that the little girl was named Nellie – another tragedy for that name. Milton Cemetery has memorials particularly to remember all the children buried in unmarked graves within Portsmouth cemeteries.

It is close to the grave of Maurice and Marjorie.

Beyond doubt little Nellie Tanner is far from the only relative of mine commemorated by that memorial – 4 Siblings of Emma Jane Combes died young for a start – infant mortality rates were so high.

Olive's other memories about her Tanner and Combes and Jennings ancestry are as follows: -

"Grandma's sister, (my aunt does not say which sister), who had been in Plymouth, returned to Portsmouth & we met her once in North End. She must have been in the sixties, & was so like Grandma, though a younger edition. Then there was great, great Uncle George - Jennings - Grandma's Uncle. He, & Aunt Maria, lived in Nelson Road, a road somewhere between All Saints Church, & Kingston Crescent - I wonder if it is now demolished? At least the church is still there.

"Uncle George had a beard & a rheumy eye. We went to tea at Nelson Road once, when I was about 6, I suppose it must have been. I remember thinking what a little house it was, & one could hear the people next door."

Jane Jennings was Emma Jane Combes' mother and born in 1845. Her siblings were called William (born 1850), George (1852), Richard (1854), Thomas (1856), and Ellen (1858). Maria was George's wife.

"Occasionally, until he got too old, Uncle George would go to the football match, & call in on his way, so he could go with Dad & Grandpa. When asked how Aunt Maria was he gave the same answer always "Very poorly, very poorly." Years later I heard that he had died & she was still living."

Wally and Ethel Tanner lived in Alverstone Road, which was about a minute's walk away from Fratton Park – the home of Portsmouth Football Club - so Uncle George calling in on the way there was very natural.

I will return to the Tanner family later, but it is time to move on to the Hale and Cripps families from whom came my maternal grandmother.

William Richard Tanner & his beloved dog

Emma Jane Tanner fishing - probably at Hayling Island

Caroline Edith Tanner & her daughter Ena Edith
(Marjorie's cousin Nene)

Wally & Ethel Tanner with Olive & Marjorie

CHAPTER THREE

Hales & Cripps

According to my Aunt Olive, my great-grandfather Athwell Matthew Hale was known as "At" to his friends, while a book given to him by his aunt said "to Attwell", but in the Navy his fellow sailors called him "John" because they found 'Athwell' difficult to pronounce. It seems to be an old Hale family name because the family trees researched by my brother Richard record that Athwell Matthew's father was called either 'Athwell' or 'Hathwell', and Athwell Matthew's grandfather is recorded as 'Hathwell'.

An internet search found 'Atwell' as a boy's Christian name of Anglo-Saxon origin meaning 'lives by a spring', and Hathwell only as a surname. Maybe the use of the name in the Hale family goes back further than my brother has been able to trace, but returning to known family history I once again quote the memories of my mother and aunt and the genealogical researches of my brother.

Firstly my Aunt Olive: -

"My grandfather was the eldest of 16."

I only know the names of 7 of his siblings: Maria (born 1853) James (1857) Alice (1859) Jane (1861) Emily (1863) John (1865) and Eliza (1867).

"The 4 youngest did not survive. - Of the others, one of his sisters, & her family went to Canada, as did another brother. Of the others, Alice married a printer, George Humby, who lived & worked in Church Road, Kingston.

"During or just after the war we met Hilda, a cousin of my mother, and her mother Alice who was approaching ninety and living with Hilda

at North End: & so I saw this great aunt for the first time, & heard that the aunt at Canada was still there & living somewhere near to Niagara Falls.

"Hilda's daughter's husband had been a prisoner of war - in Italy, I think. He was one of the first to return, but as far as I gathered was ill, & suffered emotionally from the effects of the war."

Alice would have been 90 in 1949. She and George Humby had at least seven children and Hilda's married name was Green. I do not know Hilda's daughter's name or who she married.

Athwell Matthew Hale was born in 1852. His future wife Sarah Ann Cripps was born either in 1852 or 1854. A family tree from my brother says 1852 and he has found records of two Sarah Cripps being born – one in 1851 and the other in 1852 rather than 1854. Their parents married on 7th July 1945 as James Cripps and Mary Ann Springle. James Cripps was son of chairmaker Joseph Cripps and his wife Sarah, while Mary Ann was the daughter of a sweep named James Springle and a Caroline Williams.

The first Sarah was born on 27th March 1851, though the census of 1851 records the newborn baby girl as Harriett, but when her birth was registered on 28th April it had become Sarah - but this Sarah died on 21st September 1851.

Now we contemplate the mysteries surrounding the second Sarah – born Sarah Ann Cripps and becoming Sarah Ann Hale.

Olive thought Sarah Ann Cripps was born in 1854, and apparently Sarah herself believed that her birthday was in July 1854 but when Old Age Pensions were first made payable to people over 70 and she applied she was told that her birthday was in April. She worried thereafter that they might discover that they had made a mistake and ask her to repay the extra money. To complicate the mystery more, Richard traced a birth certificate for a Sarah Cripps born on 6th July 1852 – so unless Sarah Ann Cripps was a third Sarah in the family and both previous Sarahs died I do not see how Sarah Ann could have been born in 1854 - which leaves me to wonder whether her deprived and orphaned upbringing might have meant that she grew up misinformed about her real age? Could that have been possible? Yes - according to Olive's next line.

"It seems that my grandmother's parents died when she was young,

& she was brought up by relations who had several children. It could not be afforded to send the children, she told me, to a 'dame's school' - no 'board' schools till 1871, though St Luke's opened as a church school in, I think, 1865. Grandma was born, as far as she knew, about 1854. In later years she, with the help of her husband, taught herself to read."

My great grandmother was an unschooled orphan who married before she had learnt to read. Maybe the relations were also illiterate and unable to record her date of birth. That is just three generations back, and yet her granddaughters – my mother and aunt – both became teachers – my mother even taught at St Luke's, which was a comprehensive when my mother taught there but had been a Church of England school – though according to a commemoration mug that my mother acquired St Luke's actually opened in 1864 not 1865.

Among family papers was a cutting from a newspaper of a letter saying that the school known as St Luke's was started by a Mrs Esther Taylor as a school for poor children, and she became the first headmistress of St Luke's - the writer said that she was Mrs Taylor's granddaughter. According to the Portsmouth History Centre there were two separate schools for boys and girls from at least 1946 until it became co-educational again in 1975 when it became a comprehensive. Recently it has become a highly regarded Charter Academy.

It may be pure coincidence but there was a Mrs Esther Taylor born in 1827 as Esther Ann Buckland who in 1858 married a William Michael Taylor who had a sister named Emma Jane Taylor while Athwell Matthew Hale's mother was born as Emma Jane Taylor before marrying his father Athwell Hale in 1850.

The 'board' schools to which my aunt refers originated from an Education Act in 1870, and were built in cities throughout Britain until elementary education was taken over by local councils in 1903. The 1870 Act made elementary education compulsory, provided by locally elected school boards & paid from local taxation. They were known as 'Board Schools' and intended to cater for children from deprived areas so making education universal.

The fact that Sarah Ann Cripps could not go to school emphasizes both the poverty of her upbringing and the reason why Board Schools were created. It symbolises the many ways in which the Victorians produced enormous changes in the way of improving the lot of the poor – not only by government action but also by charitable activities. Many great charities were founded during the reign of Queen Victoria. I remember reading that, whereas once orphaned or homeless children living on the streets were commonplace, by the end of the century they had virtually disappeared, chiefly by the efforts of charities like Barnardo's and the NSPCC. Many Acts of Parliament were passed to improve conditions for workers in many industries. 'Victorian Values' in action.

Resuming my Aunt's memories of Grandma Hale: "*I don't know at what age she went to work, but she worked at Love's butcher's shop in Albert Road, & at a house on Yarborough Road for two maiden ladies of the name of Brothers.*"

As far as I know Sarah Ann Cripps had four siblings (including the other Sarah) of whom two were older. Sarah Ann Cripps married Athwell Matthew Hale on 10th June 1877. The groom gave his profession as an Engine Room Artificer in the Royal Navy – and his father's employment as a boiler maker and carpenter.

Athwell and Sarah had four children in the next ten years - all girls – spaced out more than many families in this history, probably due to Athwell being away at sea. As far as I know they had no infant deaths, so considering Sarah's family history could consider themselves fortunate – unless you were wanting a son.

Returning to my Aunt Olive's memories: -

"*My grandmother married & had 4 children - all girls. Her husband, my grandfather, was a boilermaker in the Dockyard when she first knew him. It seems, as I have been told, that a contribution would be taken from pay to fund pensions - so he & his friend, Mr Bull, went into the Navy. Grandma told me that she threatened to have no more to do with him if he was in the Navy, but he went - & they married. I think he was an E.R.A., engine room artificer.*

"*Grandma never said anything about her parents. I don't think she can have remembered them much as she was quite young when orphaned.*"

At this point I can add some memories from my mother Marjorie – again about Grandma Hale

"Grandma had not had an easy life. She was in service, at an early age, to a lady living in a road off Kings Rd, Portsmouth. She met Athwell Matthew Hale, who was in the Navy. They married & went to live in Milford Rd. They had 4 daughters who became - to me - Aunt Nell, Aunt Min, Aunt Lil, & my mother, in that order. Men in the Navy often had much longer periods away than nowadays. Apparently he arrived home to find my mother had been born, & apparently cursed. "Not another girl!"

"He insisted that this one would be called SARAH, after her mother. So she was called SARAH ETHEL. Apparently Gran did not like her name, & Mum was always known as ETHEL."

As to why Sarah Ann Cripps might not have liked her name, my brother's genealogical researches produced the following interesting previous usage of the name Sarah in the Cripps family.

Firstly the Sarah Cripps who became Grandma Hale, whether born in 1852 or 1854 would surely have known her father James Cripps' mother – another Sarah Cripps who died in 1870.

Secondly, there was the previous Sarah Cripps who was born in 1851 and died at six months old of whooping cough and pneumonia.

Thirdly, the record shows that there was another Sarah Cripps, daughter of James' younger brother George – and this Sarah Cripps was born and died in 1864, so the future Grandma Hale would surely have known about her, too.

Did these three deaths contribute to the future Grandma Hale's dislike of the name Sarah? Did she not like her grandmother Sarah? For the record, her mother Mary died in 1858 and her father James in 1861, so she was orphaned before her tenth birthday and motherless before her seventh birthday.

The death certificates for both parents give the cause of death as phthisis – meaning tuberculosis – then a major killer among the urban poor.

I do not know which relations brought her up, but James was the fifth out of ten siblings whose names I know about – in order of birth, Grace, Thomas, Joseph, John, James, Betsey, George, Mary, Ann, Henry. Of them Grace and Henry had four children each, and John nine – so any would fit the criteria Olive mentioned for the relatives who took Sarah into their home – not for long, I surmise, if she went into service at an early age. If it was Grace, she also had a daughter named Sarah, born in 1840 – not Sarah Cripps but Sarah Smith.

I seem to have diverted from the Hales to the Cripps, so might as well complete the information I have about them – mostly Olive's memories – though the family tree records Sarah Cripps as having an elder brother named James Edward, an elder sister called Mary Ann, and a younger sister named Harriett.

"Quite recently, my nephew Richard, who is quite interested in tracing ancestry, thinks that they, the Cripps, were chairmakers & lived in Landport, in the area of Telegraph St - near St Luke's Church area." The death certificate for baby Sarah confirms that her father James Cripps was a Chairmaker by profession in 1851 and his death certificate cites him as a master Chairmaker when he died in 1861.

"It seems that there was a brother who, for a while, continued as a chairmaker," (presumably James Edward) *"& there had been a daughter, Sarah, who died. Grandma was then named Sarah, but she hated the name, I know. Years later, it seems, she was visiting Love's during the census, & was called Susan."*

My brother Richard noted that the brother did not remain a chairmaker after his father died – or not for long – but instead became a sweep like his mother's father by 1871, and married a woman named Ann in 1875.

"I remember her sister Harriet vaguely, but she died when I was about 4 years old." (1919 according to the family tree - Olive was born in 1915.) *"I don't know how I know, but I had some idea that she married a grocer, who came from Devon. It seems this is right - she was his second wife. The shop was, it seems, in Commercial Rd, & they lived in Crescent Lodge, a house I remember - on the corner of Twyford Ave & Kingston Crescent - now gone.*

"Grandma sometimes mentioned when she was at Plymouth. I presumed that her husband was sometimes there, but was she visiting her sister?

"Harriet's husband, Uncle Gil as Mum called him, was of course older than she was - the family was Bob, Bert, Ada, May, & Gert. I met Bert the tailor once, I think, & remember May, but mostly knew Ada, & Gert."

"Uncle Gil" was Gilbert Gibbs, who had a first wife named Eliza and a daughter named Mary by that first marriage. Apparently he was born in 1825 and his second wife in 1855 so older is an understatement. Mary was also born in 1855 so acquired a stepmother her own age.

With Harriett, 'Uncle Gil' had children Lily, Sidney, Ada, Gilbert (Bert), Robert (Bob), May, and Gertrude (Gert), and Gert was about the same age as my grandmother Ethel Hale who was born in 1887 when 'Uncle Gil' was 62. Olive not remembering Lily and Sidney suggests that maybe they also died young. Mary might have married and moved away.

While Sarah Ann Cripps was fortunate that none of her four daughters died as children their survival might well be due to the development of Portsmouth's sewage system. Sewage systems were epic achievements of Victorian engineering. According to www. localhistories.org Portsmouth took over its water supply in 1858, built its first sewers between 1865 and 1870, and opened its first sewage pumping station in 1868. In 1875 a byelaw required that all houses within a hundred feet of a main sewer had to be connected to it. Such Victorian enterprises were massive lifesavers in cities like Portsmouth.

Returning to Olive's memories of her mother's relatives: -

"After retiring from business, Gilbert the father was a moneylender, according to Mum - "Financial agent" in the local directory of the times. Bob carried on the business.

"His daughter, Norah, a nursery school teacher, later trained as school teacher, taught at Petersfield, where her parents retired to. I met Norah for the first time after her parents' death.

"Bert lost his two sons - one was in the war, I think. Ada married an older man - there was one daughter, Doris. When Grandpa was building in Milton, so was a Mr Rogers. Doris married a Mr Rogers, a builder at Portchester - I think he must have been a son."

Bert's two sons were named George and Bobby, and Ada's married name was Powell.

"May's husband retired from the Merchant Service, & they kept a shop that I remember visiting, in New Rd."

May married an Ernie Summerfield.

"Gert married the son of an official at the gas works - there were two daughters, & a son. My first memory of Gert was when she used to cycle

down to Milton to visit Mum, & I remember visiting her at Crescent Lodge. Mother & Gert were about the same age, & were much together till Gert's marriage, at 18."

Gert married a Jack Ashworth, and bore children Lily, Winnie, and Jack.

"I remember being taken to see Aunt Harriet when she was ill in bed - standing with Mum & Gran holding my hands, & I fidgeting, wanting to get to play with Gert's children. Later we went again, Gert & family were still there, There was a front garden, with a tiny little hut, a round one, on the Kingston Crescent side, a little glass porch with plants in front of the door, & the garden at the back was on two levels.

"We children chased each other up & down the slope, along the paths, climbed into the kitchen through the window, out the door, & along the lower path. There was a square hut with a bit of furniture, & a gramophone at the far end. I've been told there was a stable, & a harness room, but I didn't see it. There had once been a trap & a pony.

"Later, the house was sold - I think to the Town Corporation, who demolished most of it to widen the road. Just the stable remained - that till all the recent changes.

"Jack Ashworth, Gert's husband, decided to go to America - they had moved to Inhurst Road. This house was sold - some furniture sold. We took Aunt's mahogany dining table, & a fender. Jack Ashworth went on ahead to get settled in, & the family moved to lodgings at Southampton - all packed ready to set forth when he was ready for them. We visited them once. I remember where it was, & have since seen that the area is now a car park.

"Then, for some reason - I never really heard why, all plans were cancelled - & Jack returned. Later he got a job at gasworks in Blackburn, & we rarely saw them, till his retirement after the war."

I remember Winnie Ashworth as a friend of Olive - as their mothers had been friends, but I was unaware that Winnie was a relative. I am awestruck that my aunt could, in her nineties, dredge up so many memories of her extended family while I rarely remember the names of former co-workers when I meet them in the street. My mother had a similar problem, but an excuse that she was active in voluntary work including working on and even chairing committees, so many people would know her by sight while they would merely have been one among many to her.

My mother used to joke that she had more of a problem with such people when they mistook her for her elder sister!

Returning to the Hales - Olive remembered more about her maternal grandmother's relatives than her maternal grandfather's relatives, no doubt due to her widowed maternal grandmother living with them for so long.

"On the Hale side of the family, my grandfather. I only met, as far as I know, Mum's Aunt Eliza, & her husband Alfred - & Alma, one of her daughters. One May Day I was taken to Victoria Park, to see Alma crowned as the May Queen, but a sudden shower & clap of thunder sent us rushing to shelter & I missed the ceremony. Later after the war (WW2) we met Alma again, & renewed contact that had been lost for several years."

Eliza Ann Hale was the youngest of Athwell Matthew Hale's sisters that I know about, and she married an Alfred Ray. Other than that, I can offer nothing about this side of the family, so return to the primary storyline of this chapter – the marriage between Athwell Matthew Hale and Sarah Ann Cripps.

They had been prospering, bought their own house, while Athwell had earned a Royal Naval Long Service Good Conduct Medal – which was sold on e-bay in 2010, as I chanced to discover during an internet search. Maybe it was sold for desperately needed cash after Athwell's death – about which I return to Olive's memories.

"Again, I think of how people can have the tough side of life. Grandma was happily married with 4 children, between 5 & 12 years old, & she & her husband were settled in their own house which they had seen being built while they were in rooms with a Mrs Henley in Carlisle Road, Fratton. Grandpa was on the HMS Marathon, & wrote saying that men were dying of cholera. Luckily he did not catch it, but next year the Marathon was again in Bombay when he died. His friend Mr Bull, who was on a different ship, went to see why the flag on Marathon was at half mast, & found it was his friend.

"It was six weeks later when the news came to Grandma. She had drawn her money in those weeks, & had to pay it back."

I assume that Athwell Matthew Hale arranged for some of his pay to be paid to his family while he was abroad, and that she had to pay it back because his entitlement to pay stopped when he died and it would have taken six weeks for the news of his death to reach home so she would have had to pay that money back – on top of the news that her husband was dead and her source of income terminated – and, as Olive remembered it, the bad news did not stop there.

"She had a family, a house, & no income or social security. This was 1892. Because Grandpa Hale had died intestate, his house could not be sold until the youngest child was 21 yrs old."

Said youngest child being my five year old future grandmother.

"As far as my mother knew, there was no money from the Navy. Grandma let two rooms, & also took in one or two assistants from Oliver's boot shop when they came to Portsmouth branches of the firm. She even took in laundering for people. Minnie & Lillie, aged about 10 & 7, were taken by the Naval Orphanage which was in St Michael's Road. I've been told by Mum that Gran worried so about them - would go & stand outside the building to hear the children playing, to hope that they were happy there."

My great grandmother endured that – just three generations ago.

"Nell, at 12, went to work, half-time, at dressmaking - later doing her dressmaking at home, or at people's houses."

My grandmother's sister had to go to work at 12 years old – just two generations ago.

In *"Memories from Ninety Years"* the following memories were added by my mother Marjorie.

"When Mum was very small, & I've imagined not much more than 2, their father died. The ships were in some port abroad, & there was some pestilence. Mr Bull, from another ship, went on Mr Hale's ship, to ask him who had died this time, & found to his horror that it was his friend. When the ships returned to England, he came to Gran, & told her this. He also offered to marry her, & help look after the family. However, Gran refused. Now she had to earn money herself.

"Mr Tribe, a neighbour & a schoolmaster, gave her some advice, & financial grants were sent as today. Nell, about 12 then I believe, was sent to help a lady dressmaker who lived near the seafront at Southsea. Min & Lil were put in the naval orphanage. Mum was considered too young so

kept at home. Gran let 2 bedrooms to lodgers, & fed them. It seems they were usually young men who worked at Oliver's shoe shop. This obviously meant that Gran, Nell, & Mum lived in one bedroom."

A discrepancy here – Olive remembers 'no money from the Navy' but Marjorie remembers 'financial grants'. Whatever the case there was definitely a severe shortage of money, as Marjorie continues to describe.

"My sister, who stayed with Mum & Dad when I moved on my marriage, heard more of the matter than I did. Apparently Mum had the cot end opened so it could be extended to make her a bed. Mum said the men were given bacon & egg for breakfast. She had bread soaked in the fat in which it was fried."

That is disturbingly reminiscent of her future husband being given the bone to suck if his father had a bit of fish.

"When she was older at school she had to pay some proficiency test to be allowed to leave school early. She then went to a tailor. She used to have to take heavy naval officer's uniforms across on the ferry to Gosport. Any rate she learnt the trade. On the Jewish Sabbath she had to go in & get food for him as he was apparently not allowed, by his faith, to do it."

I remember my grandmother living in her semi-detached house on the slopes of Portsdown Hill on the northern edge of the city of Portsmouth – and had no idea that her childhood had been so hard – especially not as hard as shown in my mother's next memory.

"At one time I was told Mother became so anaemic that she had a job to climb the stairs. Nell's employer heard this, & took her for a week in her house to help her. She would make Mum walk along the front, first thing in the morning, so she would come in with an appetite for a good breakfast. I think that lady must have been very kind."

I regret not knowing the name of that kind dressmaker who possibly saved my grandmother's life – the young died easily of disease back then if they were weakened. Olive is right in remembering that her mother was about 5 when Athwell Matthew Hale died, rather than 2 as Marjorie remembered. Maybe just as well as Ethel was really petite – did lack of early nutrition contribute to that?

I do not know much about Ethel Hale's childhood, but I do know that she won some prizes. One was from the Sunday School

Union in 1894, when she was 6 or 7, for *'committing to memory the infant catechism'*. It was a small book entitled *Faithful Rigmor and her Grandmother*. All I have is a cover with no author name, so I know no more about it.

The second was a more substantial prize awarded to her in June 1898 as a Reward for Attendance at Circus C.E. School. The only Circus school I found during an internet search was a Sunday School for the 'Circus Church' – originally set up in the 1850's in a large tent to preach to all, without a collection, before moving to a permanent building in Surrey Street in 1864. I sourced this information from historyinportsmouth.co.uk.

The actual prize was edition XXIII of the *Sunday Friend*. I have no separate information on it other than that it was published by the Sunday Friend Publishing Company of Leadenhall St.

It is an impressive prize for an impoverished ten-year old. It is one hundred and eighty-eight pages long – full of stories and articles, poems, pictures and anecdotes – and though naturally religious in content many of the stories and articles are clearly not overly-sanitised. A random skim through found this among a list of what appeared to be letters or articles from readers: - entitled – *Is it possible?* contributed by a Gertrude Dey.

"A little girl, suffering from diphtheria, was brought to a London Hospital. To save her life, a little silver tube was inserted in her throat, through which to breathe. The child improved rapidly, and the mother begged very hard to take her home. The physician gave permission, but before the day was over, resolved to visit the home next morning. He found the child dead, and the neighbours informed him that the mother had pawned the tube for eighteen pence, and was out spending the money on drink."

Is it possible? Sadly, it was – and more sadly it still is, though such a mother today would more likely be buying drugs than drink. But on second reading it does not specify that the child did not die before the mother removed the tube. And not all stories are like that. The article above it, contributed by a Grace King, is entitled *A Sheet of White Paper*.

"A schoolmaster once said of a certain boy that he had never known a boy do less work in more time. Was it the same boy, we wonder, who,

when the "Result of Idleness" was given as the subject of an essay, handed to the master a clean sheet of white paper?"

Humour among the serious stuff. 188 pages. An impressive prize for a poor child. There is no price shown so it was probably paid for by the advertising – for cocoa and fountain pens.

Coincidentally, her future husband Walter Tanner would also win prizes. The first was in November 1895 from the Portsmouth School Board and for Good Attendance, Conduct, and School Work – in his case a book called *A Blind Pupil* by *Annie S Fenn,* published in 1886. In November 1897 Walter would get another prize from the same source for the same reasons – *Tales of the Coastguard & Other Stories,* a collection of short stories with no quoted authors published by W&R Chambers, with some stories recorded as written in 1849 including one entitled *Confessions of a Bashful Miss* which includes what I thought was a quotation from Abraham Lincoln. *"It is better," answered I, "to be mistaken for a fool, than to open my mouth and prove myself one."*

In 1901 a third prize from the same source for the same reason was *In Savage Africa* by Verney Lovett Cameron, a Commander in the Royal Navy, subtitled *The Adventures of Frank Baldwin from the Gold Coast to Zanzibar.* According to Wikipedia Verney Lovett Cameron was an English Explorer in Central Africa. After time in the Royal Navy, including involvement in the suppression of the East African Slave Trade, he was selected in 1873 by the Royal Geographical Society to lead an expedition to assist Dr Livingstone, but when they found Dr Livingstone he was already dead.

Returning to Ethel, another book given to her on Jan 1st 1899 by persons unknown as *a reward for neat writing* was called *Moffatt's Explanatory Readers Book 4* – a series of books from Victorian times full of short stories written to encourage older children to read.

At Christmas 1906 Ethel was given *The Master of Greylands* by Mrs Henry Wood – an internationally bestselling Victorian novelist best known for the novel *East Lynne.* This was a Christmas present from 'Gertie' – presumably cousin and close friend Gertrude Gibbs.

The family also retained two prizes won by Nell, Ethel's eldest sister, under her actual name of Ellen Hale. The first was from the Wesley Chapel Sunday School as *a Reward for Regular Attendance,*

Good Conduct, and Attention to Study, for 1889. It was *Ivy, a Tale of Cottage Life*, by Silas K Hocking, a Methodist Preacher from Cornwall whose writing career spanned 50 years, with Ivy being published in 1881. The second was from the Wesley Sunday School, Landport as a *First Class Prize* for the year 1893. It was *Twenty Minutes Late* by 'Pansy' meaning Isabella M Alden – a prolific American author of Christian books and Sunday School books.

I have no direct knowledge as to how well Min and Lil fared in the Naval Orphanage. I once read a newspaper interview with a lady who was sent there after her father died in the Battle of Jutland in 1916. She said that children from a nearby school which they attended used to taunt them for being orphans, but local sailors and soldiers were very generous to them.

I remember 'Aunt Min' better than 'Aunt Lil' (due to Aunt Min living nearer), and Aunt Min seemed very confident and forthright so I do not suppose that her experiences in the orphanage could have been that terrible.

The closest I could find in Aunt Olive's memories is the following – the home asked Min to go into teaching but she chose otherwise.

"Min & Lil went into service. Min was taller and thinner & got taken to serve at table etc. Aunt Lil was envious – being dumpy, she was put to work in the kitchen.

"At 16, Min was asked by the home to go into teaching, but she wanted to get out into the world. She got into good service in the Knightsbridge area & later worked for the Wares. This was Fabian, later Sir Fabian Ware - who, if I remember rightly, used in the earlier days of broadcasting to speak on Armistice days - I think, not sure, about the War Graves."

Sir Fabian Ware (1869-1949) was the founder of the Imperial War Graves Commission, now called the Commonwealth War Graves Commission.

Interesting that Min considered going into service to mean 'getting out into the world' rather than going into teaching, as both Ethel's daughters would become schoolteachers, but maybe the Orphanage meant teaching at the home rather than outside schools. I read a small book entitled *The Reminiscences of a Portsmouth Dockyard Shipwright 1901-1945* by Edward Lane, who was made by his parents to leave school directly at the age of 14 after passing the Dockyard exam – to his great regret as he would have liked to stay on at school for at least another year. According to Edward Lane *"For working class people, in Portsmouth the great achievement was passing the Dockyard Examination."* He added that if boys failed, *"fathers would say the only thing left for you,"* was *"to become a teacher".*

Teaching clearly lacked prestige as a profession in those days, and both Walter Tanner and his brother would go into the Dockyard as shipwrights.

"Lil also went into service, working for a Town Councillor, I think, Councillor Allen."

An interesting parallel to Ada Hollingdale also being in service before her marriage. No great coincidence – a significant proportion of the female population would have found employment as servants.

Time to return to the Burwood family – and the marriage of Will Burwood and Ada Hollingdale.

Athwell Matthew Hale

The Hale sisters - Nell (Ellen Alice) in the middle holding Ethel (Sarah Ethel) with Min (Minnie Gertrude) on her right & Lil (Lily Maria) in front of Ethel

Athwell Matthew Hale's sister Eliza Ann with her
husband Alfred Ray & 4 children - probably
Alma, Alfred, Elsie & Harold plus an older man

CHAPTER FOUR

Will & Ada

Will and Ada married on 3rd September 1900 - Will having ended his Naval career in May.

Ada's father attended the wedding, but her mother Clara had died in childbirth in 1895. Will's mother also died in 1895, and his father had died in 1888.

Will's father had an interesting life himself. When born at Emsworth on 4th December 1841 his birth certificate gave his name as William Burward, son of grocer John Burward – probably a clerk wrote the name down according to how it sounded – hinting at the accent of John 'Burward'. Shortly before his 16th birthday William was apprenticed by the East India Company to the Marine Society. According to the British Library website the Marine Society apprenticed over 25000 boys to merchant vessels between 1772 and 1873 and the East India Company was the biggest employer for the Marine Society.

As a result William received this certificate in 1865:

MARINE SOCIETY
BISHOPSGATE STREET, LONDON
This certificate testifies that William Burwood was apprenticed by this Society on 7th October 1857 to the Hon'ble the East India Company and having faithfully served his Apprenticeship, has been rewarded with the Medal of this Society for Good Conduct.
Signed _____
Chairman
Dated 25th February 1865

William spent two more years on merchant ships before returning to England in 1867 to marry his first cousin Hannah Burwood. Will was their first born son, but Hannah already had a daughter Annie born in 1865 with no father named on the birth certificate, but Annie's middle name being 'Williams' suggests that William Burwood was the biological father and he entered himself as father on Annie's marriage certificate (calling himself William John). William Burwood gave his profession as mariner when marrying in December 1867, but thereafter worked at a public swimming baths in Brighton as a bath attendant and swimming master before dying of pneumonia in 1888. Family legend claims that he taught Winston Churchill to swim, but I cannot prove that. However, Winston Churchill did attend Brunswick School at Hove in Brighton before going to Harrow in 1888 and he did learn swimming while at that school.

If so, William was only the first of three generations of the Burwood family to come into some proximity to Winston Churchill, because Churchill was among the troops taking part in the relief of Ladysmith, and Will's son Eric would work in Churchill's Cabinet War Rooms during the Second World War. Olive Tanner, incidentally, would in 1950 find herself on the same passenger ship as Winston Churchill while sailing from Southampton to Madeira.

According to www.burwoodpark.co.uk there are mentions of a manor called Burwood in Surrey dating back to the eleventh century, but that may be unconnected. My brother and his contacts have found references to Burwoods or Burwards in Woodbridge in Suffolk in 1524, and Southwold in Suffolk in 1672, while family legend is that the family came from the Lowestoft area, where numerous Burwoods still live. However, the earliest definite ancestry identified by my brother is a William Burward who lived in Hermitage in Sussex in 1814. He lived from 1787 to 1829, married Elizabeth Giles in 1811, and among his sons were William and John, who *both* became grandfathers of Will Burwood.

While official records showed inconsistencies in spelling the surname Burwood, with both Burward and Burword appearing, what is consistent is the name William. Will's great-grandfather was also called William, who had two sons John and William – and John's son William married William's daughter Hannah and my grandfather Will was their son – Will's parents were first cousins. Will's first born was christened William Eric but always called Eric, and Eric's first born was also christened William but always called Bill so at least six successive generations of the Burwood family had a William Burwood, and in the last five generations William was the eldest son.

Interestingly, the name William also passed down generations in the Tanner Family – as did association with the Navy or its Dockyard or the sea. Hannah's father William spent most of his working life as a coastguard, and Will, of course, joined the navy.

This letter is specifically about the wedding of Will and Ada - written by Ada's father, Richard Hollingdale, a journeyman carpenter by profession:

9/15/1900 9 Richmond Hill
Brighton

Sussex

Dear son & daughter, just a line to let you know we are all right. Thank you very much for the nice way you managed everything on your Wedding Day. It was a real treat and we have seen the proof of the photos. I think they are very good indeed. Everyone has come out lovely and I hoped you will like them it will make a nice picture.

Edie & Alf went to enquire about them & they gave the proof to them already packed and directed so we saw them before you. Edie posted them last night (Friday) it had to go by Parcels Post they would not take by letter or book post, hope you have received it all right. Am sending you the Southern Weekly News to let you know about Brighton affairs – its old news to us but will be fresh to you - it's the weeks news & the best to send away, I think.

Am very glad to hear you are so happy there is no reason why you should not be as happy as doves with a bright future before you & you should be happy. I could not come to the station when you went to London. My mate was away on his holiday and one of us had to be there. I should very much have liked to come but could not.

Had a funny adventure after I left you at the station - in the Queens Road pulling out my pocket handkerchief a cloud of confetti flew all over the place and there was a roar of laughter – in which I had to laugh too. One lady says there's a giddy old kipper what are you going to treat us too but it was a good tempered crowd & is seen. Dodged them and went off & had a decent smoke & a walk & enjoyed myself. I will now conclude with best love from

Dad

For Ada xxxxxxx
PS should have come on platform with you but I thought your sister Nellie had left a parcel at our house & I had the latch key but it was your sister Edie's parcel not Nellie's so it was all right with love from Dad
Good night
God bless you
The kids have gone blackberrying.

Richard Hollingdale was born in 1843, married twice, and had children by both wives. The first wife was Elizabeth Foice (1841-1870) whom he married in 1863 and by whom he had three children – James Richard (1863-1946), William Walter (1864-1894) and Emily Elizabeth (1865-1870). Poor Emily died in the same year as her mother. Possibly the same disease?

Richard's parents were another Richard Hollingdale (born 1816) and a Harriet Pannett (born 1817) who married in 1838 and had nine other children that I know about. Eliza (1838-1876), Walter (born 1839), Lucy Jane (born 1841, married name Thomas), William (1846-1846), William Jesse (1847-1849), Ellen (1849-1920, married name Stepney and known as Nell), Harriett (born 1851, married name Jones), Emily Maria (1853-1923), and Edwin (1836-1932).

I assume that Richard's sister Emily was the Aunt Emily who gave Ada a Bible as a 12th birthday present on 18th January 1888.

Richard's second marriage was in 1872 to Ada's mother Clara Marchant (1853-1895) by whom he had children Clara in 1872, Ada Alice in 1874, and Edith Annie in 1878, but Ada's mother died in childbirth in 1895, along with the child.

Returning to the letter, Ada's younger full sister Edith or Edie married Alf Tyler in 1903. I assume the Nellie mentioned is Richard Hollingdale's sister rather than Will's sister. The Edie he mentioned in his letter was probably his own daughter, but Will also had a sister Edith or Edie – not only plenty of Williams but plenty of Ediths around.

This touching little poem was written even earlier by a friend of Ada's. I know nothing more about the friend than her name – not even her full address.

To Miss A Hollingdale on her Wedding-day Sept[br] 3rd 1900
Let not any friend though now a Bride bid all her cares Adieu
Pleasures there are in married life but there are crosses too.
The one that's lately claimed your hand cannot induce content,
Religion forms the strongest bonds, but love the best intent
I do not wish to mar your mirth with an ungrateful sound
But yet remember Bliss on Earth no mortal ever found.
Your prospects and your hopes are great
May God them all fulfil;
But you will find in every state some difficulties still.
No anger or resentment keep, whatever is amiss.
Be reconciled before you sleep and seal it with a kiss,
Since you must both resign your breath and only God knows when
To live that you may part in Death with joy to meet again.
With best wishes from your sincere friend

S Earwicker
_____ Street
Brighton

This next letter was written to Ada by her father written a few months later.

Jan 16th 01 9 Richmond Hill
Brighton

Sussex

Dear Ada just a line wishing you many happy returns of your birthday. Hoping you may have a hundred and we all live to witness it have sent you a small order to buy a little present for your birthday – thought you would know best what to buy. Hope you and Will are quite well & Warwick also.

Dear Will your kind letter tells me exactly where your place is tell Ada I am going to take a snap shot with my camera so she must look out & see the land rises very fast as you go inland rising to over two thousand feet in a very short distance it looks very mountainous.

Hard work for your going to your work this dark mornings it don't get light so early where you are but you get it at night you are a little west of Longitude. But I say what about the coal the middle men are having fine games with us rose coal 5^s/- a ton last week this week they have lowered it 2^s/- a ton. Happened to buy ours the week before it rose so that was lucky. My mate bought his coal last week when they had rose now he is savage he did not wait longer years ago coals were very much dearer than they are now I remember one winter they were much higher.

Hope your Ada & Warwick are getting on alright & comfortable. We shall soon get longer days & better weather. Have started work earlier myself this week so that is better hope now we shall be able to keep it up & must now conclude with best love & good wishes

From Dad

P.S. Look out for my snap shot is my hat on straight.

The marriage was in Brighton, but Will gave his parish of residence as Abersychan in Monmouth and his occupation as electrician. Following their marriage Will and Ada did not waste any time in acquiring two sons. Their first son Eric was born on 23rd May 1901 – 11 days less than 9 months after the wedding. His birth was registered at Pontypridd.

Their second son Maurice, my father, was born on 6th November 1902 at Talywain in Monmouth - technically in Wales, but Ada was adamant that her sons were English, not Welsh. Will had obtained employment in the mining industry – as an electrician according to his marriage certificate. The above letter confirms that Will's brother Warwick was living with or near Will and Ada, though the first address I know of for Warwick was Phillip Street in Pontypridd when Warwick was married on 3rd September 1906 – 6 years to the day after Will's marriage - to Harriett Louisa Hamer, known as 'Lu'.

Will moved to Talywain for his first employment on discharge from the Navy. A torn cutting from a newspaper, unfortunately undated, referred to the *Abersychan Technical Instruction Classes presentation of prizes to last year's students*. The article refers to Germany getting ahead of us in Chemical industries, and commending the standards of so many young men and women who were taking advantage of their classes, then gives lists of prize winners in Shorthand, Mining, Technical Arithmetic, Dressmaking, French, Practical Plane & Solid Geometry, and Building Construction.

There were thirteen prize winners in the Mining category, twelve described as 2nd Class and just one as 1st class, but that 1st Class prize winner was *Mr Wm. Burwood of Talywain*. Yet Will only stayed for a few years before moving to Fulham in December 1907. I found a few letters from those years which provide insight into their life.

This first letter is another from Richard Hollingdale, Ada's father in Brighton, dated May 24th. Ada's father signs himself as Dad while addressing it to *Dear Daddy & Mummy* and refers to Ada coming off allright and 'son & heir & mother doing well'. Eric was born on 23rd May 1901 - strongly suggesting that the letter was sent on 24th May 1901. They must have got the news to Brighton very fast – maybe Will sent a telegram – or their post was faster then!

I surmise that 'the Nook' was the address of one of Richard Hollingdale's other daughters, Clara Brown, who gave birth to daughter Edith Ada May on 2nd June 1901. Probably Clara was expected to deliver first. The Edie to whom Richard Hollingdale refers is probably his daughter Edith who did not marry Alfred Tyler until 1903.

May 24th 9 Richmond Hill
Brighton
Sussex

Dear Daddy & Mummy

Very pleased to hear its come off allright and the son & heir & mother are doing well. Have been waiting to send you some good news from the Nook but it hasn't come off yet. Think the train has got snowed up and can't get here yet with the baby. Perhaps its gone off in a balloon to find old Kruger or someone its been coming this month or mini but has not arrived yet.

Edie came running out to meet me & says hallo Grand Daddy so I shouts Hallo Aunty I thought it was the Nook at last but am glad to hear Ada has come off allright it's a great comfort to me. Send post card & let me know you are getting on allright just read in Argus of explosion in Coal Mine in South Wales hope it doesn't turn out so bad as stated in Argus.

Post is waiting so must conclude now with love to all from

Dad

PS will write again soon

Dad

Hooray for Little Willie
Hooray and Bravo from Edie will write tomorrow.

The *Kruger* to which he refers is Paul Kruger, President of the Transvaal during the Boer War – thus a symbolic enemy figure like the Kaiser after the First World War.

The Argus has been the main local paper for the Brighton and Hove area since 1880, though back then officially known as the Evening Argus.

The Universal Colliery in Senghenydd in South Wales suffered an explosion on 24th May 1901 which killed 82 miners - according to a national archives site on the internet. Will's new job had its own risks.

The next three letters were all written to Ada by Will from Talywain while she was elsewhere. I vaguely recall hearing that Ada disliked life in Talywain, but maybe Ada just disliked being so far from her family. In 1938 she would write that she could not think of anywhere other than Brighton as home as far as locality was concerned, and in old age her desire to return to live in Brighton would cause real problems.

I think that this first letter was written after Eric's birth but while Ada was pregnant with Maurice - making it 1902. It confirms that Will is still very religious because something to do with 'electric' requires much prayer. As he was an electrician maybe he was hoping for some new employment? Or maybe hoping to have electricity installed in his house?

Most of all, it really displays how Will was still deeply in love with Ada.

Home

My own darling <u>wife</u>

Empty is but a shade of the feeling one feels when I look around. I could almost beg of you to come to me but that the holiday will do you good. I see your thimble your book dear. Boots & shoes under the bed no one to use them. They are in order and I could almost cry out with love for your dear shoes your dressing gown skirts your hat I brought back your work basket the quilt placed over the little cot all helps to remind me of your absence would that my arms could reach you where you are. I would cry never, never again the place is so still just the ticking of the clock as fire <u>desolate.</u>

I must not go on like this or you will think I am sad – not that only that I love you and the boy. His mail cart his little bouncer and shoes. God bless both your hearts.

Well may Warwick say I am glad you come back poor fellow. I would not have stayed in his place again nor for worlds and I know he won't stay again. He managed to spend nearly 1£ in the week for food and today he had a dinner for a friend fried chops cabbage & potatoes & Blackberry tart.

I have been out tonight and done the shopping got our meat for Sunday and some apples. Warwick tells me to tell you one disadvantage we have got we are not able to clear our pipes with your hat-pins and no one to tell him to throw out his water. I was late as per usual waking up this morning. William came and banged the door. I took a jack of cold water a sardine sandwich and some bread and butter only eat the sandwich and bought a bottle of tea up at the house by the pub. William Evans goes on his holidays tomorrow Saturday but comes back on Thursday.

I have some good news to tell you. I was talking to Mr Maggs of the stores (the manager) about the electric at the stores and he tells me he will let me know about 2 months before the machine is put up so that I can apply for it. I am sure he will do his best for me. These things require much prayer. You will remember me.

I know I arrived very late last evening about 5 to 11 when I got home. There is no train to this – until 9.23 in the evening after – the train from Paddington arrives so I had to wait at Newport that accounts for me being so tired this morning.

So my dear you will have to leave earlier than I did. There are one or two trains you could come by. The best one would be 12 o'clock from Paddington arrives at Newport 5 o'clock and then you could catch the 6 o'clock train from Newport to Aberyschan Low level otherwise you will have to come earlier still the 10.45 from Paddington arrives at Newport 10 to 2 then you have to wait until 4 o'clock to come to Talywain or you can catch one to Aberyschan 28 mins past 2. So this is how it seems.

10.45 from Paddington catches 2.23 to Aberyschan same train wait until 4 o'clock to Talywain.

12 from Paddington catches 6 o'clock to Aberyschan *but you have to wait one hour for* it can you understand the programme now my darling love. I must conclude with love deep love to you & baby well this is all those who know me have come to the conclusion that it will be a son - dutiful one to dad. Good night darling

Your affectionate husband

Will

Good prediction – the second baby was a son, my father Maurice, who would prove a devoted son – doing his best to care for his mother to the end, even after acquiring wife and children. That end would not come until 1963.

Both my parents were second children of two-child families – very different from the massive families of previous generations in the nineteenth century, but I remember a television programme which highlighted the statistical global norm that falling infant mortality rapidly produced falling family sizes.

This second letter is sent while Ada is apparently on holiday with her two babies, so would be 1903 or later.

7 Emlyn Terrace
Talywain

My own darling wife

Glad to say I arrived safe and sound but how quiet everything is. I caught a train to Abersychan Lower level so had a pretty good weight to carry up. Arrived about 11 p.m. and had a good night's rest as I was tired. I had a look round, and I saw everything was alright and being observant I saw traces of you and the little children a cup and spoon underneath the high chair. The mark of the baby's head in the pillow of the pram, and several other things as soon as I got home.

I made myself some cocoa and begged a piece of bread off old Johns so I done pretty well. Fed on eggs and bacon today. Barwick has come home and looks well and he had one sweet stay which he enjoyed very well so he says. The baker left a small loaf so I have got another one and a piece of mutton for Sunday and a butter and a jam sandwiches from the stores we are going to live in the back kitchen while you are away it already seems so strange to hear.

You would feel dull without but I shall be all right as I have plenty in so I have already got 2 pairs of trousers done. You can thank Joe and tell him so but don't say anything to the other people about it.

I see your ruffle is on the front room table. Am I to send it on, and now for yourself I did not like leaving you – it is not very nice to part even for so short a time but never mind sweetie one must look forward to the reunion. I hope you will lose the new rallie (how do you spell it) pains and that the little ones are not very tiresome but try and stay.

You will feel the benefit of a holiday and must have the rest at home. It has been a fearful day here raining all the time and blowing hard. What sort of a day are you having. Enclosed you will find 5/- for present expenses don't worry or trouble about me whatsoever. Mrs P___ has not sent for her baby yet. I don't know about nice but I have had a letter from Nell. She sends her love and so do I send mine with heaps of love to you and the Babys. I will pray earnestly that you may have a good time and so with Xs to you and Babys and love to all friends I close from

Your ever affectionate husband
Warwick sends love
Will

Mrs P__ is a name I could not decipher. The Nell mentioned is probably Will's sister. Joe means Joe Brown – husband of Ada's sister Clara.

I also have no idea what Will meant by 'rallie' pains. I may be misreading his writing but cannot guess what else he might have written.

With this third and much shorter letter we find that Ada is staying away a further week. Possibly it is a follow up to the second letter above.

7 Emlyn Terrace

My Darling Wife

I have just got your letter. I am glad to hear you are going to stop until Saturday week for your and the childrens sake, but for my sake it was a great disappointment. I have been looking forward to tomorrow (Saturday) but now another week of solitary confinement. I should not attempt to come before. We can manage all right don't worry yourself am sending 10/- on to you with a telegraph 10/- sent Friday night to you & all that I can send you now that I have got from Warwick. I want to get this off will write again on Monday you do not say if the babies miss me. I don't expect they will know us when they come home love to all kisses to Babys & yourself

Your Affec Husband
Will

I have a postcard sent from Will at Talywain on 21st Aug 2006 to Ada at a care of address of Mrs Tyler (Ada's sister Edith) at 35 Sandown Road in Brighton in which he refers to missing her and the boys as 'the abomination of desolation'.

The last letter in this group is from a neighbour in Talywain after Will and Ada have moved in December 1907. It shows that Will and Ada moved when Will obtained a job with a new 'master', and hints that Ada's health rather than Will's might have precipitated the move from Wales to Fulham.

It also shows that Will was involved in the local Baptist Chapel in Wales, called the Pisgah Baptist Chapel. It was a family involvement because Maurice received a prize from the Infant Department of Pisgah Sunday School for Xmas 1906. Presented for faithful attendance it was a small booklet called *The Broken Window or Keep to the Truth* with no named author but published by 'The Tiny Library' for four pence. The Pisgah Baptist Chapel continued to be a working chapel until 30th June 2019 when it was forced to close after 200 years due to the old building requiring repairs which its congregation could not afford.

> *Jany 21 1908*
> *5 Emlyn Terrace*
> *Talywain Mon*

Dear Friend & Brother

I was very pleased to receive your letter a week last Saturday morning, and my first word must be in the nature of an apology for not having replied to you earlier; however I feel assured you will bear with me when I say that between attending meetings & other matters my time has been somewhat limited.

I am delighted to learn of your success, and although, in common with all the other friends of Pisgah, I have been sorry and loather to part with you and your little family, yet I feel grateful to God for his goodness towards you, undoubtedly it is His hand that has guided you, and it must be very gratifying to you to realize your prayers have been answered, as it is also to have friends who have remembered you in their supplications of who, I may say in passing, I am one. I hope your new master is good not only in his relationship as master but also good as a man.

I notice you say in your letter "please pass these notes on & etc" but it was only one was enclosed namely for Mr D.K.Williams, I handed it to him the day it came. I also conveyed your messages to Andrews & Wyles, to those who met at the prayer meeting a week last Monday evening, and last but not least to your (or should I say "our") class, all were glad to hear from you and wished to be remembered kindly to you. I am glad you & Mrs Burwood & the boys will soon feel a decided and permanent improvement in her health.

Things are much the same here as when you left. Our Sunday School at Pisgah seems to be looking up, we were only 2 short of 300 last Sunday.

Miss Ball (who is at service at Mrs Shipman) is going to be baptized next Sunday evening. Mr John Powell, who lives in Albert Road, where the Britannia public was formerly, was injured a week yesterday – a fractured leg.

This morning two young men were killed on their way to the workings at Llanorch by a fall of roof – one the son of John James near Rock & Fountain bridge Garn, the other a son of Mrs Williams (formerly Flynn) of Manor Road Aberyschan.

I note you have not definitely joined any place of worship so far. If there is a Baptist chapel convenient we shall be glad to send a transfer letter on hearing from you, or from the minister or secretary.

I shall be most pleased to hear from you again at your earliest convenience. Mrs Jones and all my family also Mr Roberts & Mr Price wish to be remembered kindly to yourself & Mrs Burwood & the boys.

> *With kindest regards to all*
> *You're in the hands of Christian love*
> *Joe Jones*

Prior to leaving Wales, Will obtained a Testimonial dated 1 November 1907 from Varteg Hill Colliery near Pontypool giving 'with pleasure' 'testimony to the good character of Wm Burwood'.

Will sent two postcards on 19th Nov 2007 to his sons Eric and Maurice - sent with Wimbledon postmarks to Talywain, telling Eric to look after his Mum and Maurice to be a good boy to Mum. Will had gone ahead looking for a new job in London, and been successful.

His brother Warwick stayed working in Wales for a while, because my brother traced him working as a Colliery Blacksmith at Llandradach in 1909. He did move later, because in 1914 he was working as a Colliery Blacksmith in Kent, and in 1927 is recorded as a Colliery Goods Clerk. It may not be related to his moving but Warwick and Lu's first born son Harold was born in 1907 only to die in 1910 of whooping cough. They had other children named Nellie (born 1909), Bertha (1912), Max (1914), Glyndwr (1918), and Greta Mifanwy (1927).

Will's new job in 1907 was as a chauffeur - early days for motor vehicles. Will sent postcards to Ada's address at 196 Lillie Road in 2008. One was sent from Brockenhurst in the New Forest on 28th April 2008, and refers to bad roads and encountering 2 foot of snow just outside of Basingstoke. Another was sent from Brockenhurst on 2nd October 2008 and begins *'we are coming home on Saturday not sure of the road yet'*.

Only the wealthy could afford motor cars, so they employed chauffeurs as they would previously have employed coachmen.

The family lived at Lillie Road in Fulham from December 1907 to February 1909, but my brother has noted Will as having an address at Rose Villa, Boscombe, Bournemouth in August or September 2008, and a third postcard from Brockenhurst dated 24th September 2008 says that Will had much more comfortable apartments than he had at Boscombe. The card also asks how the boys are getting on at school and *'did you find the place alright?'*

Not sure what the last question means, but it could mean the school. Maurice's first school was Lillie Road in Fulham, before moving to Valley Road, Shortlands, in the London Borough of Bromley. They remained at Valley Boys until 1912.

Will and Ada and their children moved to a new address of c/o Clements, the Corner House Garage, Shortlands Road, Shortlands, Bromley, Kent, in February 1909, and remained there until September 1912. Presumably 'Clements' was Will's new employer and 'Garage' the chauffeur's quarters.

(Digressing briefly, Will and Ada's great granddaughter Julia and her family would live at another address in Shortlands a whole century later.)

It does, however, seem that Will and Ada's move to Shortlands did not involve a 'transfer' to another Baptist Chapel at Shortlands – maybe it had no Baptist Chapel - because this letter shows his devout Christian faith taking the family to a different non-conformist church.

> *Congregational Church*
> *Shortlands*
> *Kent*
> *Dec 11 1912*

Dear W Burwood

At our Communion service last Thursday it was felt that we ought to send you a message of loving greeting and to let you know how much we miss you and your dear wife from our midst.

We remember with gratitude to God your faith, your zeal and your prayers and we deeply regret your removal from Shortlands.

We pray that God will verily bless you and your family, that He will guide you day by day and we shall greatly rejoice if, in answer to our prayers, He will guide your steps towards Bromley before very long.

We are asked to send this letter from the church and we beg you to remember us and our labours in the Lord whenever you approach the throne of His Heavenly Grace.

We wish you every blessing for the coming year.
Signed on behalf of the Church.

> *Arthur E Abel*
> *Benjamin Bryant*
> *George T Russell.*

Will sent further postcards to Ada at 'The Garage'. From Hindhead dated 25 May 1910 and 17 June 1911, and from Llangollen on 21 July 1910. The card from Llangollen refers to having 'very nice drive' and 'comfortable quarters' but also to leaving tomorrow 'I think for Shrewsbury' and to sending a card from their next 'stopping-place' and 'so on right through the journey'.

Will is also pictured in chauffeur's uniform with car and family, taken while living at Shortlands.

Later addresses supplied by my brother Richard are:

From September 1912 – c/o Saunders, 19a Ludbrook Grove, Fulham Palace Road, Fulham.

From May 1913 – c/o Crossley, Putney.

From May 1915 – c/o Henderson, 10 Cornwall Mews South, Grenville Place, Cornwall Mews South, Kensington SW7.

From May 1917 – 44 Cornwall Gardens, Kensington, London SW.

From May 10th 1919 – c/o Charrington, Ashburton Lodge, Putney Heath – at this address my brother notes that Will was employed as chauffeur to Mrs Charrington, of the Charrington brewing family. As other addresses were c/o addresses I believe that Will was a chauffeur for different employers throughout this period.

I also have an addressed envelope to Mrs A Burwood at 48 Courtfield Gardens, London, SW5 – but the only date given is Dec 6th and it has a George V postage stamp. Clearly they lacked a settled long term residence while their two sons were growing up due to the nature of Will's employment.

Will's death certificate, issued October 1926, gives his profession as Chauffeur (domestic) - so he was probably a chauffeur for the last 18 years of his life - neither a prosperous life nor a settled one, but in one way Will and Ada were fortunate. Will was too old for active service in the First World War, and neither son had reached the age of 18 before the War ended so neither were called up. The war ended 6 days after Maurice's 16th birthday – no doubt a great relief to Will and Ada, but both would have done what they could to help the war effort. The only direct contribution I know about Will making was through 1st East Putney Scouts, which I will mention later, but Ada did acquire certificates for passing a First Aid elementary course in 1915, and a First Aid advanced course plus a Home Nursing elementary course in 1916.

Will and Ada also acquired a certificate issued by a newspaper 'Ideal Picture Competition' certifying Mr and Mrs Burwood to be 'admirably representative of married happiness'. It was issued in 1922, when they had been married over 20 years, and beyond doubt it was a successful marriage if not a prosperous one.

Unfortunately by 1922 it had less than five years left.

Will & Ada marry - Will's brother Warwick on his right & Ada's father Richard on her left - Clara & Joe Brown in front & Edie Hollingdale behind her father

Will & Ada outside 7 Emlyn Terrace, Talywaun where Maurice was born in 1902

Maurice & Eric with their first cousin Pearl Tyler

Chauffeur Will & Maurice, Ada, & Eric at Shortlands with car own by the Clements

Will's brother Warwick Burwood with wife Lu & children Nellie (by Lu) Max & Bertha

CHAPTER FIVE

Last Years

As the 1920's began Will was having health problems, judging from this letter clearly sent while he was working for Mrs Charrington. The underlined gaps are words I could not decipher, but congratulations to Maurice were probably about his school career which led to him winning a place at Cambridge, but I will tackle that in later chapters.

> *C/O Mr Shaw*
> *1 Church Square*
> *Westcliff*
> *Whitby*

My dear sweetheart

Congratulations for Maurice _____ are going on all right and that you will not have trouble with Gertie _____ concerning her holiday. I am rather in a rush to catch the post as if I don't go out now you won't get my news until Monday morning. Well there is no post here on Sunday we are leaving here for sure on Thursday and as far as I am concerned I have had a jolly enough time.

I am attending a surgeon for my nail on about the size of my little fingernail and have only had a little exhaustive sleep each night since Monday – bodily health very well only the throbbing at night is bad but today for the first time I have lost the pain out of my head so I have great hope of a good night's rest tonight.

Don't worry about me I only tell you this because I have felt oh how I wish my sweetheart the haven of rest. It will take some days to get properly well now.

I hope the boys are all right in camp and that the food is better also that Pearlie will be some little help to you. I see you have the three of them with you.

Thank you very much writing to Edie for me - I am afraid she is hopeless. I hope she won't blab too much about family affairs to Mrs Genoe although on one side or the other there is nothing we are to be ashamed of - if you answer this letter do so quick then I shall be able to let you know what we are doing. Don't worry about money for me if I want it I must ask Mrs Charrington – now will form at local Tremain.

Your ever faithful husband and sweetheart

Will

I know of no relative named 'Gertie', but Maurice's diary refers to a Gertie Speakman visiting on 1st July 1929. Nor do I know who Mrs Genoe is.

References to 'Edith' or 'Edie' in these letters are always problematic because both Will and Ada had sisters with that name. Will's sister Edith married Sam Sparshatt in 1904 (though Sam later deserted her), but 'Pearlie' was the daughter of Ada's sister Edie Tyler, so I assume Edie means Edie Tyler. Possibly 'the three of them' refers to Pearl and her two elder siblings: Alf (often called Alfie born 1904) and Cyril (1908). Their younger brother Victor was only born in 1915, though before him there were twins who died presumably at birth as I do not know their names.

Maurice's diaries record Pearl visiting Ada and Maurice many times – and Pearl's close relationship with her beloved Auntie Ada is proven by this extract from a letter sent by Pearl to Ada during the Second World War.

Even now, comfortable as I am I would be home like a shot if I felt that Mum really loved me & wanted me. Parents & home ties are too deeply rooted to be broken away without hurt. All the time something in me is longing to be home again.

It would have been different if I had come to live with you, because

I have a love for you that goes right back to my childhood. You have always been my very special Auntie, & I have such wonderful memories of holidays & week-ends spent with you, that I shall never forget. You are such a homemaker, there is always comfort & happiness where you are. If I could only at this moment sit down in one of your comfortable armchairs, by the side of the bookcase, & just laze & read. One of the joys of staying with you was that one could relax.

I do not know what the problem was between Pearl and her mother, but possibly Pearl's imminent arrival precipitated her mother into marriage. Or it may be that, to quote a letter from Ada in 1951 *"No-one on earth could ever put up with Edie"*. Pearl was 37 when she wrote that letter, so the hurt she was feeling must have been very long standing. Maurice's diary records numerous visits from Pearl before Pearl's death in 1943 so clearly there was a very loving relationship between Maurice and Ada and Pearl, and especially between Ada and Pearl.

The camp, referred to in Will's letter was scout camp. Many photographs survive of scout camps including pictures of Will as an assistant scoutmaster - so this was clearly a major side-line when Will was working as a chauffeur until 1921. We also have two letters from Maurice sent to his mother from scout camps at St Helens in the Isle of Wight. He attended camps between 1919 and 1923, but I cannot confirm which years these letters were sent, though the first was 1919 or 1920 because Will was still one of the scoutmasters at the camp.

> *1ˢᵗ East Putney Scout Camp*
> *Recreation Ground*
> *St Helens*
> *I.O.W.*
> *Wednesday*

Dear Mum

Received your letter yesterday. You asked for news of what we were doing. Our routine is this.

6.30 Reveille which is usually played rottenly. Everyone hops out of bed like lightning, chucks pajamas, puts on shorts and shoes only and dashes to the wash house. Water is scarce so it is only turned on at 10am. Accordingly about 30 chaps wash in clean water obtained the night before. Rex & I go in the officer's place so we are all right. After passing inspection by Dad (Rex & I don't), we rush back after hanging towels up & tidy tents for breakfast. Fold up all blankets the same size, remove all paper, grass, etc. around the tent.

Cookhouse gong, every boy dashes off at once to his position. When all the tent are in place, the leaders dash up to the officer of the day to report. We march into the marquee after raising the flag to the tune of the general salute in the order in which we report so you can imagine the rush. Orderlies serve at the top near the officers first so the first tent gets the best place.

After breakfast prayers & camp announcements (orderly tents etc.) (orderly tents work for one day 1 2 3 4 etc. 11. Guard tents 6 7 8 9 10 11 12 etc. orderly officers etc. Dad's scran bag everything lost goes in there & comes out on payment of 1d towards the efforts. Tent inspection. Defaulters under the flag for punishment, usually spud peeling, knife cleaning, clearing up etc. After that we do what we like in the camp till bathing up till now about 11-1. Then dinner. After dinner we do what we like until tea at 5. We can go to the beach or to St Helens just as we are, slipper, shorts, & shirt. To Seaview etc. we must have uniform, play football, cricket, hot rice etc. write letters etc, after tea do what we like until supper biscuits & cocoa. (Tea at tea, coffee at breakfast).

First post blown, leaders of tents get lights. In half an hour last post blown get into bed. In 10 mins lights out blown. Not a row must be heard between lights out & reveille. That is the routine now for details of me & my tent.

No 9 tent. We have had 20 meals at 10 of them we have been first for cookhouse, at 3 we were 2nd, at 2 we were 5th. At 5 we were later. We have already made a name for ourselves. At the last inspection no-one came near us. For all the others we have I think been first or 2nd. The only days I know of are 2 when we lost ½ mark each day. Today I don't think we lost a mark. Only one other tent has finished tidying up. Playing football I was the only one to hit the top of the flagstaff. I split my right shoe right across at it. Can't play in boots too slippery.

The tongue has come out of the other one, and its beginning to split at the back.

All the chaps are fearfully sunburned on their legs & chest. It hurts. Mine are brown already but not sunburnt (i.e. red & raw). We haven't seen a cloud yet. It is boiling hot today in the bell tents. Rex is in our tent. He never does any work in the morning for inspection. Mowle in our tent is as bad as Swanbourne for trouble but he always does what I tell him. Our tent is the noisiest lot in the camp but at night they are never allowed to speak a word by me. Then they are the quietest of the lot.

Mowle helps me but we have a cub J Higgins in our tent who is as good as all the rest put together. This morning we couldn't get a broom to sweep the grass out of the tent so he swept the whole tent out with his hand. At night only one blanket is necessary except just in the morning. You ought to see the way our chaps turn out at reveille.

Bertha is coming Thursday. Rex is most troublesome at nights. We had a recent sermon Sunday by Gillingham the Cricketer. Our brass band is greatly admired by the villagers. They say it is much better than the one they had over on Peace Day. We went to Seaview as we knock about in camp with the brass band one evening. Yesterday we had a concert to which we invited villagers. We do get through the money. Eric has written home for more, I expect. Some chaps have spent 10s already.

The cooking is fine but there might be more grub. That's about all. Hope you are all well. Hope Pearlie & Cyril are enjoying themselves.

With much love & kisses to all.

Maurice

P.S. Don't worry about mosquitos. Only seen one. Had a flea last night. Earwigs are not half so common as before. Spiders & woodlice are more common. Have killed a lot including wasps, flies, fleas (not biting ones) etc. We are quite all right.

Rex was Maurice's cousin Arthur Rex Cook from Portsmouth – Bertha presumably Rex's mother, Will's first cousin and daughter of Hannah Burwood's brother Charles Burwood. Pearlie and Cyril Tyler were Ada's niece and nephew. I know that Maurice played the euphonium for a while and I think it was with the scout's brass band.

The second letter is probably August 1921 or later, as Will is not mentioned and Maurice is now in the Officers' tent. Bert will be Will's nephew Bert Sparshatt, Ethel presumably Rex's first cousin, daughter of his father's brother Hugh.

> *1st East Putney Scout Camp*
> *St Helens*
> *I.O.W.*

Dear Mum

Just a line to let you know how we are getting on. Things have passed off quite smoothly & nothing of note has happened except that Rex had 5 bits of treacle pudding today. We went to about 100000000 church parades yesterday & played about 1000 hymns. Bathing is all right. That old pair of plimsolls has just gone west. Hope the other last. I am writing this on the soap we found at Portsmouth. The weather is fine & hot but a little windy & so not too hot. There is no difficulty about water but the provision merchants let us down a little. However that was straightened out because they sent stuff ordered for next week. If you see Bert tell him I will meet him at Seaview if he lets me know the time of the boat etc.

I am having a slack time of it in the Officers tent. Get up & wash in comfort before the boys get up. Go to bed when we like (half past ten seemed like 2 o-clock). We are waited on at meals. All I do is to issue & light the lamps at night, collect them in the morning and cut up the bread for meals. I can cut up 14 quarter loaves in about 7 minutes with the bread cutter. I also dished out the grub till now, but after today we have 3 different officers doing it each day. The tent leaders take it round to the boys.

We've got decent cooks, Jacob's son-in-law & his son. They make decent cakes, but their coffee & tea not so good. Their stew is fine. We have a cup of tea at half past six in the morning. We have crowds of clerical johnnies dropping round after the band, by the way. That tart Dad bought was fine.

I tried serving in the canteen, but although it is very fascinating it costs too much. You find yourself eating lot & paying for it. Haven't run across

Mabel yet. Rex says Ethel is coming over one day. He is going to see a London girl staying at Parkhurst tomorrow.

Well, I shall have to stop now, got some bread to cut up.

With much love & kisses from
Maurice

Had one wasp sting up to now but they are quite harmless & rarely sting.

When Will resigned from 1st East Putney Scouts he was given a testimonial to which people subscribed, and this letter was sent on his resignation.

1st EAST PUTNEY (ST STEPHEN'S)
BOY SCOUTS
30 Jan 21

Dear Mr Burwood

At a Committee meeting held last evening your resignation was received with the greatest regret by all & a note of thanks to you for all you have done for the troop, proposed by Mr Keighley seconded by Mr Buxton & unanimously carried was passed.

Although included in the above, may I add a few words of personal thanks. We shall all miss you very much. A very large part of the success of our troop has been due not only to your ideas & suggestions, but what is of far greater importance, to your splendid influence with the boys, who will be very sorry when I break the news to them.

We have retained your name as a member of the committee, so that we may not entirely be deprived of your assistance & if at any time circumstances should change, so that you can resume active operations, you know that you will be received with open arms.

Yours very sincerely
Th A Delcomyn

Mr Delcomyn is an interesting character, and I think that Ada was his family's housemaid while Will was in Ladysmith, but I cannot prove it.

According to records of Will's younger son, Maurice, Th A Delcomyn was the Scoutmaster of 1st East Putney Scouts when Maurice joined them on 20th September 1913. An internet search located, on the Total Giving website, a reference to registered charity number 303872 called "T A Delcomyn Bequest in Connection With 1st East Putney Scout Group." Even better is my discovery of www.EastPutneyScoutcentre.org from which I quote these extracts on both the group and Mr Delcomyn.

The Group originated in 1908 with four or five boys advertising in the local paper for a Scout Leader.

The advertisement was answered by two people, a homeless man who wanted to know how much he would be paid, and by Mr Delcomyn who at that time was helping at another Scout Troop. The Troop prospered under the leadership of Mr Delcomyn and in 1909 he purchased "The Red House" on West Hill, SW18 for their gymnastics, band practice and concerts etc. It was around this time that the Boy Scout Organisation had been formed and the troop was officially registered and the official name became 62nd South West London.

The troop continued to prosper and with all the Scouts younger brothers 'hanging' around the hall, Mr Delcomyn saw the necessity to cater for the younger boys and in 1912 he started what was probably the first Cub Pack, and named them Junior Scouts.

This changed 62nd South West London from a Scout Troop to a Scout Group.

In 1914, like many other troops, we lost a large number of Scouters to the various armed forces; but with the help of elder Scouters, fathers and several mothers the group continued in its activities. During the war, in addition to the usual Scouting activities, the Group supplied "patients" to R.A.M.C for their training, collected paper for the war effort, did guarding at the reservoirs to prevent damage by saboteurs and also trained and supplied buglers for the air raid warnings. They also entertained wounded soldiers at the Gifford House hospital.

Towards the end of 1918, owing to an unfortunate disagreement with the local Scout Association and the District Commissioner, the group left the B.P. Scout Organisation and the name changed to 1st

East Putney. This didn't have a detrimental effect on the numbers and in fact the group continued to increase, so in 1922 Mr Delcomyn had a new HQ built in Oxford Road SW15 on the site of an old chapel that had burnt down.

Mr T A Delcomyn was prosperous enough to buy buildings for a scout group and create a charity for them, so I believe that his family were former employers of Ada who were either reacquainted with or kept in touch with his former employee and her husband, and must have known about Will's service in Ladysmith. Mr Delcomyn died in 1955 at the age of 91.

I have found some later family references to Mr Delcomyn. The first is in a family cash book giving a Christmas list for 1952 where the name Delcomyn is one of the entries, and an even later reference to Th A Delcomyn comes in a letter from Maurice's cousin Bert Sparshatt (Ada's nephew) in Jan 1955.

"I don't know if I ever told you but I have met old "Delcy" once or twice. (Mr Delcomyn – 1ˢᵗ East Putney Scouts) Among my many activities I am a member of the Battersea Rotary Club and while visiting the Putney Club have met him as he is a member of that Club. It seems strange that after all these years I should meet him as a fellow Rotarian – he still remembers you all."

I do not know what 'circumstances' prevented Will from continuing 'active operations' with the Scouts. Probably it was health problems, and possibly Ada was also having health problems, as indicated in this next undated letter from Will to Ada from Putney Hospital – the address itself proves that he was seriously ill. As to the nature of Will's illness, his death certificate in October 1926 gives a cause of death as an operation on a gastric ulcer and what appears to be 'anorexia'.

It seems an odd wording by modern connotations – maybe we would say 'malnutrition' rather than 'anorexia', and according to an NHS website a gastric ulcer (or stomach ulcer) can cause loss of appetite and weight loss which would weaken the body and make it more vulnerable. It could also cause indigestion, heartburn, feeling sick and bloated – possibly the 'dreadful feelings' he mentions in this letter:

                                                    Putney Hospital

My own dear Sweetheart

In spite of seeing you yesterday I am dropping a line to you to let you know that I am allowed to take fruit – so I have got that - best to get me 4 oranges. I have had a letter from Cyril at Chatham and am answering it now. I have not had any different – diet – only fish but I am glad to be able to take potatoes and other things without those dreadful feelings. I have had a nice lot of butter and I hope that in a day or two I shall be on my feet – don't be alarmed my dear I won't overdo it.

I should send for my clothes. When you bring them down bring my best things. I want to look tidy and if you can prepare for us to go away that is yours and my things.

I hope you got on all right out with Mr Price to-day. Let me know how you got on with the Convalescent Home at Worthing or wherever you decide to go – anyway you and I are going together – both of us getting better than we were – and we are going to have a nice time because God has been good to us – now with fondest love I remain your affec sweetheart & husband.

                                                            Will

I am unsure when this was written. If it refers to Will's last illness it was 1926, but a later letter from Maurice written, I think, in 1924 suggests it might be then that Will was in hospital. Alternatively it might have been written 1921 or 1922 and be related to Will resigning from the scouts. In that case Will must have recovered sufficiently to resume work.

Cyril was Cyril Tyler, Pearl's brother.

Several letters were exchanged between Will and Ada and Maurice while Maurice was at Cambridge between 1922 and 1925. Many of the letters have no dates, and some are incomplete, so I cannot guarantee the order, but I start with one that had a date - October 1922 - sent by Ada when Maurice had just started at Cambridge University.

Oct 6th 1922

My Beloved Son

I thank God that he gave me the gift of your dear self. You have always been such a comfort to me. You will live in my heart for ever. I pray God that he will guide your steps & keep you in that path that leadeth unto everlasting life. May he keep you under the shadow of his wings.

Never do anything you would be ashamed of your mother to know my dear son however greatly you may be tempted to do wrong you will always be kept in the strength of the Lord Jesus. God bless you & keep you in his care for ever.

Your loving Mother
He will never leave thee
nor forsake thee

Not much substance to this letter, other than to prove that Ada shared Will's devout Christian faith and loved her son.

I can date the next letter to November 1922, because it refers to a general election when the Conservatives won 330 or so seats, which I think refers to the election on 15 November 1922 when the Conservatives won 344 seats in the first election held after most Irish seats left to form the Irish Free State.

Clearly another letter sent by Ada - showing how big a fan she was of Gilbert and Sullivan operettas. They were massively popular in days before television and talking cinema, because they provided great live theatre with catchy tunes and plenty of laughs.

Ashburton Lodge
Putney Heath
SW15

My darling son

We are all up in the clouds at the results of election. There is a mandate for the revolutionaries, (big word) now our beloved country can settle down to a stable government. We all tried for the P.M. Prize – the nearest Eric put 330 Conservatives or thereabouts.

I went to Gondoliers, had to stand, then a gentleman offered me a seat in the second act. Dad went to Iolanthe, & Dolly & Eric went to Pirates. They did enjoy it. We are having overture from Yeoman tonight. Dad was in rapture over Iolanthe, we must save up & go to all of them when they have their next London season, & I hope my beloved Maurice will be here with us.

<u>Sunday</u>

It was such an appalling night last night we did not go to Yeoman. We are having part overture from Patience on Tuesday, so they are looking up.

Next week will seem quite flat after the past one of excitement. I shall send you a parcel I hope on your birthday, shall not send football boots unless you send word that you need them.

What a <u>boring</u> experiment you had to do, I'm sure it needs patience. That reminds me the character of Patience as far as I remember were of course the usual stars.

W Lawson	*Patience*
H Tyson	*Bunthorne*
B Jones	*Lady Jane*
J Millage	*Archibald*
E Sharps	*Lady Angela*

Saphis Ellen Davis I believe she is rather short & a voice something like Elsie Gold in Ella (don't know)

Major Sydney Pointer. Goulding was one of the three ascetic men who say "you hold yourself like this, etc. Glad to hear Joe has got a job, is it a teaching one.

Do you happen to have programme of Princess but there it doesn't matter old dear. I enclose one of Gondoliers. Dad gone to Auntie Edies, shall not stay to write much more in a day or two. Take care of yourself & don't get kicked feed up my dear old boy.

I must close with my dearest love God bless & keep you ever in His care. A nice message on the wireless, every soul striving to live up for all that is good, & true & beautiful is a saint of God). He is on their side. Keep that strait path before you & ever look forward to that Blessed Hope & the glorious reappearing of our Lord & Saviour Jesus Christ. Goodnight dear love of my heart.

Your loving
Mother

Dolly was Florence Gertrude Stevens, born 1902, who married Eric in 1926. The 'Auntie Edie' mentioned could be either Edie Tyler or Edie Sparshatt.

It is possible that the second page (from *'Major Sydney'* onwards) is not part of the same letter, but the line *"you hold yourself like this"* does come from *Patience*. Either way, it confirms Ada's love for Gilbert and Sullivan - and Jesus. The former was shared or possibly inspired by Maurice as shown by these next two letters sent from Cambridge – possibly in May 1924.

Dear Old Things

I'm writing rather early because I shall be rather busy this week-end. I'm afraid there is not a lot of news but I suppose we can utilise that accomplished art of talking a lot about nothing. However, will answer your letter first. About time you did write. Here was I coming in after a hard morning's work to see – blank day after day, wondering whether you were alive or dead, whether you had arrived safely. Oh! By the way, are you aware that travelling in the train is about 10,000 times as safe as travelling in London streets. Figures show this indubitably. Poor old guy, talk about pouring, it has been doing so since the beginning of term with intervals of ¼ hour per 2 hours. Cricket practice match has been postponed from Thurs → Fri → Sat → Mon → Tues, ½ hrs cricket on Wed, none on Thurs. League match Fri & Sat, so they had no guide for choosing team. Match probably won't be played. Haven't got very thick vest. According to weather, shan't need thin ones.

Don't be downhearted by criticisms. You won't see any weak point in the opera & the weak points the critic takes are not very tangible & certainly detract nothing from the enjoyment of the play. As for money its all rot about affording it. You can get in for 2/6 the two & fares 2/0 – 4/6 all told. You know the cast (its in Tuesday's Telegraph). Take the money out of what you send me & so send me less. As for seeing the Yeoman its about the best & its different from all the others. It is essential for you to see it. If you go to Sorcerer next week, here is the cast.

Sir Marmaduke Poindexter	*Darrell Fancourt*
Alexis Poindexter his son	*Charles Goulding*
John Wellington Wells - Sorcerer	*Henry Lytton*
Dr Daly - Vicar	*Leo Sheffield*
A Notary	*Joseph Griffin*
Lady Sangazure (Blue Blood)	*Bertha Lewis*
Aline (her daughter)	*Elsie Griffin*
Mrs Partlet (Pew Opener)	*Anna Bethel*
Constance (her daughter)	*Eileen Sharp*

(you will find this correct though I haven't seen the cast) & Trial by Jury as well. You know whom

Judge	*Leo Sheffield*
Usher	*Sydney Granville*
Defendant	*Leo Darnton*
Counsel	*Henry Millidge*
Associate	*Ivan Menzies*
Foreman	*Penry Hughes*
Bride	*Kathleen Anderson*
1st bridesmaid	*Aileen Davies*

I hope you will excuse the writing – I am doing it in bed & its late & the blanket is leaning on the end of the pen & I'm too lazy to lift it off. Thanks to Eric for the budget but it did not include one of the import things viz what films to ask for so that it looks as if I am an old hand.

Question? Does Quaker Oats keep. I have some left from last term. It looks & smells all right. It has been covered but air of course can get to it. It is dry. Very important this. I think you ought to write & tell me if I can use it so that letter reaches me by Monday. I think that as I have to work so hard I ought to get 3 letters a week to cheer me up. Dyer used to get 7.

Funny about Madgwick. Browne was asked by him to send me on some Elasticity notes after he had used them, so he did so. Anthem was "Dear B, please return the E & M notes by Monday at 7pm". This he had written on some 6 months before. So I started dashing round sending them back in a great hurry as you know. Well you put in the next a little piece, about 3 ins say, of that very, very fine wire that Eric's got, the finest wire you have got. We are not editing this in maths lecture. This is continued in Mineralogy lecture.

I can give you the cast of Yeomen

Lieutenant of the Tower	*Sydney Granville*
Sergeant Meryl	*Darrell Fancourt*
Wilfred Shadbolt	
(assistant head jailor & tormentor)	*Leo Sheffield*
Jack Point (strolling jester)	*Henry Lytton*
Dame Carruthers	*Bertha Lewis*
Elsie Maynard (strolling singer)	*Winifred Lawson*
Phoebe Meryl	*Eileen Sharp*
Probably also the following	
Colonel Fairfax & Leonard Meryl	*Leo Darnton & Charles Goulding*
Kate (niece of Dame Carruthers)	*Elsie Griffin*
	Possibly Kathleen Anderson

Had a Latymer meeting. Ellis read a characteristic aesthetic paper. Ellis is a true aesthete & the paper is admirable taken off by "Patience". Nevertheless it had points of interest. I induced Pars to go & we had a fierce discussion at the meeting. Cobban wanted to push through a request from the Old Man changing his status from Vice-President (with Tubby) to an Honorary Member. Pars was violently opposed to it & the rest of us disagreed too. However, I will tell you more later.

Love from Maurice

This second letter appears to have closely followed, and refers to Delcomen by the name 'Delcymine'.

Dear Mum & Dad

I shan't be coming home this term. The school are not playing the college, at least I don't think so. In any case I shouldn't have time. I'm writing early of course. Here's to the millionaire. Cluck, cluck. I think going to Delcymine in a deputation will put his back up at once. Cox has asked me if I will ride his bike down so I shall probably do so. If I do I will send my luggage down. Luggage in advance on Schur's ticket. Hope Eric got through; my Exams commence Monday fortnight. Please note the look of the above sentence without the semi-colon.

The D'Oyly Carte are giving a departing season so that I shall be able to see Iolanthe, Yeoman, Ida, Pinafore, Sorcerer, Ruddigore. Booking starts next Monday. Don't book. Can always get in for 3/-. Eileen Sharp is leaving the company before August to act in "confession" at St Martins. Of course you know what a repertory season means.

Dixon is up here today swimming for Imperial College against the Varsity. Joe is not in the varsity team but I hope he will get in. I had to waste an hour or two carting Dixon round. The Old Boys F.O. have sent me some 1/- tickets for a sweep on the Derby which they want me to get rid of. Would you like one; I am getting one myself. The 1st prize is £20, the second £10, the third £5, & the 4th £2 10s. Also the sellers of the 4 winning tickets receive £1 each. They are sending books of tickets to Murphy & Salter so I had to dash round early to the Old Latymerians. Then I hit on the brilliant wheeze of asking them to get tickets. Neither had received their tickets yet & I got two from Joe & one from Murphy. They will be peeved when they get their books. When you go to the Yeoman get the timetable of the Repertory season.

Went to a lecture by a big American chemist, Noyes. In a lecture two days before Palmer said "There are two Noyes in America". Tremendous applause.

I expect I shall be glad of a thin vest later on because even now it is hot during the quarter of an hour the sun shines. Just at the moment it is horribly damp and cold.

Dixon passed as one of the 300 for Civil Service of whom 19 will be given jobs. I think they eliminate 250 or so by means of some ferocious medical examination & 31 of the remaining 50 by personal interview I expect. If he gets a job he will be as probationer assistant to the assistant inspector in the department of the chief engineer to the Post Office section.

You didn't tell me about the porridge. I wish you would look at my last letter when you write. Then you would not only be able to answer my questions but you would find material for writing a much longer letter than you actually do write.

Well, I can't think of anything else at present so goodbye.

> *Love to all*
> *from*
> *Maurice*

In this extract from a later letter Maurice made this interesting comparison to Shakespeare.

Saw amateurs do "As You Like It" in the Master's garden with a very pretty setting in flowers & trees. It was perfectly wonderful. There is nothing like Shakespeare anywhere unless it is G&S in a different line, but Shakespeare can stand without good acting. It needs only to be spoken with sense.

Gilbert and Sullivan were not Ada's only loves. She also owned some novels by American author and naturalist Gene Stratton-Porter – one of them a present from Maurice on her 50th Birthday, 18th January 1924. Gene Stratton Porter is described by Smithsonianmag.com as being as *famous in the early 1900's as J.K.Rowling is now.* She published *26 novels, nature studies, poetry collections and children's books,* and five of her books sold over a million copies. There exists a Gene Stratton Porter Society and a Gene Stratton Porter Historic Site where Wetland and Prairie restoration is in progress.

This next letter wishes Maurice a happy birthday and his birthday was November 6th, but I am unsure of the year. There are two words in this letter which I cannot decipher.

Ashburton Lodge
Putney Heath
SW15

My darling son

We all wish you a very happy birthday & many happy returns of the day. Eric was sending you a selection of the operas. I went up to Chapples to see if I could get that book of songs. I found that it was 15/- & as I owe you so much I thought it best to get the less expensive ones.

I shall get you later a book of one of the operas – which do you like best let me know. I thought dear, as you have a p_____ you may like to st_____ of course the separate books are 7/- I can get them in Putney. Dad sent this knife so you must give him a coin when you come up for it. I have saved 1£ & was going to put it in parcel but did not think it safe. I shall have the 3£ for you before you come up will send it or keep it until you come, which you like.

Have sent 3 prs of new socks have not washed them if you don't wear them too long they won't get holes in them. Only don't wear them if you get a wound on your feet. Have sent an old pair of pants which you need not send to the wash. If you wear it up when you come I will have a new pair ready it will save washing, hope the things will arrive alright & the pairs not bad.

Should like to have sent you more but must pay my debts, we have paid premium & the land fees since you went up, so we haven't done so bad. Dad <u>must</u> have boots next week. Fondest love from all

Your loving Mother & Dad

Why not try the bars have enclosed tutor which please do not destroy.

Clearly they are trying to help Maurice financially despite their limited monetary resources. The mention about paying land fees might be a reference to Will and Ada trying to buy a house of their own. They were seeking to buy a newbuild house. Construction began on 52 Rosslyn Crescent on 6th July 1925, and the purchase price was to be £1050. Purchase did get completed, but by the time of completion the official purchaser would be Maurice Burwood not Will Burwood because that purchase was not until 1927 after Will's death.

This next letter is from Maurice at Cambridge.

Dear Mum & Dad

I'm sorry I'm using the nice crested envelopes but I've used up all my plain ones and cannot procure any more crested ones. Therefore, after about 4 more letters I shall have to send you postcards. Of course you won't mind I'm sure. Poor Old Keighley's had a cold. How's the old "Arofless roofer" with his roofs. I don't know whether I told you they put up lab fees 1.1.0 a term & lecture fees 10/6. So my bill this term will probably be £68 if not more.

Sad to relate I have to go to tea today with Mrs Mills. She has two daughters who, I am told, look as if they have been run over by a steam roller. I shall probably have to come up in the long vac next year, which will be a bit expensive. As far as running goes, I am doing so in the college sports on Tuesday. Monday, Wed & Sat are football matches. We won two league matches last week Clare & Sydney 2-1 & 6-1 which is a good start. The Varsity team don't seem so dusty. They've found two good backs freshers & a good wing half. Forwards are still weak. I have been playing back in the last two matches. If you are keen on sending groceries you can send cheese, bacon, sugar, sardines, biscuits, little salt, anything you like in fact but don't forget it costs money.

I may not be coming home during the term because the Charterhouse match is off, the Oxford match if it occurs will be on our ground. If they get a match with Lancing I may get home. I shall ask Salmon to get a match near London if he can. Did I tell you Salmon, Wright, Dyer, & Powell played in the Seniors trial. I've broken the glass of my watch. I've stuck a piece of cardboard across the hole in the case. Is that enough to keep the dust out or shall I get a glass put in. By the way, another question for Eric on the intricacies of digging in the grave. Does one push the jolly old instrument upwards or downwards.

We are playing Wellingborough in a week or two but we don't go through London, alas. The Rugger people have lost all their matches up to now. By the way do you know how the phrase "Hobson's choice" was derived. It was the result of the efforts of a man named Hobson who had horses for hire in what is now called Hobson's of Cambridge. The undergrads used to go in & pick out the good horses so that they were worked to death & the poor ones not used. So he arranged his horses in order & the men who came had to take them in order. The stables is not a garage of course.

Have you been looking for my press links & silver pearl. I hope not because I've found them here in Cambridge. How did they get there? Latest scientific problem. Next time I hope to give an interesting lecture on "Osmosis & its relation to life". But don't worry, it won't be technical.

Kearsey's brother was up here a week before I came up. He stayed in my rooms & was highly interested in my clock. During last vac Kearsey went to work in the chem lab at school. He isn't going again, Georgie kept telling him was a - - - - - - - - - - nuisance or words to that effect. Did you see the old boys lost last Saturday 2-1 in the A.F.A. cup. Well, I must stop now

Love from loving son
M R Burwood Jesus
College Cambridge

Very good of the Old Lady. Don't expect gown is any use.

This next letter definitely dates to November 1923 as it refers to Maurice qualifying for a 'latch key'. Traditionally a child was awarded a 'latch key' to the family's house on their 21st birthday - 6th November 1923 for Maurice.

When I was a child in the 1960's one of my earliest memories of what one might term 'political scandals' was a report that increasing numbers of children had their own front door keys and let themselves into their own homes after school because mothers as well as fathers were at work. It was considered to be a 'scandal' that 'housewives' should 'have' to work.

It also mentions Will and Eric getting or building radio sets, and wiring in electric lighting – electricity in houses was still comparatively new. The BBC began broadcasting in late 1922 after the government decided to authorise a single broadcaster – fearing that private broadcasters would interfere with government and military radio communications.

The Lodge
Ashburton Lodge
Putney Heath
London SW15

Sunday
Dear old chap

Just a line or two to wish you many happy returns of the day, and incidentally to inform you that you are now allowed a latch key and also to pay your own debts. We all of us wish we could have made you a nice present but as circumstances are you must accept the wish as the deed. Anyway we shall think of you on the 6th. I am sorry you did not get a look in at the Cam Trials, but we must look on the best side if it was not meant to be, so you must put your back into your work things will pan out alright in the end. Don't forget to send us a list of your fixtures. I bought The Sporting Life giving the results of the college sports.

I see Edie and Sam other day she has got her furniture up here and she seems jolly glad but Alma would not come down because Maurice was not there. You spoke of Hobson's Choice in your letter, but I am afraid there are many versions of tale – mine is that during the American Spanish war a young Lieut named Hobson's done a very brave thing and all the girls in New York on his return to that place made a fuss and kissed him so ever after when a girl (E lam?) I know for a fact that such was the case because the papers were full of it.

So there any chance of seeing you before the end of the term as I am anxious to know if you are playing Lancing if you go there to play Guy. Roebuck will no doubt make himself known, but you will not allow any patronage to take place for you are his superior. I have mentioned it although I don't think with you it is doing the dole kick but no matter – let us know all about it we have been having great doings in the lodge lately. I finished putting in the conduits and wire for lighting purposes and we use them tonight for the first time.

At this point Will input a small sketch of their residence including bedroom, kitchen, small room and scullery as if only one floor, but the picture of Ashburton Lodge shows an attic window. Will had worked as an electrician before so was probably wiring it himself with Eric's help.

Ashburton Lodge was in the grounds of Ashburton House, a large house on Putney Hill to the north of Putney Heath.

Continuing Will's letter -

Black line is conduit pipe

2 lights 1 switches and the doors

Of course it is out of proportion and another thing you will be glad to know we have got a wireless set and Eric has also made one but he had got to improve it a bit before we can use it. Mine cost about 30/- altogether. We are having it tonight? Notice the query? Bert sends his best respects to you Edith was over the other required. I see the Premier has been making some fine speeches lately & hope you have been able to read them. Quite food for thought and also there has been some nice articles about Bonar Law well worth anyone reading.

I don't know that I have any more to say. Kind love. Best wishes and success is the desire of your _____ Dad

W J Burwood

I hope the _____ is of use. Anyhow you shall have the other 3 volumes of the Plays soon. Hope you will get this old dear. What a lovely budget am so excited at your coming tomorrow. Aunt Polly is here again fond love & kisses from all Mum.

Another couple of words that I could not decipher.

The Prime Minister making fine speeches would have been Stanley Baldwin who became Prime Minister after Andrew Bonar Law resigned in May 1923, due to having terminal throat cancer, finishing the shortest term as Prime Minister in the Twentieth Century. The 'nice articles' about the latter were probably because he died in October 1923.

Aunt Polly is Will's mother's sister – actual name Mary Ann - born in 1858, and therefore another first cousin of his father. She married a Charles Thomas Hughes in 1879. The Edie mentioned is Will's sister Edie Sparshatt because her husband was Sam and her third child and second daughter was Alma (born 1913) – she had two older children: Albert Edwin Robert (1904) and Winifred (1908). Another daughter Edie was both born and died in 1915.

Ada would maintain contact with the Sparshatt family: a letter from Bert Sparshatt (Albert Edwin Robert) was written to Ada after the death of his mother Edie in 1951, which includes these interesting extracts:

The suddenness of Mum's passing came as rather a shock although I had told myself that it would come someday but I am glad that she did not linger. To go peacefully in her sleep was just as she wanted it to be. She had had a hard life and not a great deal of fun and happiness.

And

Yours and Uncle Will's hands came out to help me in 1920 at a very difficult time and I want you to know that I have always remembered that it was your kindness and encouragement in those days that put me on the right road. I have often said to Mum in the past that it was due to the efforts of yourself and Uncle Will that I stepped off with the "right foot". Had you not helped me to get a job in London and then urged me to go to Evening School I might never have acquired sufficient ambition to go on with my studies.

The 'hard life' which his mother suffered probably involved her husband Sam Sparshatt deserting her. A much later letter to my brother Richard includes this extract *"I was greatly helped by your grandmother who gave me temporary lodgings until I found others about 12 months later. Both she and your grandfather also gave me much encouragement in urging me to study (I was only 16 at the time) and I shall ever be grateful to them"*.

In 1933 Bert married Lillie Florence Toten and had one child Derek Edwin on 9th July 1935. Possibly Bert's 'difficult time' in 1920, when he would have been 16, was caused by problems in his parents' marriage.

The next letter was probably sent in May 1923. It refers to dropping a line to Eric for the 23rd, and Eric's birthday was the 23rd of May, and also refers to Maurice's going into lodgings next term.

> The Lodge
> Ashburton House
> Putney Heath
> S.W.15

My dearest Boy

I have looked at one of your previous letters, in which you said you were going to kick off 20th for exams on Chemistry, so that is why I thought it began yesterday. I trust you will get a First. Oh dear one thing we did so want to see your rooms & if you go into lodgings next term I suppose we shall be unable to see them I suppose.

Don't forget to send Eric just a line on the 23rd. I am afraid we cannot give him anything more. He was highly amused about the pretty girls photo. Good wheeze. How did the examiner find out about list of kings hall. Another look I suppose. Well done. Going he is getting at. First you will get something of the sort.

How soon does the result come out – just after you come down, I suppose as we must see the 'Times'! then about the description you wrote concerning programme etc. of opera, my dear boy. You should have heard the comments about your faggery to write out all that – we fairly gasped. & even Dad say where does the old chap get his information from.

I was worried a bit as I know you are busy & it must have taken you a long time. I have had a look at the programme of the Rep. season & fancy me. counting up Gon. as tops. well anyhow Gon. comes next & I chuckled after I posted my letter & remembered I had left out the Mikado. I knew I should get told off. You can put Mikado as 3rd on the preference paper. In fact one wants to put all of them top, as the old lady commented they are all lovely.

I like Patience because of the lovely music & songs, the Gondoliers because of the rollicking gaiety, & the plot of the Mikado is good & yet Ruddigore is so spiffing & yet again Yeoman was so feisty fine & British & I suppose Pinafore is British. Are not these storms frightful nearly every day we get them, the old lady at the meeting will say it's the Lord speaking to the nations to amend their ways.

How many tickets in a book did you sell them all.

The time will soon pass now for your return, you will be thankful when that time comes. Don't worry about finding money for term in Long Vac. as if needs be we must take it out of bank, you <u>must</u> have the money dear if it is going to help you, all your future career depends on it, & now take advantage of everything that will help you to gain the highest honours you can, we <u>must</u> let you have everything we can that will help you, so don't let finances worry you, even give you a pound a week if you need it, as no doubt you will.

I must close now. Mrs Cooper coming to dinner & must go shopping so with all our fond love & earnest prayers that God well bless & aid you in all you undertake.

> *Your ever loving*
> <u>*Mother*</u> *A Burwood*

This next letter is incomplete but clearly sent in 1923 because a minority Labour Government was formed after the Election on 6 December 1923. Once again G&S operettas dominate, but the letter includes advice to Maurice to vote both in Cambridge and in Putney. It was then legal if you were a student to vote both at home and at university, and possession of property in more than one place could confer the same entitlement - not made illegal until 1948.

> *Ashburton Lodge*
> *Putney Heath*
> *SW15*

My old darling

I went to see Iolanthe this afternoon & herewith I enclose programme. Couldn't get Eric from Golders Green, no doubt we shall in due time, most extraordinary scenes this afternoon. I arrived about 1:30 thought it strange, only 2 small queues & chuckled according at the prospect of a good seat. I went in the gallery found to my dismay half full of early door people, it was <u>high</u>, higher than Princes, & such a frowsy crowd, I couldn't hear very well, no backs to seats.

Eileen was splendid & sang that last song fine, we are so disappointed we couldn't see Pinafore we couldn't get a full programme before &

now as you see they are only doing it once & not doing Sorcerer at all, disappointing, so I hope to see Gondoliers, Patience, Pirates. Dad has gone to see Princess Ida tonight you see Dad must go when he is in early.

I heard people saying they waited half an hour in the pouring rain & then couldn't get in & when I came out at 5 people were lining up with their stools & the streets crammed with cars. Goodness knows if we shall get in. I might try Ruddigore or Yeoman, wish you were here my dear old boy. You are inspired, God bless you! Glad to inform you have A.E. Jones receipt safely, he is disgusted with the Labour government, but there. I sent that news this morning, I have ascertained that you are entitled to 2 votes I here & 1 at the Varsity use it, its essential. Did you leave the third series of Gilberts plays at home. It's good to read it at home let me know

As I said, that letter is incomplete. The next letter is complete, but hard to date, and again topic number one is Gilbert and Sullivan.

Ashburton Lodge
Putney Heath
SW15

My darling Boy

This is a G&S letter. I am sending you my lovely souvenirs without delay.

When I read a queue had formed midnight Friday night my heart went into my boots & I wished I had gone in the week but none of us had enough money until Friday. Then I thought I would risk it on Sat. so you can imagine my dismay when I read that on Sat. morn. As it happened Dad came in about 3 Sat afternoon, finished, so we conferred, and arrived about 4 at Palmers.

Great scenes of enthusiasm & little crowds all round princes & police stationed all round. We lined up & found the police giving out tickets when they got to us. They talked a little then the attendant said oh yes give the lady and gentleman one each. They said its only starting. We didn't hear as we were the last of the line to know how many standing tickets. He said you can go away now an hour or two, be here not later than 7 o'clock.

Dad & I talked it over. I wondered if it was possible for one of us to give up our ticket to you then we said well its risky seeing the crowds & as you are going to see them in Feb, I really felt, old dear. I couldn't miss it on the chance of your being in time as they only let in a certain number.

They started at 8 oh dear. I never saw anything like it. My head aches at it all. I felt your spirit near me, it was a secret performance, no programmes, some of the ticket holders didn't turn up in time we went in early, so consequently Dad & I just squeezed in the last seat but 2 at the back, oh we were packed of course as many as possible stood.

We had Trial By Jury, last act of Pirates, & the last act of Iolanthe much to Dad's huge enjoyment as he had seen none of those. They brought the house down with the applause, & at the last they screamed for Henry Lytton. He had to come to the front – in his dressing gown, quarter of an hour after it was over & make a speech, he began in a weak voice, oh I shall be late for my party & so on.

Perhaps my dear next time you will be with us. It is something to be remembered in the speech they said that they may be coming again in 2 years time to London at which some shouted its too long, then he said they may play Utopia at which Dad went frantic & stood on the seat & waved his arm & shouted hooray Hear Hear you know how he can shout – not one left before quite 20 minutes after it was over. We arrived home at nearly 1 o'clock too tired to get any supper. Eric may go on his tour.

Men were trying to trade in the tickets some paying pounds, when we lined up hundreds were turned away on the chance of about 30 lined at 6 o'clock up abreast with the ticket holders 4 lines. The Police & attendants came & said its no <u>earthly</u> use you expecting to get in they stuck there & wouldn't budge, & ladies came up in cars & taxis & to try at the box office & went away some sneaked in our queue, but they were turned away, as our tickets were numbered, mine & Dad's were 401 & 402 & we were lined up singly when we went in a police looked at our numbers & had to give in our ticket at the booking office. There were different coloured tickets & the colour pasted up at different points we were excited to see (line up here for the <u>Cambridge</u> ticket) Cambridge being underlined. Dad enquired if they were for the Undergrads but it was only the colour.

It was a great day. The only regret was that my old darling Maurice wasn't with us. Next time we will go to <u>every one</u> & you will be there for the <u>last</u>. Here's a long letter. I must go & have a nap to get refreshed. How I longed for you to be there – too precious to miss perhaps both you & I losing *a place. Dad's fancy trip is cancelled – cannot get any accommodation at the Tyrol only one chance & old lady won't risk it passports & all got most annoying*

> *That all*
> *Your tired*
> *Mum*

Will lost out on a trip to the Tyrol after getting a passport. The date of this letter is probably 1922 or early 1923 purely on the strength of a postcard sent to Ada from Will at Amiens and date is, I think, 3 July 1923, but the post office stamp is not clear and it might be 1920 – or even 1925. The stamp also mentions the Somme as well as Amiens. Another postcard with no date was sent I think from Calais and mentioned visiting Ypres. Did Will's employer have him drive her on a trip visiting First World War battlefields or cemeteries?

This next letter is Maurice's reply to the last letter – referring to Maurice not taking one of their tickets and to paying for the 'Long Vac'.

Dear Mum & Dad

Thanks for souvenir. I expected it would be photos. I'm frightfully pleased you got in. Bet you enjoyed it. Wanted to go not so much for the intrinsic worth of the performance but to join in the excitement. Of course I should not have dreamt of taking one of your tickets, though I could have come down pretty speedily easily in time. You seem to be under the impression that I should have gone back to Cam on Sat. Of course not; next day is the day. Gandar wasn't sure if he was coming back on Sunday. Last train on Sat is 10.10.

*I hope you will like the enclosed fag card. You were lucky to get in. Of course you see they have a month's holiday & open at Brighton on the 25*th *or so. I saw one girl has been 110 times. So would I if I had the ooftish. There are two G&Sists in our lab working next to me both cursing because they couldn't go. They are, as a matter of fact, extreme Eileen Sharpists & were frightfully annoyed when I said she was leaving. Then when I gloated about having a souvenir one of them produced a book 2/10 including postage containing pictures of all the operas, good pictures too by the*

Sphere people. You write up to the Sphere. I can send you address if you like. If Eric has to work on Monday he had better come Wed. If he bikes & arrives about 4 I will have just arrived from labs. I can manage my luggage & he can bike home with Waddams.

With regards to coming up on Sunday the Porter tells me the day ticket is 6/8 so you might as well come up. You need not bother about having good clothes. My suitcase will be about 5/- to send. Tommy says I am going to see if these facts are right & if they are you had better come, both of you. Mum can leave Aunt E & Uncle A if not Dad can come. Will Dad want camera now? He does not need the suitcase so importantly now does he? I shall not send suitcase till I hear that you won't come down. If I sent it on Friday it will arrive Sat I expect

With regards to money thanks for 10/- but I did not mean you to send any. Elliott is the tutor you understand & my £25 college money is just taken off the bill, but they will give me money if I want it, which is put on the bill as "cash". I have enough money to pay you, if you are short, for the trip on Sunday. That is to say, I shall be able to pay for Long Vac term so can walk safety get the money from Elliott. If it is the last Peacehaven I can let you have the money for that too. Please enlighten me on all these points implication above letter & excuse scribble. Hurry.

Love from Maurice

Man in Railway tells me this. Week end tickets (- any train Sat return any train on Sunday Mon or Tues) 9/3. Suitcase 5/3.

A shorter letter next, once again mostly about G&S.

The Lodge
Ashburton House
SW15
May 15th

My darling

Will and I had a glorious evening at the Yeoman last night. It was <u>fine</u> & I so enjoyed Eileen. I think I must write to tell her she must not leave the company. Leo Sheffield & Eileen in "If I were thy bride" was really fine. We *hurried away at the end as I didn't want to miss the last bus. It is thundery weather. This is an order of preference as far as I am concerned. I like Patience 1st*

Ruddigore
Gondoliers
Yeoman
Pirates & that's all I've seen.

I don't know when you come down but I should like to go with you to the 3 I have marked. We must see old dear. The only thing it's so warm in there & I have got a raging headache unless the thunder is the cause of it excuse parental.

I hope you are giving yourself some breathing spaces between the swotting. I will write next after I have received an answer from you.

Fondest love & God's blessing from your loving Mother.

You will notice they are giving The Gondoliers more times than any of the others. Did I tell you we are having a Sullivan evening on Sat. You must see the Yeoman the cutting I've enclosed is writing of it. – of Yeoman the cast is sent was all correct I enclose programme.

I've got a good deal of pain today in my face I'm sure its nerve pain 'cos I got hot up in the gallery & excited shall go in the pit for the future, better crowd of folks. I shall go to a Doctor in a week or two if the pain don't go.

Pit is 2/- Amphit 1/6 which is about 5 seats attached to gallery

Bye bye dear love
From Mum

This next letter can fairly clearly be dated to just before the general election on 29 October 1924 because of the reference to the 'dreadful red letter', which must mean the Zinoviev letter leaked to the Daily Mail about four days before the election. Zinoviev was the Head of the Communist International. Now believed to have been a forgery - though forged by who is unproven – it alleged that treaties then planned between the Labour Government and the Soviet Union would be used by the Communists to assist a Bolshevik plot against the country.

The letter allegedly lost Labour the General Election. Not provable, but the Conservatives did win a large majority.

Ashendon Lodge
Putney Heath
SW13

My darling son,

I'm dashing off a letter quickly as I am so busy. On Monday I went to Wembley to have a good book to study on my very own, & to my great annoyance Auntie Edie & Alma saw me after I had been there about an hour, of course they had no money for anything. I paid for their tea and Alma had the sulks because we did not stay long enough in the Amusement Park, Alma wishing she could go on this or that. I turned a deaf ear to each appeal.

Then last night Dad & I went to see Patience when I tell a queue was as long outside the pit as far from here as the Green Man or even longer. Just where we joined the queue was split to allow people to go in the entrance & about 20 people came in by twos and threes & insisted to the police that they had been there a long time & the first two girls at the back one a red hat and one white so that's how he kept them out. He said he was queuing up on Friday himself. Then I had an altercation with a lady inside. We got 2 seats in the second row – she resented us pushing by, must tell you all about it. Anyhow, all passed off happily, the pit was full of early door people, I must say.

Now Patience _must_ come first in order of preference, then Yeoman. Dolly Dad & Eric going on Thursday to Pirates evening, I must go to Gondoliers on Thursday matinee, I feel it too much to stay for evening too, but think I must go to yeoman, why don't they stay longer say the people by the way, was disappointed that Glanville did not play Archibald, it was Milligan, he sang well, but not so clear as Glanville, all the other artists were the same. _Why_ didn't I go to Ruddigore. I like them better than ever. come with me in spirit to Gondoliers.

I enclose Princess Ada Dad went

Congrats on a good game at Wellingborough. _Do_ tell us what you want for your birthday.

We have got the deeds of the land – at last signed & sealed. It is 26 feet by 15.5 ft, we have to put up a fence within 6 months. Went to labour meeting did I tell you I had a small audience of reds with their flaming *rosettes outside, they really <u>could not</u> answer some of my questions. I pray there will be a big majority for a stable government. Mrs Temps called yester morn (hassas). Iris called, she said, to ask someone's advice about the dreadful <u>red</u> letter, Dads away. I'm liberal I was going to vote labour, don't think I will vote, sequel. Think I've got 3 votes for Conservatives. Samuel himself is not much good; (this is <u>my</u> personal opinion, Maurice, but his policy is alright. She said Mrs Burwood can advise me better than anybody, she begged me to go down to see him, that requires thinking about.*

Old boy, the money <u>this</u> week is going to D'Oyly Carte, can't resist, but will soon pull up, enclosed, poor Mrs Price letter – sent me a paper – terrible hooliganism in Wales. I see I've missed a side of paper – you see – I want to write a lot but am too busy so I'm a bit excited got to vote, buy a licence, etc, etc, etc.

Dad was charmed with Patience, yes off to Mikado tonight, I might go. People lamenting on bus last night wish I could afford to go to Mikado, shall go to every one when they come to London.

Must really stop will write again fondest love

> *From all*
> *Your loving mother*
> *A Burwood*

The Edie mentioned must be Will's sister Edie Sparshatt because her daughter Alma was born in 1913 so the right age to sulk about not spending long enough in an Amusement Park. Having 'no money for anything' could be because of her husband deserting her.

I assume that getting the deeds of the land and putting a fence up refers to their planned future home at 52 Rosslyn Crescent. £125 was the deposit paid, and a loan of £900 would be applied for towards the purchase price. Will and Ada were hoping to become property owners after so many moves. Sadly, Will would not live to see that purchase completed, so there would be no happy joint retirement for them – nor had there been for their parents, nor would there be for their children and grandchildren.

The next letter from Maurice is one I cannot date, but once again G&S feature largely.

Dear Old Things

I am too busy, alas, to write a long letter & I've really got a lot to talk about. I shall have to make notes & sing them forth when I come down.

I have wasted a lot of time seeing Patience, Yeoman of the Guard, and Princess Ida. Henry Lytton, Leo Sheffield & Darrel Fancourt were the good itself, the former (who is about 50-60) being easily the best. Winifred Lawson's singing was absolutely wonderful. Her opening song in Princess Ida is in Gems from Sullivan's cornet solo, which they never play right at the Scouts. Eric will play it on the cello. I knew the tune was a fine one but – well, they applauded & cheered for about 5 minutes. "Love is a plaintive song" from Patience, sung by her was equally applauded. I was at the back of the gallery & yet hardly missed a word in any of the plays except in "Ensembles" where several different songs were sung at the same time. The other leading ladies were very fine, too. Catherine Ferguson does not sing as well but is the best actress. Bertha Lewis does both well. The great thing is that you can hear what they _all_ say. In amateur performances the ladies are usually not too clear. The song – "I have a song to sing-O", "Sing me your song-o" etc in the Yeoman was one of the best!

Everybody up here is raving about "Ruddigore". They say it is almost as good as the Mikado. Now the D'Oyly Carte visit is over everybody is going about wearing a haunted worried look. I have suddenly woken up to the fact that I've some work to do. Thanks for the money. Tried measuring a crystal the other day. It's a terrible job. The measuring takes half a minute, the adjusting about an hour & a half.

Did you see how Lowry & Wright between them nearly beat Lancs. Will you send up to me some of your many camphor balls so that during the long vac the clothes I leave up will not be eaten up.

By the way, the Yeoman of the Guard is almost a tragedy

Watkins is getting married & the Latymer Club is giving him a present also. Hope it won't be more than 2/6 each.

We had an interesting lecture on distance of travel of sound. Long distance records have always been made against the wind. Velocity of the wind has no effect. What is effective is the gradient of the wind velocity as you go up. If it is blowing faster higher up then underneath, the sound waves are bent down into ground (if going with the wind) & are absorbed by the ground. If going against the wind they are bent up & so do not dissipate their energy by friction with the ground & therefore go further.

If the velocity is less, going up, the opposite occurs. At midday in hot weather the bottom layers of air are hot & the top cool. Then sound is bent up both ways. Now if the length of the arrows (diagram of 8 horizontal arrows with the middle arrows longer) *denote the velocity of the wind the sound rays travel like this* (diagram of sound wave curved up about surface of earth) *and so a zone of silence is obtained & then further away from the source of sound is heard again. Also moving to varying gradients the sound can come different ways & so several repetitions of the sound can be heard at intervals. This had actually been observed in the case of loud explosions.*

At the Silvertown explosion as many as 5 were heard. Many experiments were made during the war. At Silvertown a diagram of audibility was obtained. 20 miles north of it no sound was heard. In Cambridge & Suffolk & Norfolk (in part) no sound was heard. But at Stowe it was heard plainly. You can look up Stowe on the map. At two places in the silent zone it was heard. These were on high ground. It may not have been the sound however.

Hope Dad is bearing up bravely against the pressure of work. Its quite easy when you know how to do it. The best thing is not to do it (the work). I met Fordham (a soccer player from Sloane School) at Princess Ida. He said Latymer had won a schools championship. He said it wasn't a cross-country so I think it have been the inter-schools. Anyhow he said Faithful won the quarter. (Claridge, by the by, left at Easter). The chaps up here say the inter-schools was next Tuesday but that may have changed it to last Tuesday. Anyhow you had better find out before you go. It may give it in the West London Gazette. If not you have better go to the school if you want to see it.

I must close not with love to all from

Maurice

'A' team drew with Cranwell R.A.F. 4-4 most exciting match tell you next time.

The Silvertown explosion was a munitions factory in London which detonated in 1917. The comment about Will 'bearing up under the pressure of work is another hint that Will's health could be in decline, as the next letter mentions. Aunt Nell is probably Will's unmarried sister, though Ada had an Aunt Nell whose married name was Stepney.

32 Goodwin Road
Cliftonville
Tuesday

My Beloved Son

You will be sorry to hear that Aunt Nell was operated on last night for appendicitis so I had the 2 of them to look after, it has upset poor Dad of course it is comfortable here in the flat if Dad gets worse. I shall not move him from here now. I hope you are getting on alright & that you are looking after yourself. If you see Eric tell him the news, I will write later. I called at the hospital this morning & she was fairly comfortable.
With fond love
From Dad & Mum
Had a bad storm last night my dearest.
Warwick is here – he told me not to take the letter he sent to heart – he <u>had</u> to write and send it to please Nellie. He knows you and Eric have given your last cent. I didn't want you to hear when we arrived either. She asked as she was frantic because we came, she made herself ill but I cannot tell you all myself. Warwick still thinks highly of you both. We have been relieved of the worry now by Nell being in hospital. God works in a mysterious way, His wonders to perform. She was really unkind to us & said we ought to go to Brighton, but no doubt she was ill and we must forgive her, send me Warwick letter, fond love & write soon dear.
Love from Mum

Will's sister Nell would live until 1956 (this is not the only hint that she could be 'difficult'). As we approach Will's last illness, there was one bit of very happy news for Will and Ada before that. On 25 February 1926, their eldest son Eric got married.

The bride's name was Florence Gertrude Stevens, born 1902, but always known as 'Dolly'. Eric and Dolly would go on to provide Will and Ada with their first two grandchildren. First was William John – named exactly the same as Will so probably in tribute to Eric's father because 'Bill' was born in 1927 after Will's death. Bill would acquire a younger sister Marianne Frances in 1930, who would go on to become a top fashion model in the 1950's, and wrote that she once turned down a date with a too good-looking young male model who would go on to become an actor – named Roger Moore!

Sadly Will would never know his grandchildren.

Will left his employment with the Charringtons in June 1926 due to being unable to continue with his duties – clearly due to illness – which leads to his last letter to his beloved Ada dated on the day he died - 3rd October 1926 – and clearly knowing he was about to die.

My Dear Sweetheart.

All that I have and own is yours.

I want to leave just a few lines that will help you to bear the burden.

We have loved each other from the beginning and each moment has not been too much and as we are on the wrong side of 50 we cannot be parted very long. You do know that I believe absolutely in the Lord Jesus and I know you do so. We have that consolation we are saved for eternity and since it has pleased the Lord to take me first, you know I am safe in his hands.

Now my love you would not have me back to pass through all the pain again. I am sure you do not, and as its me first its better because without you I should be like a tree without its root, a child without its mother, a husband without his wife and of such a wife I have had as one would look after me like you have done.

I am all too uninteresting to anybody else except to you. I am your all and you are my all. It may be selfish of me to be glad to go first but I was in pain let that be my excuse.

You dear heart have someone to love you not quite like me but nearly so. Your two boys I know because for any mother I would have given all and our sons are the same the love for their father is not less keen but there is the feeling in a son that the father does not need. The sympathy and protection from that which would harm. Like a mother so dear sweetheart there is their love and mine that is now intensified through Jesus Christ so with us it is not goodbye just Au Revoir my love. I am in Jesus hands. I leave you in his also.

Your own affectionate
sweetheart
Will

Don't wear weeds just a hat.

Buy a small bunch of flowers. Violets if possible. Put half of them in my hand and keep half yourself.

That is all my dear heart. I am at rest. I promised you that I would come to you sometimes if Jesus allows it.

The Valley has been dark but Jesus helps you through it.

<u>*Will*</u>
X

Once again Will faced death bravely – putting his faith in Jesus.

I do wonder if Ladysmith, with its unhealthy diet and contaminated water, contributed to his hernia and eventual death, but I can only wonder.

The following letters are all letters of condolence on Will's death, starting with two relevant to his time as a scoutmaster.

East Putney,
SW15
30th October, 1926

Dear Mrs Burwood,

Just a line to convey to you and your sons, my sincere sympathy & grief, on learning of the passing of your beloved husband & my old dear friend & chum. I learned of his illness in the Putney Hospital, months ago now whilst recovering myself from a month's sickness & then of his removal to north London. I called at Oxford Rd on several occasions for news but had no idea until this last week of the sad news of his loss. I was so grieved & hurt that I was not informed of the serious turn in his condition & of his removal to Brighton. My brother Frank, & several of my scouts who knew Mr Burwood at camp in the Isle of Wight – also join with me in sending their sincere regret & sympathy for you all. We can only trust that his release was a merciful one from further suffering & that you may be given comfort & courage to bear up under his will & the knowledge of his love.

Mr Delcomyn told me of his visit to him at Brighton & many of us will always cherish the memory of him as a truly Christian gentleman & a true Scout. He has been & always will remain my ideal scoutmaster.

> Believe me,
> Yours very sincerely
> Arthur V. Atkinson
> to her family.

The name Delcomyn appears again as the sender of this letter.

> Feldheym
> Wimbledon Common
> S.W.
> 4 Oct 1926

Dear Mrs Burwood

I was grieved to hear your sad news from Maurice this morning; will you convey my thanks to him for letting me know. At the same time we must be thankful that your dear husband's sufferings are at an end. His name will for ever be linked up with our group & be honoured & revered by all who knew him, for no one has done more for the boys than he did. He is now at rest. May God's blessing be with you all & please accept my heartfelt sympathy.

> Yours very sincerely
> Th A Delcomyn

This last condolence letter is from Will's brother Warwick. Lu is his wife, and little Glyn was Warwick's son Glyndwr born in 1918.

My dear old Sister

Lu has said all and has expressed my feelings to the letter. But my dear girl there is that terrible loss of a dear brother and my only one at that *which I shall never forget him and I know he has gone to His Father. The loss is yours and mine Ada but the gain is his.*

I pray God he will bless you after the noble fight you have made to save him & in your sorrow may you feel the comfort of knowing that you have done all that has been humanly possible to do. I should have loved to have spent the last moments with him But am thankful that he had you all by him. Thank God for that just kiss his dear old face for me as the last from his broken-hearted Brother he has been longing for. I wrote to you this morning dear one our letters crossed I wish I hadn't now – telling you of little Glyn. You have quite enough. Anyhow don't worry he is going on nicely. Try and be still brave as you have been all through. God will still give you strength only trust in him. I wish I was nearer you, but you have your dear sister – she had been good to you now. Do Bear up a little longer and then you will be able to have your well-earned rest. Good night dear, much love and deepest sympathy from us all.

> *Warwick & Lu*
> *The children are very*
> *upset – they loved their*
> *Uncle Will.*

I have an address of 6 Harcourt Terrace, Mill Hill for Will and Ada after leaving his employment due to ill health. After Will's death Maurice, my father, took over the responsibility for looking after and housing his mother, and fulfilled that pledged duty until her death – but all that is for future tales.

Ada at Ashburton Lodge, Putney Heath

Young Eric Burwood

Ada's niece Edith Ada May Brown

Eric and his parents in Kensington garden

Eric Burwood marries Dolly (Florence Gertrude Stevens) in February 1926

Edie Tyler with her children Pearl, Cyril & Vic

CHAPTER SIX

Tanners & Hales

Time to leave my father's parents and return to my mother's parents – again mostly relying on the memories of my mother and my aunt because I have no letters between Wally and Ethel during their courtship. They were never separated by Naval Service or job hunting, and the Hale sisters communicated with each other by postcards. Wally, like many Portsmouth men, worked his whole life for the Naval Dockyard - he was indentured on 27th February 1902 and served well enough to receive a letter from St James Palace dated 8th August 1947 awarding him an Imperial Service Medal. Ethel lived all her life in Portsmouth.

Walter Richard Tanner married Sarah Ethel Hale on 30th May 1914, and their daughter Olive was born on 11th April 1915 – so they did not waste any time, but a major event impacted their lives between those dates – the outbreak of the First World War on 4th August 1914, Ethel's 27th birthday.

Wally was not called up to fight because he was working in the Naval Dockyard at Portsmouth. He worked long hours for the next four years, and it may not be chance that my mother Marjorie was not born until 11th December 1919 - after the war was over.

They were luckier than many who lost close family members in combat, but they did not escape tragedy. Wally's elder brother Bert died in 1917 of natural causes, and a second loss was caused by the War's most horrific aftermath: the influenza pandemic of 1918-1919. Here I return to quoting the memories of my mother and my aunt.

"I had an Uncle Laurie, the husband of my mother's eldest sister, Nellie. I have been told that he came from Mevagissey - in Cornwall, & had - as was the way, in those days, been apprenticed to a trade - in his case to an undertaker. Not liking this, he had come to Portsmouth with his mother & sister. This was the time of much shipbuilding, & he had found work in the Dockyard.

"Aunt Nell was the last to marry. As Laurie had mother & sister & their shop to look after. They stayed at Milford Road, when married, until they could get tenants out of their house - then Laurie died within quite a short time."

Laurie left a bible from the Congregational Sunday School in Mevagissey, on its centenary in 1904, inscribed with the name L S Edwards - remembering a life cut tragically short. Olive described her memories of the tragedy as follows:

"I was being washed by the fire one night when my father came in and said "he's very bad". Next I remember the blinds drawn, and mother putting on a black necklace. I was told that Uncle Laurie had died. Flu, I have later learned, had turned to pneumonia, and the doctor could not get the oxygen he needed. This was March 1919.

"I suppose it was 1919 when, one morning, mother was standing at the kitchen table stirring something, and said "I don't feel very well, Olive." Next, she was in bed, and my father was home from work, taking her hot drinks. My next memory is of both Mother and Father in bed ill, and both grandmothers there looking after me and them. They were given Bovril, and I was wanting some too. Apparently I had it slightly, first, but I don't remember much about it, unless it was the time I had a cough and was given melted butter and sugar by one Grandma. The other one suggested vinegar and sugar. That was not so nice!!"

Laurie died a victim of the influenza that killed more people than the entire First World War. Between June 1918 and December 1920 it probably killed at least 50 million – about 3% of the world's population. In Portsmouth the outbreak was so serious that schools closed and hospitals only admitted emergency cases.

Lawrence Edwards was not the only one infected. Olive and her parents also fell ill, with both Grandma Hale and Grandma Tanner coming in to nurse them. The pandemic was particularly unusual in that the elderly were much less affected and the worst fatalities were among younger adults – notably many young soldiers - so Laurie died and Olive's parents were really sick but Olive was only slightly ill and the grandmothers may not have got sick at all.

Nell had only been married for two years before being widowed, and she never had a good life, for Nell before her mother and long before her sisters – as Olive recalled.

"Aunt Nell found it difficult to keep her house. There was no pension for widows back then, except for those with children under 16. She took a job of housekeeper, but it was too much. She had had a tough time, since she was twelve, & she was ill for a while. Later she sold the house, & lived in rented room, but was again ill & died at 31."

Nell was actually 51 when she died as she was born in 1880 – so Olive probably meant 1931 as the year of death – though it was actually 1932.

"Nell went into lodgings, but often came to a Sunday meal with us. I remember her taking us occasionally by ferry to Gosport, & giving us some treat in the way of food there."

Among family possessions is a little book entitled *The Pronouncing Pocket Dictionary Illustrated* devoted to describing phonetically how English words are pronounced. It is annotated as owned by Marjorie Tanner, but includes the touching penciled entry *"Nellie Hale, My aunty – she gave"*. A more lasting treat than food – a present from a loving Aunt to a loving Niece.

"When she became ill, Mum & Aunt Lil took turns in spending the night at her lodgings to care for her. Mother had some infected tooth, but did not get to the dentist till after Nell died. Her tonsils became swollen & she was under treatment by Dr James for some time."

Time to return to Nell's mother, whom my own mother and aunt called Grandma Hale. As Olive recalls:

"My maternal grandmother lived in Milford Rd, Fratton & I can remember visiting her there when I was very small - I must have been three years old. It was a flat-fronted house, & had, I think, one of the old fashioned foot scrapers in the wall by the door. My grandmother lived in the middle downstairs room, & it had a fire with an oven next to it."

Just 'middle downstairs room'? I am unsure whether Olive means that one room was all Grandma Hale had to live in or if it was all visitors saw.

"My next memories are of Grandmother (Hale) living with us, in Alverstone Road, & Aunt Nell & Uncle Laurie in Teddington Road, Milton.

"Because Grandpa Hale had died intestate, his house could not be sold until the youngest child was 21 yrs old. Now she was able to sell it, & she came to live with us in Alverstone Rd. There was the spare bedroom - quite a big one, & there she had a bed-sit, with bed, little Victorian dressing table, & washstand, table, couch, 4 chairs, basket armchair, sideboard, & built-in wardrobe, & a fireplace. Still room to move around - Until we had the electricity lighting put in, I remember the big oil lamp on her table.

"We used the gas jets on the walls. She would be helping with washing, cooking, & various little jobs, then retire to her room later in the afternoon, light her fire, & spend the evening there. Regularly, on Saturdays, she would sweep & dust her room, till the last few months, when she was ill. She lived until 1935, when she was 81."

A hard life – orphaned young - little education – widowed with four young daughters – forced to let two children go into an orphanage – seeing her youngest suffering physically due to poor diet - up to and including watching the tragedy of her elder daughter's life and death. A patient and undemanding soul, who settled for her little bed-sit and did her best not to intrude on her daughter and son-in-law's life while finding some security and comfort for her final years in their care.

My mother had very fond memories of her.

Her other daughters were more fortunate, and here I return to quoting the memories of my Aunt Olive – and another chauffeur in the family!

"Lil, who married Will Hutty had 2 sons - Vic, who went into the Army, & Ed, who worked in the Dockyard. Will Hutty went to the war, as a driver. He had been a chauffeur, & once the driver of the Mayor's car. Later he returned to the family occupation of gardening, then took a shop near Sevenoaks. We went to visit them there several times, & went to both Vic's and Ed's weddings."

According to a postcard dated 27th August 1936 Ethel visited Sevenoaks without Walter but with her sister Minnie instead, and wrote to tell Walter that they were going to the zoo before taking a coach home to Portsmouth from Victoria. Another postcard from both Walter and Ethel at Sevenoaks was dated 1958.

Will Hutty served as a driver in the First World War. Vic would serve in the Second World War – of which more will come in a future chapter.

"Min & Bob returned to Portsmouth. They had one son, Bert. Bob, who never had good health after the war, died in 1942. Bert, who had known what unemployment meant before WW2, then was in the RAFA on the balloons. He married Daphne, then was in the RAF & was in the Desert & crossed to Italy, & at the end of the war was up in North Italy at Udino. His marriage failed. After the demobbing he returned for a while to the RAF, then left & had a happy marriage to Kathleen."

'On the balloons' would mean the barrage balloons which guarded against low level air attacks.

Marjorie wrote similarly but with other details.

"Min married Mr Robert Holton. I gathered that she worked in the household of Mr Addison, a solicitor, at first, & that he had a house in Maidenhead. Later he was part of a firm of solicitors at Hampshire Terrace in Portsmouth. That was when I knew them. They were given the top flat, & had a son Robert. He was known as Bert, & his father was Bob. During the Second World War they used to go down in the basement, where the safes were. One day, during a raid, they were frightened by a sudden sound as of bricks falling. Bob was especially worried because apparently he had been practically buried in the trenches in World War 1.

"Later years, when Bob had died, Min came to live in Bramshott Rd, off Winter Rd, in a house offered her by Dad. It had a narrow alley beside it where Grandpa used to keep his ladders etc. when he & his workers were building around there."

Min's husband Bob died in 1942. The Grandpa mentioned here is William Richard Tanner and the Dad Wally Tanner – as I return to Olive's memories of her family – and yet another chauffeur. Involvements with the Navy and the sea on both sides of my family – and now involvements with driving cars for a living, too.

"One more memory of this side of the family. A few years after the war, we were contacted by Alma (whom I went to see crowned as May Queen, when I was about 5). It seems that her daughter was at the school where my sister was teaching. We visited Alma & Albert, & talked about old times.

It seems that Albert was the driver of the official car for the Dockyard. After the big blitz on Portsmouth, he drove Churchill around when he visited the town, but unfortunately had a puncture in the badly blitzed Kings Rd, & another car was brought up immediately. Albert had driven many important people, in his job, including royal princes. He once had a slight accident, but as the occupant was Ribbentrop he was not worried!!!"

This is the Alma mentioned in chapter three – daughter of Athwell Matthew Hale's youngest sister Eliza who married an Alfred Ray. Alma married a husband called Albert whose surname I do not know, but I believe that the daughter was named Audrey. Alma herself had three younger siblings – Elsie, Alfred and Harold.

Time to return to my mother's and aunt's memories of their parents Wally and Ethel Tanner.

"When they married, my father & mother were given a house in Hollam Road, & the one next door. Actually, there was a mortgage to be paid, but the down payment for the mortgages was paid for them. I can't, of course, remember living there - we moved to Alverstone Road when I was two. The house, on a corner, was bigger."

There were good family connections to Alverstone Road in Milton, Portsmouth - as Marjorie remembers.

"I realized that our three terraces were built by Dad's father, who also built in Vernon Avenue. There are still (writing in 2009) tablets on the house walls. On the west is Battenburg Terrace - 1909 W R Tanner. On the east is Comeragh Terrace - 1910 W R Tanner. On the long Alverstone Road is Beresford Terrace - 1907 W R Tanner."

Returning to Olive's memories of 88 Alverstone.

"There was a spare bedroom, which was let to a Mrs Johnson - I remember her - she had a canary, & a cat killed it. I suppose it was a cat. We had a black & white cat - there was the cage door open, I remember, & just a few feathers left. I must have been about 3 years old. I have clear memory of my father coming in by the back gate, & showing him the empty cage."

I wonder if the spare bedroom let to Mrs Johnson was the room later given to Grandma Hale – maybe Mrs Johnson left because of the canary – it might explain Olive's memories of going to see Grandma Hale at her previous address. 88 Alverstone Road still exists. It can be seen from the entrance to Milton Cemetery where Wally, Ethel, Maurice, and Marjorie are buried. It is a corner house on a terrace so maybe bigger than others in the road.

"One evening, in December 1919, I was sent into next door, where there was an older girl, Edie, & no-one came to take me home, for such a long time. It was quite late when I was taken home. Next morning I was told that I had a baby sister, & was taken to see her. I was just disappointed because she was not in long clothes with bonnet & veil like my doll."

That evening was 11th December 1919 – the birth of Olive's sister Marjorie.

"I remember the doctor coming to the house by bicycle - when my Baby sister was born at home - doctor & 'nurse' came - the nurse was actually someone on the doctor's list, of people who went to help at the birth, & stayed for a while to help the mother & tend the baby. I remember calling her "nurse". No hospital births, & private homes & trained nurses too expensive.

"Then Mother did not come downstairs until Xmas Day, & I was sent to play by myself in the hall while they got her comfortably settled by the fire, & saw to the baby - I was quite hurt about it. But we had an Xmas tree that year - the only one we ever had, I think."

Ethel was in bed and convalescent for a long time after giving birth to my mother, Marjorie. Maybe Ethel found it a struggle. Ethel was quite petite, and had suffered poor nutrition as a child – but maybe that was normal for the time. Supporting that theory is what Marjorie wrote about her birth.

"I think Gran was living at Alverstone Rd, before I was born. I was told the Dr. visited my expectant mother & said 'Oh you're not ready yet. I'll get my dinner & come back. When he came back he apologized & realised mother's event was urgent.

"Mother said she came to feeling as if boiling water was being poured on her. Dad had been sent round the neighbours to borrow hot water bottles to try to rouse her. Any rate we were both O.K. She was only allowed to have gruel at first. She was surprised to learn, when my first son was born, that I was offered a proper meal straightaway."

'Gruel' sounds unappetising, but it is just a form of cereal boiled in water or milk – like a thin porridge – traditionally a staple diet for peasants and sustenance for the sick. The latter tradition was clearly being adhered to in Ethel's case, which reinforces the theory that Marjorie nearly lost her mother at birth, as her mother's mother had.

Wally and Ethel may have had good reason to refrain from trying for another baby in that case. In the meantime they had two little girls to bring up, as Olive remembers.

"The baby's pram was quite big, with a seat at each end, & though 4 years old I was often sat on the seat near the handle when Mother wanted to hurry. Somehow I managed to tuck my legs into the well, & avoid the baby's.

"I seem to remember that babies wore long clothes for quite a while, then, but one Sunday I came home from Sunday School, & found that my sister was in a short frock - the baby was "tucked".

"Then there was the Christening - this service took place later in the afternoon on Sunday.

"I went to Sunday School, & children could, after school, go to the Church service, in charge of the deaconess, & sit in pews at the side. I wanted to get out to join my parents at the Christening, but in spite of explaining this, & Edie's help, was not allowed to get out of the pew, & could not really hear or see, so I missed the Christening. No-one in the family seemed to have missed me!!!"

Time to shift to Marjorie's memories of the household in which the sisters grew up.

"As long as I can remember, my mother's mother lived with us. She sold her house in Milford Road and gave some help to Dad for his mortgage payments.

"Mum and Dad had the front bedroom looking over open ground north to St Mary's Hospital. Mother said that she sometimes saw a, presumably young, doctor doing his keep fit exercises. Olive and I had a three quarter size bed in the small bedroom. Gran had the back bedroom where she liked to sit in the evenings beside a fireplace where she could warm herself in winter. She used to take a little scuttle of coal upstairs with her. In the daytime she helped Mum downstairs. I used to hear her say "Oh, that Marjorie! she's pinched one of the little potatoes I've just scraped." There were some tiddlers among the potatoes from Dad's allotment. I liked raw potato.

"I remember that my mother would often invite Gran to spend the evening downstairs, but she would say that 'Wally' and her should have some time alone, & Gran would then retreat up to her bed sitting room.

"When we went into her bedroom she was usually reading, mouthing out the spelling as she read. I think that she had more or less taught herself to read. There was a glass dome containing artificial flowers on her sideboard and this, I always remember, would quiver whenever we passed by. Many years later, Mum, Olive and I were returning along Vernon Ave when we were horrified to see her sitting on the window sill cleaning the outside of her bedroom window. Immediately below was the glass roof of the greenhouse where Dad kept cacti and a fine grape vine that produced lovely bunches of black grapes that he very carefully thinned out at the right time.

Many years later Marjorie would try growing grapes in the greenhouse at the back of her marital home. Unfortunately changing the glass roof for a safer material did not suit the grapes at all.

Returning to Olive's memories of her family:

"We had a children's party. I must have been about 6, & I remember that children from the family came. Nene Tanner, my cousin, & cousins Ed & Vic Hutty, Bert Holton, & the Ashworths - Lillie, Winnie, & Jack. We played 'pin the tail on the donkey' when blindfolded, & there was a sheet run across the corner of the dining room. We each dangled a string over the top & pulled up a present. My father was behind the sheet."

Nene Tanner (Ena Edith) was born in 1915 like Olive, and was the daughter of Wally's elder brother William Herbert Tanner – known as Bert probably because his father was also a William, who died in 1917 leaving a widow Caroline and Nene as his only child. Olive used to play with her first cousin Nene when they were children. Olive provided memories of them playing together at their shared Grandma Tanner's house.

"There was a female cat at Grandma's - Trixie - & sometimes little kittens. Also there were some chickens. Sometimes my cousin Nene was there.

"I suppose, living near Milton Cemetery, we had seen many funerals in the 'flu epidemics, & one of our games was giving "Katy", the rag doll, a burial. When Dad & Grandpa were digging we would watch for worms, & take them to the chickens.

"One day we were in the spare bedroom, where there was only a big wardrobe, & playing some imaginary game, & I remember Nene saying "This is my house," stepping into the big wardrobe. It promptly toppled over, with her inside!!

"I rushed to the stairs calling "Auntie. Grandma!" They came rushing up, & scared, lifted the wardrobe, expect to find Nene hurt, & Nene just looked up saying "I was like a bunny in a hutch" & quite unhurt or frightened."

William Victor Hutty was born in 1912 and known as Vic probably because his father was William Hutty (yet more Williams) who married Olive's Aunt Lily Maria Hale in 1911. Edward Athwell Hutty, born in 1914 and the last Athwell in the family that I know of, was Vic's younger brother.

Bert Holton was Robert Arthur Holton, born 1912 and son of Minnie Hale who married a Robert Holton in 1911 – there are many Berts around as well as Edies and Williams.

The Ashworths I mentioned earlier – Grandma Hale's sister Harriet's daughter Gert was married to Jack Ashworth and Gert had always been a friend of her cousin Ethel Tanner née Hale.

Wally Tanner spent his entire working life in Portsmouth's Naval Dockyard – not unusual in Portsmouth during his lifetime as the Navy and the Dockyard were the main employer for the city not only then but for centuries past. When he was awarded the Imperial Service Medal in 1947 the local paper described him as a shipwright and local chargeman.

That brings me to Olive's memories of what that employment meant for her family – starting with the important matter of remuneration.

"Dockyard wages - shipwright, about £150 per year, counting in any overtime, or extra for danger work, e.g. up by the top of a mast.

"No pay for sick leave - men joined clubs - the Broken Bone Club, the Jury Club (no pay if out on jury service). Accidents at work treated by the dockyard surgery, & if necessary a stay at the Naval Hospital at Haslar. Any money left over in the club was shared out at Xmas. I remember that family presents were bought then, and once or twice on Xmas Eve, or a day or two before Xmas, we would visit Charlotte St where the market continued after dark, by the light of flares, for a few Xmas extras.

"In those day people had their own favourite remedies - I remember eucalyptus for nosey colds, put on handkerchiefs I think, and camphorated oil rubbed on the chest. With no National Health Service visits to the doctors could be expensive. My father paid into National Deposit for my sister and I, which in case of illness paid out part of the bill. I think that there was some state scheme into which employees paid. This, I only remember vaguely, meant that they could go to the doctor named, and get the medicine from the chemist (as is done now by everyone). For other patients, most doctors had their own dispensers, or made up their own medicines. One usually had a bottle of medicine, not often tablets."

In the next paragraphs Olive reminds us that even though her father had a good and regular job they were still poor by modern standards – though well off compared to the childhood Ethel had known. Ethel left school at 13, and went into tailoring. Even though Wally had a good job, the family finances would be stretched – as Olive remembers.

"I cannot remember the years of the First World War, but I have been told that very long hours were worked - Mother has said how the porridge oats for Father's supper would be waiting & waiting - for Father to get home. Dad was on night work the night that I was born.

"My memories are of post war, when times were tough. For a few weeks Father did not work a full week. I have since read that this was done in an effort to prevent discharges, but there were, later, many jobs lost. I remember Father coming home one Friday night & naming one man as having had his notice. Thankfully, Dad was established, & so kept his job. I did not know that at the time, & was old enough to feel a bit scared that it would happen to us."

There was a very large recruitment of workers in the dockyard during war time, and inevitably peace massively diminished the work required on warships and many less staff were needed. The short time working was to enable more men to be kept on for longer, but it only put off the evil day when many skilled men were let go and had to find whatever alternative work they could.

Even as late as the early 1980s, when there was a big row about cutbacks in the Dockyard, many people seemed to assume that there were no alternative employment options for Portsmouth. Time has produced a myriad of new businesses and job opportunities in the enterprise economy that has developed since the 1980's, so Portsmouth's prosperity is no longer heavily tied to the Royal Navy and its Dockyard.

There was a state unemployment benefit scheme in existence at the time, but it was limited – so the threat of losing employment must have been scarier.

"Dockyard hours were from 7am-12noon & 1.30pm-5pm. There was no official morning break, although men usually managed to get a cuppa & a sandwich, unofficially, but had to be careful not to be caught at it.

"'Float Time' gave the men a short dinner hour, when it was not possible to get home from the job & back at lunch time, but an earlier ending to the day.

"One could get to work, if late, until 7.30am, but lose 1/16th of a day's pay. There was no holiday, apart from bank holidays, until 1928 or thereabouts. New Year's Day was not a Bank Holiday, even though all banks did close that day.

"Friday was pay day. There were, in early days, stalls outside the main gates with vendors hoping to sell on pay day. I have been told that my great grandfather, when retired, bought a sweet making machine. He made sweets down in the cellar of his house in Surrey Street, & sold them at the Dockyard gates. No pensions in those days, & he had had 16 children, of whom 12 survived. Couldn't have had much chance for savings!!"

Olive does not say which great grandfather had 16 children. William Clark Tanner was the father of Olive's father's father, and married three times, but I only know of him having three children. William Combes, father of Olive and Marjorie's Grandma Tanner (and yet another William) only had eleven of which I know the names, but I do not know the names of four who did not survive – I presume Olive means that they did not survive birth. Athwell Matthew Hale's father, also called Athwell, only had eight for whom I know the names, while Sarah Hale's father Joseph Cripps only had five and did not live long enough to retire, but Olive earlier described her 'grandfather' as the eldest of 16, which must mean Athwell Matthew Hale, which would make his father Athwell Hale as the retired sweet maker – and having had another eight children of whom I know nothing.

Returning to Olive's memories of family financial stringency.

"When money was tight I was sometimes - not often, sent to Highland Rd to buy butter at the Maypole - it was cheaper than Pinks, in Milton.

"Also on Saturdays, when a fried fish shop opened in Milton Rd, I had half a crown to buy five 5^d pieces of fish - plaice, usually, and 5 pennyworth of chips.

"Afterwards, no pudding, but occasionally an orange, or the once a week cup of coffee. Red, white, and blue brand coffee and chicory.

"One day, I dropped the fish and chips. The greasy paper split & the fish came out. I was scared - the family dinner - a whole half-crown - I wrapped it up, & said nought. Nobody got food poisoning. I kept quiet about it."

No pudding, an occasional orange, and a weekly cup of coffee – sums up just how poor they were.

Five pieces of fish - for Wally, Ethel, Olive, Marjorie, and Grandma Hale, but Grandma Hale died in January 1935 after being ill at Christmas. Grandpa Tanner (William Richard) then died just after Christmas in 1936, and Olive remembers that *"Grandma Tanner moved from Drayton to North End a year or two before the war. She also bought a bungalow in Purbrook, when the fear of war came, & later moved to it."*

Purbrook is on the northern side of Portsdown Hill, which hill marks the northern boundary of the City of Portsmouth on the mainland – most of the city is on Portsea Island with the Dockyard – prime target of the Luftwaffe, being on the south west corner of Portsea Island, so when the Blitz came many families would find ways to stay on or over the northern side of Portsdown Hill for safety, and the Tanner family would be glad to sleep in Grandma Emma Tanner's house in Westbrook Grove, Purbrook when their house at Milton (in the south east of Portsea Island) was first endangered and then damaged in the Blitz.

Milton was where the Tanners lived before the war. It had been a village all of itself until late on in the Nineteenth Century, and when the Tanners were living there locals still called it 'the village'. Many Dockyard workers lived there and cycled to and from work twice a day – like Walter Tanner.

Going everywhere by bike was not without risk – even when there were few cars on the road. When young Marjorie was being taken by her father up to Bedhampton, where Grandpa and Grandma Tanner had a house, Marjorie was allowed to sit on the handlebars in front of him. One day her foot got caught in the spokes. Luckily the spokes were rusty and they broke instead of her leg.

Demonstrates how old and well used that bike must have been, and their holidays were not extravagant. Walter & Ethel went to Midhurst in Sussex for a week in August 1926 and to Hambledon, only a few miles from Portsmouth, on another occasion. Money was clearly tight before Marjorie's grandfather died – and the Tanners only went on holiday occasionally – as Olive remembers.

"We had not been away for a holiday week for 4 years, rather having day trips, but in 1939 we went to South Devon at Torquay. The 1935 holiday had been North Devon at Combe Martin."

Photograph albums were created from the holidays at Combe Martin and Torquay, showing that the holidays involved visiting Watermouth, Ilfracombe, Lynton, Lynmouth, Clovelly, Tenby, Woolacombe, Westward Ho, Wells, and Babbacombe as well as Combe Martin and Torquay. A real treat for a family compared to what would have been possible for their families not many years earlier. I remember my mother commenting on how amazing they had thought the narrow country lanes of Devon - only to discover, decades later when she was driving her own car, that Hampshire had equally narrow country lanes as close as the north side of Portsdown Hill.

But to return to the West Country holidays – these were not luxury tours, as Olive explained.

"It was a case of "bed & breakfast". Prices then ranged from 4s 6d to 6s 6d, including a cooked breakfast.

"Before that our other holiday had been a week at Hambledon, not far from Pompey. Unfortunately there were several damp days, but we had some country walks. We had to do our own food shopping in village shops, but it was a change for Mum - no cooking or washing up. That was in 1924 or 1925."

I remember once, when I was driving Olive and Marjorie through Hambledon, Olive remembered that holiday in 1925 with her sister and their parents had a holiday in Hambledon – and recalled that they had to purchase cream and milk from an ironmongers.

The Tanners' holidays were much less adventurous than the holidays of Marjorie's future husband during the same inter-war period – as I will be covering in a future chapter.

Next to cover in the Tanner story is the education and early employment of the Tanner daughters, but before that I will return to the educational career of Marjorie's future husband, Maurice Burwood.

Young Ethel Hale

Minnie Gertrude Hale

Lily Maria Hutty née Hale

Ethel's cousin & close friend Gertrude Ashworth nee Gibbs

Olive and Marjorie as children

CHAPTER SEVEN

Schoolboy & Athlete

Maurice Burwood was a good student.

He was a student at Valley Boys School in the Borough of Bromley in Kent for three years from the autumn 1909 term to the summer 1912 term. In nine terms he was late only four times and absent only 14 times, while his school reports show that he rose from 13th out of 34 scholars in his first term to 1st out of 51 scholars in his final term. His teacher's comments on him in the 9 reports went as follows:

1. *Arithmetic very much improved.*
2. *Much improved. Much more careful.*
3. *Maurice does his parents and teacher great credit. I am very sorry to lose him for the year.*
4. *Maurice is a careful and intelligent boy & has done excellently all through the term.*
5. *Maurice has done very well & got a well-earned high position in the class. He has kept up a high standard of work in all subjects.*
6. *Maurice is a bright intelligent boy. He does his lessons thoroughly, & likes them.*
7. *Well behaved; very intelligent. He deserves his high position.*
8. *Maurice is to be congratulated on reaching the top of his class, & thoroughly deserves his position. Very intelligent & a credit to his class.*
9. *Maurice is to be congratulated on reaching the highest position in his class again. His work & behaviour have been excellent throughout the whole year.*

The list of subjects reported on is interesting: Scripture, Reading, Handwriting, Composition, Spelling, Grammar, Recitation, Arithmetic, Drawing, History, Geography, Handwork, Science, Singing, Drill, and Conduct. I suppose Recitation would now be Drama, Singing would be Music, and Drill would be P.E.

Clearly both Eric & Maurice did well, and the school impressed Ada enough to send a letter which produced this response

> *Valley Boys' School*
> *Bromley*
> *July 26th '12*

Dear Mrs Burwood

I was very pleased indeed to receive your letter with the kind words of appreciation. It is a great encouragement to a teacher to receive such a letter,
It has been a pleasure for me to have such boys as Eric & Maurice in a class as they are so well behaved & keen on learning,
I wish them every success in the future & feel sure that they will be a credit to Mr Burwood & yourself.
Again thanking you.

> *I am*
> *Yours sincerely*
> *A Beavan*

On Maurice's departure from Valley Boys, the Headmaster supplied this letter to support the teachers' assessments.

> *Borough of Bromley, Kent*
> *Education Committee*
> *Valley School Boys Dept*
> *Nov 15th 1912*

Maurice Burwood who is leaving the above school is a boy of above average ability.
He stood a very good chance of winning a Kent County Scholarship here, and his parents are anxious that he should if possible have a chance of competing for a scholarship in his new school.

I can definitely recommend him on the grounds of character, industry and ability.

> *J J Webber B.A.*
> *Head Master*

The head master also responded to another letter from Ada.

> *Valley Boys' School*
> *Shortlands*
> *Kent*
> *Dec 12th*

Dear Mrs Burwood

I am very pleased to hear that the boys are settling down in their new school and hope that Maurice will meet with success when the Scholarship exam comes.

If I get the medals and prizes early enough next week I will post them to the boys at Kingwood Road School. If they do not reach there before the holidays commence, the boys will be able to get them by applying to the caretaker I presume.

Your good opinions of the school and staff here, make pleasant reading – and show us that some, at least, of our work has not been in vain.

I shall be delight to see the boys if they ever find the opportunity of paying a visit to their old school.

With kind regards & the compliments of the season to yourself and W Burwood, and all good wishes to the boys.

> *Yours sincerely*
> *J J Webber*

I do not know what the medals and prizes referred to were, but I do know that Maurice earned a school prize awarded by the Borough of Bromley Education Committee - awarded Christmas 1911 for "Good work and conduct". It was a copy of *Cook's Voyages* – the story of Captain James Cook's three famous voyages to the Southern and Pacific Oceans, and mostly told in Captain Cook's own words nearly up to his death - an exciting read for an intelligent nine-year old boy whose father had been in the Navy.

Maurice recorded being at Valley Boys School for 2 years and 7 months, after previously spending 1 year and 2 months at a school at Lillie Road in Fulham. I know little about Eric at this time, but a book was given to Eric for Xmas 1910 by an 'Auntie Scoops' – a nickname for a Mrs Cooper (I do not know her connection to the family). The book was Tom Brown's Schooldays by Thomas Hughes, and has colour illustrations. Probably Eric passed it on to his brother.

Returning to Maurice, after Valley Boys School he attended a school at Kingswood Road in Fulham for 1 year. After that he attended a London County Council School in Wandsworth called Hotham Road. His school report for the term ended 31st March 1914 records him coming top of the class again, and winning a Scripture prize.

The prize was from London County Council, and was awarded *'under the gift of the late Mr Francis Peek and the Religious Tract Society for Excellence in Biblical Knowledge'*. It was a copy of the New Testament from the *Pocket Paragraph Bible* and is *'According to the Authorized Version newly arranged in paragraphs and sections with a preface and marginal notes containing improved renderings of many words and passages etc. Also references to parallel and illustrative texts, chronological tables and maps'*.

A serious work of biblical scholarship for an eleven-year old boy. I do not know how much he read it, but he kept it until his death.

Hotham Road School came under London County Council so Maurice got London County Council Scholarships enabling him to attend Latymer Upper School from 1914 to 1922. On 30th August 1918, the London County Council Education Offices at Victoria Embankment sent him a letter saying that:

I have to inform you that the Council has provisionally awarded you an Intermediate County Scholarship tenable as from 1st August, following your sixteenth birthday.

The award is subject to the condition that you satisfy the Council's regulations in all respects at the time when the scholarship is due to be taken up. You must continue in regular attendance at school for the period preceding the date on which the scholarship is due to be taken up, and your school reports for that period must be satisfactory.

If you are <u>not</u> holding an award from the Council, I shall be obliged if you will forward an official copy of your birth certificate which be returned to you as soon as possible.

This was followed up by a letter dated 6th October 1919 saying that:

I have to inform you that the award of an Intermediate County Scholarship which has been provisionally made to you is now confirmed, and that you are authorised to attend the school or institution named on the enclosed Form No. H154 as from the beginning of the Autumn term 1919. The form must be presented to the Head Master or Principal as soon as possible. In the event, however, of you being found subsequently to be ineligible for the scholarship, the Council reserves the right to withdraw the award.

Your parents' (or guardians') annual income has been assessed as not exceeding £160, and a maintenance grant will be paid on this basis (see summary of regulations which accompanied the letter of provisional award of the scholarship).

The assessment of Will and Ada's annual income proves that Maurice needed a scholarship. Latymer Upper School was set up at Hammersmith in 1624 when Edward Latymer left funds in his will to educate eight poor boys in the local area, since when it had a long tradition of taking pupils from all backgrounds, but was not a state school.

Maurice's reports continued to be good at Latymer. His Midsummer 1915 report in Form 2A quotes *Excellent* for Reading, Handwriting, and Drawing and *V Good* for Holy Scripture (Old & New Testaments), Spelling, Composition, English (Grammar, Literature, and History) Geography, French, and Algebra – with *Good* for Geometry & *Mod* for Arithmetic. Homework and Punctuality were recorded as *V Good* and Conduct as *Excellent*. The final remark was *A Very Good Pupil* and he is placed as 10th out of 31 pupils.

Christmas 1915 in form 4C sees fewer *V Good*s but a long list of *Good*s, *V Good*s and *Excellent*s and adds Chemistry to his subjects but ends with him placed as 1st out of 30 pupils and described as *An Excellent Pupil*.

Midsummer 1916 in Form 5C sees him drop back to 8th out of 30 with a couple of *Weak*s in Arithmetic and Algebra, some *Fair*s and *Very*

Fairs, adding Physics and optional German to his subjects and a return to *A Very Good Pupil*.

His reason for taking German as an optional subject despite the War might be because, as my brother Geoffrey explained to me, studying German was considered important if you wanted to study Chemistry because so much Chemistry research literature was written in German.

Christmas 1916 in form 6A drops him down to 17ᵗʰ out of 32 and to *A Good Pupil*. A couple of *V Weaks* appear in Chemistry and Spelling. Making me wonder if he had been promoted to a higher stream with stiffer competition from other pupils and higher standards expected by the Form Masters.

Midsummer 1917 in form 6A and there are no *V Weaks* and he is rated 13ᵗʰ out of 29 and described as *a capital worker*.

Christmas 1917 in form 7A the number of subjects plummets but he is rated as 9ᵗʰ out of 24 and doing Latin instead of German as an optional subject and rated as *doing satisfactory work*.

Midsummer 1918 finds him rated as 4ᵗʰ out of 22 and described as *a very good pupil*.

Christmas 1918 brings a complete change of report style – and a reminder that Maurice was sixteen and just getting seriously involved in playing football. The report simply reads: *Maurice Richard Burwood has done a fair term's work & there has been at times some indication of talent. He will however have to realize more fully that the only way to success is by the union of industry with intellect: he has been inclined to take things too easily.*

Chemistry Fair; Latin Good, Mathematics & Physics certainly improving.

The selection of courses emphasizes that Maurice had chosen the sciences for his academic career.

Midsummer 1919 produced this report: *Maurice Richard Burwood has done a good six months' work. The Higher School Examination is designed to be a suitable test for pupils after the completion of a special two year course at a secondary school. For certain reasons we wished to ascertain what could be done at this examination after one year of the course; in that we have not been very successful. His Latin & Mathematics are reported as being good, while he works hard at his Chemistry. Physics fair, Conduct good.*

For some reason I have no reports for 1920, but Midsummer 1921 provides this letter: *M R Burwood has been working well at his Chemistry & Mathematics & with fair success. On the other hand, in Physics I have been unable to detect any energy or much ability. In English he is fair & his conduct is good.*

His subsequent report letters are different, because they reflect the fact that Maurice had succeeded in winning a place at Jesus College Cambridge in 1922 - winning a State Scholarship and a College Exhibition.

An Exhibition in this context is a financial grant to an individual student awarded on merit – usually outstanding results in examinations – but it is not a full scholarship, which is where the State Scholarship came in.

Maurice did not only do well academically at Latymer. He left Latymer in 1922, which is the date of this interesting letter from someone whose signature I could not read.

62 St. Helen's Gardens
North Kensington W.
May 21st 1922

Dear Mr Burwood

You certainly had good cause to feel that justice had not been done to Maurice.

With regard to the records stated in the programme, I pointed out to the General Secretary the omission you have stated and it certainly will be rectified next year. There were other mistakes & omissions in the list of records & they have undoubtedly been kept in a very slovenly way.

It was regrettable that Claridge should have got all the credit for the 100 yards run, when the performance of your son was of greater merit. But paper reports must always be taken cum grano salis.

I should like to say how much we all appreciate the whole-hearted & splendid way in which Maurice has gained glory for the school as well as in other directions. Personally I think he is the finest runner we have ever had at the school and I shall look forward with the greatest interest to see whether he will not be the first of our boys to win a 'blue' at Cambridge.

Yours very faithfully

C.E.Gr----

"Cum grano salis" is Latin for "with a grain of salt" – or 'not to be taken literally'. Describing my father as the finest runner Latymer had ever had might be hyperbole, too, but it is still evidence of athleticism.

He also had a talent for drawing. Not professional standard, but his pictures of birds, animals, tables, flowers and other things actually look like birds and animals and tables and flowers.

His sporting talents were more important. He regularly participated in athletics, soccer, rugby, and hockey - not all at Latymer or even at Cambridge - and on occasion played cricket, tennis, and bowls. Even in his fifties he participated in team sports.

A schools Athletics championships was held on Tuesday May 10th 1921. Six schools were competing: - Aske's Hampstead; Aske's Hatcham; Latymer; St Dunstan's; Strand; and Wilson's. The same six schools met for at least two annual competitions with Maurice competing for Latymer: school colours black, white, & blue.

On 10th May 1921 the tenth event was the 100 Yards Open (open to all pupils regardless of age) and comprised two heats and a final. M R Burwood won the 1st heat in 11 seconds while the second heat was won by fellow Latymerian N F Claridge in 11 and a fifth seconds.

Oddly enough the final, event 15, was won by Claridge in 11 and a fifth seconds but with Burwood not in the top three - implying that something went wrong. Maurice is next recorded as being one of four in the winning Latymer team for event 18, the 880 yards relay (open). As the time given is one minute 42 & two-fifths seconds I assume that each runner ran 220 yards.

The final entry for Burwood is event 22, the 440 yards (open) and he finished 2nd (with Claridge 3rd) – the winning time being 56 & four fifths seconds.

Latymer dominated the Championships - winning easily for the 2nd successive year.

The Schools Championship for 1922 - between the same

schools - records event 10 as the 100 yards open heats with M R Burwood and N F Claridge winning both heats in 11 seconds, but in the 100 yards final this time Burwood wins in 11 seconds with Claridge second.

As this 1922 championship was held on Tuesday May 16th 1922 this may explain the letter above.

Burwood then appeared in event 19, the 880 yards open relay, but Latymer did not finish in the top three.

Finally Burwood appeared in event 23, the 440 yards open, and again came 2nd behind a winning time of 55 & two fifths seconds.

Latymer comfortably won the Championship for a third successive year.

In addition to that I have a record of Latymer Upper School's 24th Annual Athletic Sports day on the school playing fields on Friday June 2nd 1922 - Maurice's last year at Latymer.

The first entry is the open mile, denoted as 'decided previously'. Burwood (running for Bradmore House whose house colours were crimson) came 4th.

He also competed in the open long jump – again decided previously - but was not placed in the top four.

He then ran in event 1 - the 100 yards open, winning the 2nd heat and then the final, pushing Claridge into 2nd place.

Burwood then competed in the open High Jump (event 11), but was not placed in the top four.

Then he competed in heat 1 of the hurdles (event 16) and came 4th.

Then he competed in the 880 yards relay (event 25) but Bradmore are not in the top four.

Next Burwood comes 1st in the 440 yards open race (event 31) – again beating Claridge into second place, though Claridge won the hurdles final.

Finally Burwood competed in the 880 yards open (event 38) and came 3rd.

That makes two first places, a third, and a fourth. The document records that Latymer awarded a School Championship Medal to the boy scoring the greatest number of points in certain open events – including the 100 yards, the 440 yards, the 880 yards, the 120 yard hurdles, and the high jump and long jump. I am unclear whether Maurice won the championship medal – maybe Claridge did after winning the hurdles, but Maurice must have been a contender.

Maurice kept a display case with fifteen medals in it - seven of which bore the original Latymer coat of arms and the words *Praemium Ludorum* and *Paulatim Ergo Certe*. If I translate correctly *Praemium Ludorum* means 'prize of the games', while *Paulatim Ergo Certe* ('slowly therefore surely') is the motto of the school's founder Edward Latymer. I assume they were awarded for athletic competitions at Latymer.

Maurice Burwood was one of the outstanding athletes of his day at Latymer Upper School, and that was not his only sport. A record of Latymer football team fixtures for 1918-1919 indicates that Burwood was the second XI captain.

His sixteenth birthday came in November 1918, and he was captaining the second XI which played 25 matches that season – winning 19, including the last 11, while drawing 3 and losing 3. The worst loss was the first match of the season when they lost 0-6 to Isleworth County School. The best win was 18-0 against Acton County School in the third to last match of the season. That reads to me like a pretty good record for any captain to boast about – though it is likely that he got promoted to the first XI at some time during the season, if only for a couple of matches, and he was awarded First XI colours for 1919-20-21 so he spent at least three years playing regularly for their First XI – probably at left-back.

Fixtures lists and scores for Latymer for the seasons 1919-1920, 1920-1921, and 1921-1922 record that the 1st XI was quite successful. In 1919-1920 they played 28 matches winning 22, losing 5, and drawing 1. In 1920-1921 they played 31 matches winning 22, losing 7 and drawing 2. In 1921-1922 they played 31 matches winning 21, losing 5, and drawing 5.

I also have some newspaper match reports of Latymer matches where Burwood is mentioned, and have transcribed the relevant sentences.

LATYMER UPPER SCHOOL v SLOANE SCHOOL 15th October 1921

Latymer were well served by Macmillan and Burwood, while for Sloane Fordham was always conspicuous.

Latymer won by four goals to two.

LATYMER V HABERDASHER'S SCHOOL – 3rd December 1921.

Mention must be made of Macmillan, who brought off a number of good saves, and of Burwood, whose speed and dexterity at left-back extricated Latymer from more than one dangerous situation.

The match was drawn with three goals apiece.

LATYMER v ROYAL SCHOOL OF MINES – 14th December 1921.

From that moment Latymer attached incessantly, yet could not score; instead Julian broke away and scored a third goal after a thrilling race with Burwood.

Burwood was again an outstanding figure in the Latymer defence, while Dale gave an impressive display at left half.

Another game drawn 3-3.

LATYMER v CITY AND GUILDS COLLEGE 4th March 1922

The opening stages of the game favoured the visitors, and Macmillan in the Latymer goal had many troublesome shots to save, although the backs, Brown and Burwood, defended finely.

Latymer suffered their third home defeat of the season losing 2-1.

LATYMER v EMERITI – 8th April 1922.

The Latymer backs, Burwood and Brown, had defended well, and what chances had come the way of the Emeriti forwards were lost by indifferent shooting.

For some time in the second half Latymer were compelled to play a man short, as Brown was feeling unwell. During his absence Emeriti set up many attacks, but Burwood tackled brilliantly, and Macmillan, in goal, made some remarkable saves.

Latymer won 5-0, ending a season with 22 wins, 4 draws, and 5 losses out of 31 matches played. I do not know of Maurice participating in any other sports at Latymer. Football in winter and athletics in summer probably took up quite enough time when he was not studying – or reading.

There were other books inscribed to him at Latymer – besides the school prizes. The first records him in Form 2A and quotes his address as Orkney Stables, Gwendolen Av, Putney – but later amended to 10 Cornwall Mews South, Grenville Place, Kensington. The book is *The Heroes* by Charles Kingsley.

Charles Kingsley (1819-1875) was a Church of England Priest, University professor, historian, novelist, and social reformer. His novels included historical novels like *Westward Ho!* and children's novels like *The Water Babies. The Heroes* was written for children, but retelling three great stories from Ancient Greek myth – specifically the stories of *Perseus, The Argonauts,* and *Theseus.* I believe that Maurice was twelve or thirteen when he first read it.

The second book is also marked as belonging to Maurice when he was in Form 2A and is entitled *The National Song Book.* It is billed as *A Complete Collection of the Folk-Songs, Carols, and Rounds suggested by the Board of Education (1905) Edited and Arranged for the Use of Schools by Charles Villiers Stanford.* Sir Charles Villiers Stanford (1852-1924) was an Irish composer, conductor, music teacher, and one of the first professors of the Royal College of Music.

The National Song Book contains words and music of well over a hundred tunes – including staples like *Auld Lang Syne, God Save the King,* and *Rule Britannia;* carols like *God Rest Ye, Merry Gentlemen* and *We Three Kings of Orient Are.* It also includes traditional English songs like *John Peel* and *The Roast Beef of Old England;* traditional Scottish songs like *Annie Laurie* and *Charlie Is My Darling;* traditional Welsh songs like *Men of Harlech* and *Land of My Fathers;* and traditional Irish songs like *The Flight of the Earls* and *Let Erin Remember.* It also includes a list of Welsh Titles of the Welsh songs (over thirty of them) and a *'Glossary of Scotch Words'.*

Another book for Form 2A has an address amended from Orkney Garage, Gwendolen Av, Putney, SW to 10 Cornwall Mews. It is Siepmann's Primary French Course Part I by Otto Siepmann, reprinted 1913, and is joined by Siepmann's Primary French Course Part II, reprinted 1914, but inscribed with form 6A, and copious pencil notes throughout.

Form 5c provides another book *Papers on Sir Roger De Coverley from The Spectator* by Joseph Addison. Addison lived from 1672 to 1719 and was a gifted writer of humorous prose responsible for the first version of the Spectator in 1711.

The next book has a legible class name of 6a, but previous entries are crossed out and the same two addresses are in, so he probably first owned it in 2a and kept using it. The book is entitled *Elementary Geometry – Practical and Theoretical,* by C Godfrey, M.V.O., M.A. and A W Siddons, M.A. C Godfrey was headmaster of the Royal Naval College, Osborne, and A W Siddons is credited as *Late Fellow of Jesus College, Cambridge.*

Maurice also had an atlas while in form 6a – Philips' Modern School Atlas.

The last three books are marked with form 7a. The first quotes 10 Cornwall Mews. It is *Siepmann's Primary French Course Part III,* completing the trilogy.

The next book says *Thackeray's Henry Esmond* on the cover. The writer is William Makepeace Thackeray (1811-1863) – best known for his frequently dramatised novel *Vanity Fair.* The edition is dated 1917, and the full title is *The History of Henry Edmond, Esq., Colonel in the Service of Her Majesty Queen Anne, Written by Himself, by William Makepeace Thackeray.* 10 Cornwall Mews is crossed out and replaced by 13 Ashwood Mews, Courtfield Rd, Kensington.

Another book inscribed M R Burwood, Form 7A of 13 Ashwood Mews, Courtfield Road SW7, Latymer Upper School King St. Hammersmith WB is *Selected English Essays*, reprinted 1917.

Another book has Form 7a (Science) written into it, and a date 1920, but the name in it is PEF Farina. Philip Farina was an old friend of Maurice with whom he took more than one holiday, and who corresponded regularly with Maurice until Maurice's death. After both men were dead, my mother took me to meet Mr Farina's widow Edie while she was on holiday at a hotel in Chichester. The book is *The Johnson Epoch, Volume VII of Epochs of English Literature by J.C.Stobart M.A.* – the 'Johnson' referred to being Dr Johnson, most famous for writing a *Dictionary of the English Language* which was published in 1755. It contains brief biographical details of various literary figures in Britain between the years 1750-1798 and extracts from some of their work.

Maurice had one more book Form 7a written into it – though written as roman numerals VIIA – but it does not mention Latymer or any home address. The only address in it is Jesus College, where Maurice was to go after leaving Latymer. The book is *Modern Plane*

Geometry, being proof of the theorems in the syllabus of modern plane geometry issued by Association for the Improvement of Geometrical Teaching with the sanction of the Council of the A.I.G.T. by G Richardson M.A. and A.S. Ramsey, M.A.

Very serious mathematics, but Maurice was serious about his academic career – and his acceptance at Jesus College depended on academic successes to which I will turn next.

In July 1917 Maurice received a Secondary School Certificate stating that he had attained the required standards for a Senior Local Examination in the following subjects:

1. English Composition
2. Religious Knowledge
3. English Literature
4. English History
5. Geography
6. French
7. Arithmetic Geometry Algebra
8. Theoretical and Practical Chemistry
9. Physics (Heat, Sound and Light Practical Physics)

Maurice was placed in the Second Class of Honours - an overall mark which could encompass first class performances in his best subjects.

The next examinations Maurice took at Latymer were in 1918: University of London General School Examination results for the 'School Certificate' - a secondary school qualification later abolished and replaced by 'O' levels.

The certificate reads *'Maurice Richard Burwood, born 6 November 1902, has been a pupil at Latymer Upper School, Hammersmith (inspected by the Board of Education) for a period of 8 years and term ending Midsummer 1922, and has pursued a course of study in the subjects set out on the back of this certificate'.* It then adds that *'Maurice Richard Burwood, having been examined in the following groups of subjects: - (i) English subjects, (ii) Languages, (iii) Mathematics and Science, (iv) Other subjects, has passed the General School Examination held at Latymer*

Upper School, Hammersmith in June/July 1918, with credit in the following subjects:- English, Arithmetic and Elementary Mathematics, Electricity and Magnetism, Chemistry, and with Distinction in the following subjects:- French – also passed an oral test, Chemistry.

The next document is dated January 1919 and certifies that Maurice *'at the General School Examination reached the standard required for Matriculation in the following subjects: - English, Arithmetic and Elementary Mathematics, French Written and Oral, Mechanics, Electricity and Magnetism, Chemistry.'*

The next document dates to July 1920 and is called a Higher School Certificate. Higher School Certificate examinations were usually taken when pupils were 18, or two years after the School Certificate examinations – and were abolished when finally replaced by 'A' levels.

The document confirms Maurice had been a pupil at Latymer Upper School since September 1914, and had pursued a *'Course of Higher Study from September 1918'* and *'having been examined and reached the required standard in the following Main subjects: - Pure Mathematics, Applied Mathematics, Physics (with Distinction), with the following subsidiary subject, English, has passed the Higher School Examination held at Latymer Upper School, Hammersmith in July 1920.* The back of the certificate also declares that Maurice took a course of study in Chemistry, but there is no mention of him taking an examination in Chemistry.

Most important of all is probably the 'Physics (with Distinction).

Before then he had some dealings with the Imperial College of Science and Technology at South Kensington, London SW7. They sent him a letter dated 29th September 1921 informing him *"that at the Entrance Examination held at the College last week you qualified for admission to a 2nd year course of study in Chemistry."* The course of study apparently would have begun the following Tuesday 4th October, with fees of £60 per session plus £2 breakages payable in advance. Maurice did not take the course – maybe the opportunity to go to Cambridge instead had prevailed.

On 19th October 1921 Maurice is certified by the University of London to have *'passed as an External Student the Intermediate Examination in the Faculty of Science in the year 1921'*. During the 19th and early 20th centuries many students of other bodies took University of London examinations as external students. In those days the Examinations Boards used by schools were commonly run by universities. Oxford, Cambridge, and Durham, for example, and in 1902 the University of London created the University of London Extension Board to run exams. Schools could pick which Exam Board they use, and it is no surprise that a London school like Latymer should use the University of London.

Clearly the pass indicates that Maurice had chosen the sciences when he applied for Cambridge University, but that would not be a quick or simple affair, as the following series of letters demonstrates. To afford to attend Cambridge Maurice needed a Scholarship, so he had to take examinations to apply for them.

Surprisingly he was able to apply more than once. Clearly his school considered him to merit some extra effort. Maurice's first attempt to gain a Scholarship produced this response from Jesus College.

> *The Master's Lodge*
> *Jesus College*
> *Cambridge*
> *December 23 1919*

Dear Sir,

I am sorry to say that you were not successful in the Scholarship exams. Your marks were 154 and those of the lowest candidate satisfied for £30 exhibition was 215. Your work in Physics was rather better than that in Chemistry.

> *Yours faithfully*
> *Arthur Young*

As the Scholarship exam was taken in 1919, Maurice was presumably seeking to start at Cambridge in the 1920/1921 year. He could not afford the modern luxury of a 'gap year', so he tried again the following year.

Jesus College,
Cambridge,
December 1920

Dear Burwood

I am sorry to say that you were not successful in our Scholarship examination, your marks being about 40 below those of the lowest candidate whom the Examiners adjudge worthy of a £30 Exhibition: maximum marks 450. Your marks in Mathematics were very fair, and also in the Chemistry paper; Chem practical moderate; Physics paper and practical weak, especially the latter. I notice that you can be a candidate again next year.

With regret for my
message
Yours sincerely
E. Abbott

And this time it was not only to Jesus College that he applied.

Queens College
Cambridge
Jan 16 1921

Dear Mr Burwood

In the Scholarship Exam your son's Physics mark was fair. He did not do well in Chemistry, the practical being very weak. His mathematics mark was good.

Yours sincerely
C.M. Sleeman

Possibly the second failure discouraged him, and he considered leaving school at the end of the 1920/1921 year – or maybe there was some other cause like family illness, because this next letter indicates that he was remiss in applying for a scholarship to remain at Latymer for the 1921/1922 year.

Latymer Upper School
King St.
Hammersmith W6
7.vi.21

Dear Madam

I know no way of repairing your son's omission to apply in time for the renewal of his Intermediate Scholarship. I did everything in my power to prevent such a thing happening by getting my secretary to write and a Special Notice with dates & posting it on my Board in good time.

We can make Maurice a Foundation Scholar which will excuse his fees next term.

I hope he will try for a Scholarship at Cambridge next December when he should be successful. He stands a chance too of a State Scholarship & is eligible for a Senior L.C.C. Scholarship if he does well.

Yours faithfully
C L Smith
Headmaster

However, Maurice did somehow get his intermediate scholarship renewed.

London County Council
Education Offices,
Victoria Embankment W.C.2
<u>Intermediate County
Scholarships – Extension</u>

Dear Sir,

With reference to your application I am directed to inform you that, subject to the regulations and to your passing the Higher School examination before 31st July next, your intermediate county scholarship has been extended for a further period of one year as from 1st August, 1921.

The extension consists of free tuition at Latymer Upper School, together with a maintenance grant, if your parents' income is within the limits laid down in the regulations. (Vide – the Summary of Regulations

Form H.172 posted to you with the provisional notice of the Intermediate County Award in 1919.

> *Yours faithfully*
> *R Blair*
> *Education Officer*

Maurice used that extra year well – persisting in trying again – and third time lucky – he succeeded, as these next two letters confirm.

> *The Master's Lodge*
> *Jesus College*
> *Cambridge*
> *December 18*
> *1921*

Dear Mr Burwood

I have much pleasure in writing that the examiners have nominated you for an Exhibition of £40. It is tenable at first for one year, but if you continue to do well will afterward be renewed and possibly raised to a scholarship of higher value. Will you kindly tell me whether you accept the nomination?

You are apparently exempt from Previous Pts 2 & 3, but not from Pt 1. It is most important that this should be passed before you. However term begins in October. Will you please inform me of your intentions by filling up and returning the enclosed form?

> *Yours very truly*
> *Andrew Gray*

And the second letter:

> *Wellside*
> *Well Walk*
> *London NW3*
> *20 Dec 1921*

Dear Mr Burwood

I wired you on Saturday, and now write to congratulate you on your nomination to a £40 Exhibition at Jesus College. Your work in

Physics and in mathematics was better than in Chemistry, but your practical work in Chemistry was good. Perhaps you will write (or may have written) to the master, Mr Gray, to say if you accept the offer of an Exhibition; if you do accept it, I should write to you in the course of next summer as regards rooms in College or lodgings, and on other points of business.

Yours sincerely
E Abbott.

Also in 1921 a letter was received about applying for a State Scholarship at University, and Maurice applied for and received one as well as an Exhibition – as enumerated in the next chapter, but first comes this letter written to Maurice's father confirming the success of Maurice's last year at Latymer.

Latymer Upper School
KING STREET,
HAMMERSMITH W.6.
21st December 1921

Dear Mr Burwood

We wish to congratulate you on your boy's success at Cambridge & are content to let that result of his, stand as the report on his school work.
May his future be as successful as his school career hitherto.

Yours truly
George J Francis
E Dale
Headmaster

The pair of names at the end of the letter show the headmaster countersigning a letter written by another staff member – possibly a housemaster.

That same pair of signatures are attached to a letter written to Will Burwood when Maurice finally left Latymer Upper School in July 1922.

Latymer Upper School
KING STREET,
HAMMERSMITH W.6.
24th July 1922

Dear Mr Burwood

With pleasure I can inform you that your son has completed another year's work of satisfactory & successful effort. We all hope that in the future he will achieve the success of his school days.

As a prefect he has worked hard for his House & the School. We are grateful. I append the formal reports of his teachers;-

In Mathematics; - Has been giving more time to Science but has kept this subject going satisfactorily.

In Physics; - Would do well if he would wake up

In Chemistry; - Satisfactory

George J Francis
Hearty Congratulations
& all good wishes
E. Dale

This confirms that Maurice was made a prefect. Clearly he was a busy school prefect during his final year at Latymer – a year of preparation and successful application for a place at Cambridge before leaving Latymer in 1922 – which leaves one final letter about his school years – written to his parents by the headmaster – written a week before the last above, but more appropriate as a finale to his years at Latymer Upper School.

Latymer Upper School
KING STREET, HAMMERSMITH W.6.

HEAD MASTER
REV. DR. E DALE   *July 18th. 1922.*

Dear Mr. and Mrs. Burwood,

I must thank you both on behalf of the Staff and myself for the exceedingly kind letter you have written. I shall tell Mr. Smith or show him the letter when I see him next. It is one of the highest pleasures of a School Master's life to find, that what he has tried to do, however uncertainly, may be working itself out by virtue of its own spiritual force. I am hoping that the "The Honour of the School" will carry us very far indeed for many years to come. I congratulate you on your son's successes and your son. I am so very glad that I have got to know him thoroughly, and to find out his sterling qualities. With very many thanks.

> *I am,*
> *Yours faithfully,*
> *E. Dale*

Will and Ada must have been proud of their son Maurice becoming a student at Cambridge University, so that is the next tale to tell.

Young Maurice

Maurice on right of picture in Chemistry Lab at Latymer Upper School

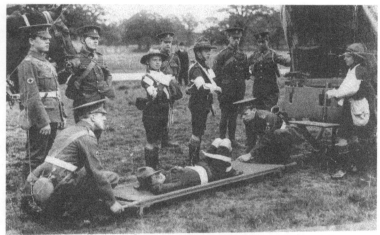

Maurice with Scouts doing training during the war

CHAPTER EIGHT

Cambridge

Cambridge University was founded in 1209 by scholars who left Oxford University after a dispute with the locals. Like Oxford its Colleges are largely autonomous – students do not apply to Cambridge University but to the specific college – like Jesus College.

Jesus College was established in 1496 by John Alcock, Bishop of Ely, on the site of a Benedictine nunnery which had fallen into dilapidation. He did so at the suggestion of William Chubbes who became the first Master of the College. The royal letters patent quoted the formal title of the College as *"The College of the Most Blessed Virgin Mary, Saint John the Evangelist, and the Glorious Virgin Saint Radegund"* but it was always intended to be called Jesus College according to *A History of Jesus College, Cambridge* by Arthur Gray & Frederick Brittain. Arthur Gray, MA was Master (meaning Head) of the College from 1912-1940 and Frederick Brittain Litt.D. a Fellow of the College. Thomas Cranmer was one of its earliest students, became Archbishop of Canterbury for Henry VIII, and played a central role creating the Church of England. Jesus College would provide another three Archbishops of Canterbury and one Archbishop of York.

It began as a small college training students for church-related careers, but today Jesus College is one of the larger Cambridge colleges - an elite college in an elite university, and Maurice won a place there on academic merit, despite being the son of a chauffeur.

According to Gray and Brittain, it was the first time that poorer students could receive government grants to attend there, and it was not until after the Second World War that working class boys were able to enter Jesus College in considerable numbers. Maurice must have been one of the earliest, winning a State Scholarship and a College Exhibition (a grant from the College itself) to Jesus College Cambridge, studying there from 1922-1925.

The Exhibition of £40 was awarded after an examination for entrance scholarships. The State Scholarship was £50 annual fees, other fees up to £10, and a maintenance allowance of £80 p.a. – awarded for 3 years to a student whose parents' annual income was assessed in 1919 as not exceeding £160.

Maurice would duly earn his degree, but earning his degree was not all he did, as his letters home record. This letter is clearly the first after his arrival.

B1
Jesus College
Cambridge
Oct 6th 1922

Dear Mum & Dad

Arrived safely 5 mins before time. Rooms are excellent. Have got some fine curtains there. The chairs we were doubtful of are jolly good but I want an armchair. That green plush deck chair would be nice. I have a Chesterfield with a few holes so could you procure or make a cover for it? If not, it doesn't matter.

Have already spent 7/- on groceries. There is a blind in the bedroom. The bedroom faces a pretty little garden in which no students can go. I think it is the Masters garden. I want a reading lamp badly & shall have to get a cheese dish.

The college lamps are 50 volt and cannot be obtained except from the college but if you can get me a stand I shall be very pleased.

Let me know when you send the bike. You had better send it to be left at Cambridge cloakroom till called for & it is best to tip the porter a 1/- or he may put his foot through the wheel. I want a writing table & so I am going to smile sweetly at the Porter.

They are building new bathrooms & lavatories. Some will be ready next Monday.

Have seen Abbott; Mills is to be my chemistry tutor with Abbott as nurse etc. I have to visit the Dean next Tuesday. Had a topping dinner this evening.

Fish filleted

Veal cutlets & Tomato Sauce or Roast Mutton & Onion Sauce with spuds & Cabbage

Apple Pie with sauce or cream of something or other.

I managed to unpack all right. Nothing badly creased. Suits & boots all right. One plate cracked. One glass broken in transit. I broke another glass by dropping the bread board on it. Have got a decent bedder, who enquired if my sheets were aired. Clocks are going all right. Perhaps a rug or two would be nice but not necessary. I do not want any pictures yet at any rate. Robbins & Marin are on my staircase. They have come up yet. Weather is fine with a tinge of dry coldness.

> *With much love*
> *from*
> *Maurice*

P.S. I wish Eric luck with his Church parade.
I want a frying pan.

The next communication was on a post card depicting the 1st Court of Jesus College – one of three lawns on which guests are not permitted to walk. It appears as a flat square lawn with college buildings along three sides.

2nd Court is nearby, and, to quote Gray and Brittain, it was in 1922 that the *'1870 conveniences in Second Court were replaced by a staircase (four sets of rooms) and a block of bathrooms. These were the first to be erected during the eight centuries of the history and pre-history of the college. Until then the only baths had been big circular tin saucers'.*

As Maurice's letter above shows - only just in time for him.

The postcard was postmarked 8pm 31 Oct 1922 and addressed to Mrs Burwood, Ashburton Lodge, Putney Heath.

Dear Mum

The window on the extreme right hand & at the bottom is one of my sitting room windows. I will explain more when I come. I shall possibly arrive by the 5.50 at Waterloo & hope to catch a Putney train at once so may be home at 6.30. Next train arrives at 7.46 so if I miss the 5.50 I shall not come. I am however, almost sure to catch it.

The last train to Cambridge is the 10.12 arriving at 11.46 leaving me just time to get in before 12. So shall probably be home on Wednesday for 2 hours. Please get me ½lb Pure Coffee & one lb bacon. I will pay you. If I do not come you can either send the things I want on or use them yourself.

& so Love from Maurice

He was planning some sort of flying visit within a month of going up. I doubt that it was only for coffee and bacon. This next letter shows him settling in.

B1 Jesus College
Camb
Wednesday

Dear Mum & Dad
I am writing another letter while I can.

Thursday

As you see I do not get much time for writing & as Sunday is the only time I can get in I shall have to send you a long one on Sundays.

We started lectures today. The first on Calculus by Fowler. He gave us a test so that he could know what type of work to do. I think he is in a mess. Some of the chaps there know nothing. Others like myself are fairly advanced & there are all intermediate stages.

We went & did 2 hours, I & a scholar named Woolley in partnership, on a simple physical experiment under Bedford. I am, I think, going to change it to a more advanced course by Serle if I can arrange the times decently.

Then I went to Sir W Pope's lecture on Organic Chemistry & it was the most absurdly simple stuff on the face of the earth. We were amazed to learn that "steam was obtained by heating up this can of water" & that "half of 64 is 32". All such statements were received by stamping & cheering. Still, he is a splendid lecturer.

I am trying to arrange Practical Chemistry under McCombie which is advanced. It will have to be in the afternoon (because every morning from 9-1 is booked up) & I have to put in at least 9 hours a week at more than 1½ hours at each visit. Up here we arrange our own lab, work & walk into what lectures we like, within limits of course. I am taking four subjects for the tripod ("trip") Chemistry, Physics, Mineralogy & Mathematics, which necessitates 34 hours a week lectures & labs & excluding private work. The Maths Johnnies have 12 hours a week & the history people 67. The science people mostly take 3 subjects except a few who are good at maths who take 4. Robbins & Mannam are both on my staircase.

The Cambridge Inter Collegiate Christian Society (pronounced kickyou CICCU) has not too good a name up here but there is another, the name of which I have forgotten which is supposed to be very good.

I have been in to tea only twice up to now & coffee only once. The air is decent up here & I am beginning to drop into the Cambridge feeding times & get thro' all meals well without stuffing it down. Breakfast at 8.15, Lunch 1.15, Tea 5, Dinner 6.30, Coffee 7.30, Supper 9.30. We have to wear our "rags" in maths lectures & whenever visiting the Tutors or any Officers of the University on business. If the cap ("square") is taken at all it is crushed up & put in the pocket.

Bike arrived allright. Have got a chain lock for it. Had an interview with the Dean. He is a jolly decent fellow. My tutor Mills is a clever chap but does not know any physics. Had a game of soccer today in the college trial match. Had to play right half in the second half – a disgusting position & the two backs were a couple of non-entities, so in the first half we scored three & they scored none (I was back) & in the second they scored three entirely due to the misses of those backs (I got a chunk out of my leg 2 inches long, nothing serious, in the first five minutes

Playford is up here as chaplain & so will not row. Oil stove works fine. They are building new lavatories with sinks & there are going to be 17 baths. Marinari says my bedder is the best in college.

Can you send me at least ½doz pictures. Any old sort will do as long as they are pictures. Do not make a light cover for the Chesterfield. It will dirty. Couldn't you put off Winnie's coat, because I want it as soon as possible. I can make use of any old rugs you can send but do not send too many. I want another little saucepan & a bigger pair of scissors. I bought a writing table 4 2/6. Chap wanted 50/-. It is mahogany with two lockable drawers & key & looks fine. I got a fairly large & decent frying pan for 10d. Can you send me a curtain nearly 2½ ft by nearly 6 with a rod too? The fittings there but no rings.

The room is cream coloured with a red baize double door at the entrance, green curtains over the bedroom etc door. This curtain is for the double door.

I am getting an inner tube new from Joe for 1/6d (Dunlop). The porter a chap name 'Oppit or something is a wonderful fellow. He asked me my name once only & every day at Hall ticks me off infallibly. Very often chaps have never been asked by him for their names. He seems to know it already. Have seen all the Latymerians except Johns who broke his wrist on a bike & is not coming up till Saturday.

I have yet to come across an undergrad without a bike. And outside Trinity Gates there are piles & piles of bikes left in a mass all night. The only inhabitants without bikes are babies under two years. You cannot go any speed you like. If you are in a road with motor cars & carts you go slow if you fall off or have to get off because it is so slow a whole crowd of about 50 bikes behind you have to get off. When however you come to a road without car or cart traffic you have to scorch to prevent being run into by about a million bikes behind & you want a good brake. If you approach crossroads you see a cloud of bykes approach from all the other three roads & they all scatter & it is nothing to see in a small square about 20 bikes going in all directions & completely intermingled. It is like a maze. I have not seen any collisions yet though.

It is very exciting to have seen Mrs Osborne.

There is no ragging of freshers & so I was right but ragging between friends occurs. Last year they ran Robbins round the Cloister Court in his pajamas to cure his attitude of high & mightiness & I think it succeeded. I believe Baxter was the prime mover. I have been in the Ghost room. In the next staircase to mine there is a black cat with ears torn in shreds & neck cut about & ripped in places which rushes about up & down the stairs once a week. Nobody has seen it or heard it though... I enclose a plan of the College.

Brown shoes are not tight but fit perfectly. Don't know why I thought they were tight. College shoes are fine. If you have any spare cushions I should like them as soon as possible and a blanket too. I am using the dressing gown at present as a blanket & it is excellent.

Friday. The weather is fine. Had a jolly humorous Physics lecturer today & he explained that unconsciously the child learnt that to keep itself upright its centre of gravity must be directly above the pt of support. "Thus," he says, "the stout man always keeps his head & shoulders well back in order that the centre of gravity may not be too far forward."

Hutchinson was decent on crystallography. In the practical I had to identify the symmetry of a lot of crystals. I told the chap that in one of them there was a dead axis of symmetry & he said there was another & told me to find it. After ¼hr I said that I could not find it & he pointed one out which I showed was not one at all & then after that he spent 10 mins examining it & found that after all there was only one axis.

I think Mrs Osborne can get me a cheap reading lamp, & so you need not trouble but I will let you know.

I have arranged Practical Chemistry 2-5.30 Monday, Wednesday, & Friday & so if a soccer match comes on those days I am done. And as for running I do not see any chance for you have to train every day.

Can you make me a pair of white shorts for running & a pair of black thin ones for football because they are 8/6 the cheapest up here. The amalgamated clubs blazer which I may find it necessary to buy is 42/- & the football shirt 16/6. Got a soccer match tomorrow & I am playing right half the most hateful position on the field. I must close now. If there is anything I want which you have will you send it as soon as poss because I want to get the place straight. There are lots of gnats up here but they do not sting.

With much love to all
From Maurice

This letter posted 11th Feb 1923 shows how Maurice lacked the money of many other undergraduates.

Sunday

Dear Mum

> *Thanks for Doosh*
> *Sorry I mistook the enclosure of your other letter. I've read the piece you've meant me to read now & taken it duly to heart. Please do not run away with the idea that I have been playing well because I have been getting goals. Quite the contrary. The only game I have played well in this term was the last one against a team from Emma in a scratch eleven. I played a really good game but I only scored one of our three goals. We drew 3-3. In another match against Selwyn Wright & I played back & they scored 5 goals. Both Wright & I had forgotten how to play back. In fact we can't play anywhere now.*
> *I saw rather a decent mirage the other day. Of course you can't see in a mirage anything that is not there but it may be a long way away. Anyway at the end of a lecture, Alec Wood said next time I hope to show you a mirage. We will rig up a desert (loud applause) & we have a certain amount of the flora & fauna of the desert, a few palm trees etc. (Applause) Owing to the uncertainty of the weather we shall have to heat our desert artificially. We shall observe the mirage with a telescope & any of you who are suspicious enough to suppose it to be a picture at the end of the telescope may look with the naked eye. It was rather decent. The desert consisted of a long tin with a little sand sprinkled & heated by four Bunsens, one of two small toy palm trees at the end. It looked like a big sheet of water with palm trees on the outskirts. He also explained how it was that at sunset the sun looked just as broad as usual but much less wide in a vertical direction. "You can see it any day in which the sunset is visible. Of course it occurred at sunrise as well, but most of us enjoy more opportunities for seeing the sunset than we do the sunrise." (Stamps)*
> *Expect Dad will enjoy his little trip & I am sure he loves learning French. Especially when I am helping him will he enjoy it. Thanks for offer of £30, but I am afraid it is unnecessary now for a time. They had the dinner last Saturday & needless to say, your humble was not there. Nor were Taylor &*

Burton & Chips so I was in good company. The dinner alone was 10/-. The old man was invited but could not come, so they invited Cod & George & Skinner. Only Skinner could come. Harling, Baxter & Lean were there but I saw them all today & had a long chat with Baxter. I've got to fork out about £2 to help in a deposit on the Jesus College Ball. I shall get the money back next term some time.

Have I told you about Tommy Watt? He is a dear old chap, the pracleator, who is so old he can hardly walk, but who comes to watch every match, rugger, soccer, or hockey, on the close. He catches hold of you & starts chatting like fury on various sports & then he tells you what he thinks of your play. He gives you the soundest advice & encouragement possible.

What is the price of Dutch cheese? We had an interesting paper in the Science Club by Mr Appleton at Johns. He had been investigating lightning flashes. He is convinced that "atmospherics" in wireless sets are due simply to lightning flashes transmitted all over the Earth. People who are trying to get rid of these are handicapped because they do not know what the lighting flash is exactly. He has been finding it out.

C.T.R. Wilson has by a clever bit of work found the quantity of electricity in a thunder cloud to be <u>20 coulombs</u> only but he was greatly troubled at first by spiders crawling over the knob he had above the hut in which he was working. They produced exactly the effect of a lightning flash.

Appleton has shown, by a simple apparatus, that the time of duration of a lightning flash is only one thousandth of a sec not a millionth as has been hitherto supposed. This means that the current in a lightning flash is 20,000 amperes (the current though an electric light is 1 ampere & potential is 110 volts) & 1,000,000,000 volts. What is more important, he discovered that a lightning flash is just a rush of electricity to earth & not an oscillatory discharge as has been supposed hitherto. Very soon he will be able to photograph his results. It is interesting, too, to observe that he will at the same time be able to photograph the ordinary wireless Marconi waves. He used just an ordinary wireless aerial. The apparatus I can explain later.

Eric will explain to you what all the above means. Oh, he also said while making these experiments he got a spark about 2½ft long from *his apparatus to the gas pipe. Fortunately he was not near at the time. He mentioned lightning conductors, he said "funnily enough, they actual work & quite well, too, but not as people suppose. They are not to attract the electricity through them so that it does not hit the house, but to <u>discharge</u> to cloud by a well-known phenomenon of the discharging action of point. Thus the cloud can be discharged to a great extent without a lightning flash. A lightning discharge is always preceding by a sudden uprush of wind. Well, I will stop my lecture now.*

Saw a good bit of work on the soccer field. Man dribbled two people, steadied himself about 2 yards from the goal, shot, hit the cross bar, rebounded, shot again, hit the goalie, rebounded, shot again, hit the side post & went to their left half who cleared. He was our inside left & would have been the winning goal. The Magdalen (Oxford) Jesus soccer photo is rather good. Will get 1 when have got some money, in the Christmas term. How is everything going. Pretty well I suppose. Send me the latest bulletin about the cat etc. etc. etc.

Must stop now.

Love to all from
Maurice

A programme card for the Cambridge University Athletic Club Inter-Collegiate Competition, Round 1 Division 2 match between Jesus College and Fitzwilliam Hall (presumably Fitzwilliam College, Cambridge), on Tuesday November 28th 1922, records M.W.Burwood (presumably a misprint) running for Jesus in the 100 yards but not finishing in the top three. Jesus won by 59 points to 21 so probably provided much stronger competition level than Latymer.

Maurice's main sport was still football – as the next letter demonstrates. Hawks Club is a Cambridge institution – dating from 1872. It still claims to represent the best sportsmen at the University. Membership is currently by election only, and the usual criterion is that the member was awarded a Blue for competing for Cambridge against Oxford in a relevant sport. Wilkinson was Honorary Secretary for Cambridge University football, and he selected Maurice to play for one match in his first year at Cambridge.

HAWKS CLUB,
CAMBRIDGE
8/3/23

Dear Burwood

You are selected to play for the Varsity on Saturday at 2.30 on the Varsity ground against R.E. (Chatham). Trial shirts & blue knicks.

Sincerely yours
FW Wilkinson
Hon Sect C.U.A.F.C.

I found a small newspaper cutting, possibly from the *Weekly Dispatch*. The title is CAMBRIDGE UNIV v R.E.CHATHAM followed by LIGHT BLUES WIN FINAL GAME.

The sentences from the article mentioning 'Burwood' are:

The opening stages of play were very uninspiring, and it was nearly twenty minutes before M R Burwood, took a pass from R P Hamilton Wickes, and scored. Burwood was the leader of another attack immediately afterwards, but Lt Osborne fisted out for F W Wilkinson to score.

And in the second half:

After 20 minutes Capel-Slaughter, who had not had the best of luck during the game, sent in a good shot, which hit the upright and bounded back into play. Burwood, close handy, sent it back again and scored.

Cambridge won 6-1 with Maurice scoring twice.

This letter provides his own description of the match.

Jes Coll
Cambridge

Dear Mum & Dad

I am writing this letter chiefly because I have actually nothing to do & because it will come as a surprise or at least you will not be expecting it. I am delaying the posting of it till I find out when I can come down.

There was another good rag in Pope's lecture the other day. There were a no of models for showing stereo-isomerism on the lecture bench, (wires with coloured balls specially arranged & tetrahedra.) Two men came right down from the top of the building and pinched these. They took them back to the top of the lecture room & placed them on the bench. Then they cleared off. Pope & his lab boy came in. Pope did not notice their absence because he did not know they were on the bench originally. The lab boy spotted it & as he whispered to Pope great applause broke out.

Oh! I ought to have said that one of our chaps, Benson, brought a lot of forget-me-nots & put them in a beaker on Pope's bench. (Applause). The lab boy dashed in and took them away. The models were then pinched as a revenge.

Anyhow, the next lecture the models were out again but the lab boy stood on guard the whole time. Then a man right at the top of the room got up, walked right down to the bottom took hold of a stool & walking up to the lab boy offered it to him. He refused (Great Applause throughout! I suppose you heard/saw that Phineas was stolen by the Caius Co-optimists a fortnight before the rag & that Scotland Yard had just traced it to Caius College the day before the rag but they could not find it.

A very amusing thing happened to the Dean of one of the colleges. A flashily dressed woman dashed up to the porter & asked where the Dean lived. The porter showed her the stairs just by & she went up. This was at one minute to ten & the porter almost at once shut the gate so that no one could get out without him knowing. Well, time went on & no woman appeared. The Porter got fidgety & when 12 had struck he went to the Master. So the Master & some dons went to the Deans room & found his door locked. Ha! So they hammered on the door & after a long time the dean opened it blinking & yawning with a dressing gown on. They insisting on searching his room & on finding nobody apologised most profusely & the Dean was very indignant. The point was of course that some chap had dressed up, gone up to another chap's room above the Dean and changed into man's clothes & come out again.

There was a grand rag at Emma the other day. A man went to the tutor and said there was too much row in his section of the building (the Hostel) to work. The Tutor suggested he should go round & ask people to be quieter & like a fool he did. The next day they got a donkey, took it up to his rooms (top storey) & somehow got a pair of pajamas on it & put it on the bed. Then at Hall a notice was sent round telling everybody to go to his rooms. So the whole college trooped there to find this donkey in his bed.

Naturally the porters were awfully wild because the donkey was upset by the noise & they had to get him down.

This is rather good as an example of how Englishmen mess things up. Kelvin & Stokes were discussing Fraunhoffer lines in the spectrum of the sun & they hit upon the explanation of them but they each of them maintained that the other had thought of it first so neither took steps to publish it. But they lectured on it & a student's notebook is still preserved with the explanation in, 9 years later Kirchoff published the explanation & so gets the credit. Of course the notebook shows that Stokes & Kelvin knew the explanation & "so" says Alec Wood & you see lecture notes do have their uses. (Great Applause)

I made a mistake when I said I was playing for a̲ Varsity team. I was not. I was playing for the̲ Varsity team and bills about the town advertised the fact. If you had been wise enough to get the Weekly Dispatch you would have seen how I got 2 goals. We won 6-1. I was playing inside right although down to play left half. I scored 1ˢᵗ & last & the second goal was practically mine. Wilkinson at centre forward got 3 & Goddard one.

This is how I got a game. Wilkinson is a friend of Savill & Powell & has been trying to get them a game for a long time. Having succeeded he asked Savill if he knew anyone who was any good. Hence my selection. Savill & I started at 11 on Saturday morning & spent 2 hours (11-1) trying to borrow 2 shirts to play in (Trial shirts). We were in his car too & let rip now & again dashing all over the town. We went round to all the blue & varsity men we could think of. I got Mustell's & Savill got Ashton's. It was a game. The shirts cost 31/- in the shops.

In the game itself all the play was on the other wing, I thought the game was slow but the paper said it was fast. We have a match tomorrow against Emma I. I think I have got a cold waiting for Savill to recover after the match and take me back in the car.

Imagine this. A friend of mine Waddington has won a 21/- pipe̲ for the best̲ set of cigarette̲ pictures̲ of the University Arms. He is now a famous man, it is as good as a blue for sure. We had a soccer dinner last Friday, & he was duly congratulated amidst thunderous applause. Abbott was there & Terry & Cohen & Sinclair etc. Cohen turned up ten minutes late in evening dress & was received with tremendous applause. You see no-one else was in evening dress & when he saw it he nearly fainted. There was *a lot of bread throwing. Bot got up & requested us not to do as the boat club did to use the <u>ices</u> as missiles.*

A.G.G.Marshall of Jesus won the 440 yds scratch race & so should get his blue. Greenhill got his half-blue at boxing but was defeated in his fight. We lost the boxing by 4 to 3 but we won the fencing so we are still up on Oxford with the Soccer, Rugger, Hockey, Fencing & something else to us, & the Lacrosse, boxing & cross country to Oxford.

I shall be coming down on Tuesday either by the 11.14 arriving at 12.37 or the 1 o'clock arriving at 2.21. If I am later do not worry.

Love from Maurice.

'Emma' must mean Emmanuel College, Cambridge. Caius Co-Optimists is a club at Caius College, Cambridge. Fraunhoffer lines are dark features in the spectral absorption of the sun, named after German lensmaker Josef Von Fraunhofer developed Newton's experiments on dispersing sunlight with a prism - according to www.chemistryworld. com. Gustav Kirchoff worked with Robert Bunsen researched further and concluded that the sun and the stars were made of the same atoms as the everyday world.

This letter, posted 5 March 1923, shows Maurice getting deep into the spirit of Cambridge undergraduate life, and highlights the University's Head of the River rowing races – apparently what would now be called a 'contact sport'!

Jesus Coll, Cam

Dear Dad

Cheers! Roars! Shouts! Bellows! Great applause! Whence this sudden outburst of energy? As far as I can recollect that was the second letter you had ever written which did not have some deadly purpose. What I mean to say is it was one of your first chatty letters. Virtue is always rewarded, however, & hence this epistle. We had a good game the other day in a league match against Trinity III. We won five two. We scored three in the first half, Wright & I one each. The other was scored by 9 of our side. The ball got mixed up with Gandar Dower & their goalie & all their defence dashed up to help. Thereupon the whole of our defence & forwards tore up

& pushed hard & the ball gradually travelled into the goal with the crowd. In the second half they scored two quickly. After that I got one & just before the end Dyer got the fifth. We are now, I think, third in the league.

I am afraid that as no one I know up here has heard anything about a swimming bath you must have seen a false report. Where did you see it. Do you know why you did not see my name in the College sports? Well, keep it dark, they didn't ask me to run. In fact, to admit all, they asked three other chaps to run against Magdalen.

Pray, do not worry about money. Your humble knows what he is doing & has the situation well in hand. I shall be able to pay the college bill quite all right. The only thing I require is your £1 per fortnight & all will be merry as a bell. I think I can wangle out of the £2 deposit I spoke about.

By the way, am I a Hindoo or a Mohammedan or what? Had our soccer photo taken the other day. Note that the football boots that were going to burst at the first kick are still as good as ever. Tara-la-la-la. How I gloat! Hear me!

Glad the car is at last all right. In my next instalment I will give an interesting account of the bells of Cambridge.

We had jolly bad luck in the Heads, I don't know if you have read any accounts but the papers are unreliable. The first boat kept head of the river easily. On the first night our 4th boat was bumped by the head boat of division 4 (Trinity Hall 2), so they descended from bottom of division 3 to head of division 4. They kept there with ease but could not catch the boat in front were at the bottom of division 3. You see the boat at the head of a division rows first in that division Y then an hour after in the bottom of the next division, & if it wants doing to bump the boat in front, then.

The Third boat was <u>the</u> unlucky boat. This is the 2nd division. First night they bumped Magdalen 1st boat & then above them were Caius 2, Downing 1, Pembroke III. Our 3rd boat was a better crew than any of these & if they had bumped Caius II on the second night they would have bumped Downing 1 & Pembroke III on the next two days. They would thus have made 4 certain bumps & would have got their "oars" (the reward of four bumps). But they did not bump Caius II. All our crews are fairly slow up to Ditton, but from then on they go at a terrific rate. At Ditton our 3rd was nearly a length behind but they gained rapidly until about 50 yards from the railway bridge they were only a foot from Caius 2. In the next 5 yards they overlapped Caius by a foot & just as the cox was swinging the boat round to bump Taylor's oar broke.

The chaps in the boat thought they had bumped & stopped rowing & they had lost a length before they started again. Even then with 7 men they got up to within half a length of the Caius. The next night they had Selwyn 1 A boat behind them & they were unable to bump Caius because Selwyn bumped our 3rd boat first. If they had bumped Caius that night before, Selwyn would not have come next to them.

The 2nd boat were fourth in the 1st division (a great distinction for a 2nd boat. No other 2nd boat is in the 1st division let alone in the first four places. On the first night rowed over the course without anything happening. 1st Trinity 1 were in front of them & they nearly caught 3rd Trinity 1. If they had caught them our 2nd boat would have gone to 2nd place on the river. In the end order of boats was Jesus 1, 3rd Trinity 1, 1st Trinity 1, Jesus 2, Pembroke 1. You will see why in a minute.

On the second day 1st Trinity bumped third Trinity. At Ditton Pembroke 1 was a yard from Jesus 2 but as I said before we are very fast from Ditton & we drew well away after that. (incidentally our 2nd boat upset Pembroke's chance of getting 4 bumps, a bit of a pill for Pembroke to be done by a 2nd boat). On the third day Jesus 2 had 3rd Trinity 1 in front & Pimmer 1 behind. Jesus 2 gained on Trinity & Pimmer gained Jesus till as they were rounding Ditton Pimmer caught up Jesus & Jesus caught up Third Trinity. Then as they went round the corner, Pimmer overlapped Jesus 2 & Jesus overlapped Trinity.

As the Trinity boat rounded the bend its stern swung out to our bow. Our bow swung in to Trinity stern & our stern swung out to Pimmer bow. Pimmer bow swung in to our stern. So the boats approaching one another & it was an absolute toss up whether our boat would hit Trinity or Pimmer hit ours first. As it was Pimmer bumped us & then almost immediately our boat bumped Trinity but of course as we had already been bumped it did not count. If we had bumped third Trinity first then we would probably have bumped 1st Trinity the last night & gone 2nd on the river, with our 1st boat already Head. That 3rd day was a most exciting day. It is some game running after the boats. You run for about a mile & a quarter in the middle a crowd on rough gravel & shouting all the time, while round the corners you have to sprint like blazes. At intervals the umpires on horseback dash through the crowd & if a man falls over, about a dozen fall over him.

Tell Mum that its no good sending up the trivet, as next term I should have a fire & this term is nearing its close. We met Selwyn on the football field & lost 5-2. We had a scratch lot out & Wright & I were playing back. Murphy was playing for Selwyn & he said how badly Wright & I played. He observed that we did not know where to go or what to do. I only did one good tackle. We are playing Selwyn this week I think & I hope we have a good team out. I have just been gloating over Chips because our 3rd boat bumped his lot.

There was a terrific row last night on the close after the bump supper. Nearly all the college was drunk, & there was a great bonfire. All the November woodwork of the college was carefully taken away by the college authorities on Friday. Otherwise it would have been burnt. You see we are still head of the river & so many from other colleges come & join in our rejoicings. In Jesus land last night about 50 undergrads without cap or gown. A Prog came along & so every bod shouted together "Well rowed Prog. Well rowed Prog etc. Well, I must close now to catch the post.

> Love to all from
> Maurice

Next a time jump to what reads like next year's competition.

Dear Mum & Dad

I am glad you are having a spell away. It won't hurt. We have had an eventful week. On Monday we lost to Pothouse in the knock-out 2-0 & we thoroughly deserved it; they are very bad. Preliminary round.

I caught a cold on Friday & had to play on Saturday v Casuals we lost 3-0. Took precautions & completely got rid of it by Monday morning the only trace being a slight bunged-up-ness in the nose for which I was very grateful as the knock-out was on Monday. Quickest cold I've ever had. Tell you what I did. After the match on Sat had a bath – hot. (Had signed off Hall & went straight from bath home & sweated hard over fire in a sweater till 3 o'clock Sunday when began to cool down slowly & carefully for Hall at 6.30. (Have to go on Sundays, or rather have to pay if don't go). Woke up Monday. Found Sunday did not need more clothes than usual.

On W, Th, F, S the Lent 1ˢᵗ boat for some reasons, one being that they were light & the head wind was very heavy, didn't row the last day & got bumped. The next day they did row & for a mile they raced after the 1ˢᵗ Trinity boat about 2 feet away. On the 3ʳᵈ day they forgot to row. On the 4ᵗʰ day drew to within ½ a length of Trinity but no more & so lost the headship gained in 1921. Most people agree they were unlucky. 1ˢᵗ Trin were not good enough to catch them normally. Lady Maggie, who were to make a bid for the headship, were bumped three times. Our 2ⁿᵈ boat bumped 1ˢᵗ Trin 2 on the 1ˢᵗ night. On 2ⁿᵈ night Queens 1 in front just escaped them by bumping 3ʳᵈ Trinity 1 who were bad. On 3ʳᵈ night they bumped 3ʳᵈ Trinity 1 & on the 4ᵗʰ night bumped Queens 1. They just missed their oars therefore (for 4 bumps or Headship oars are awarded). 3ʳᵈ boat stopped where they were. 4ᵗʰ boat went down 2 places. Benson in the 1ˢᵗ boat has rowed three times & gone down 11 places & Osborne the stroke in 5 times has gone down 15 places. Of course they got into a bad boat each time. There is usually one.

Very funny in the Physics Lab. Appleton & Rutherford are giving a lecture on Electric Wares & Oscillations. Ru Lectures for the 1ˢᵗ half of term & Appleton for the 2ⁿᵈ half. R is always used to using p to denote the frequency of the oscillation and j to denote Ö-1. But as A always uses ω for the frequency & i for Ö-1, R decided to use ω & i. But his notes were in j's & p's, & he has been using j's & p's for 30 years. So every now & again he used to remember to put ω & i but not very often. The result is that all through the term there has been a hopeless mix up of p's, ω's, i's, & j's. He would put things down in this sort of way.

$$\therefore x = j\ p\ cosA = ip\ cosA$$
$$\&\ then\ x = i\omega\ cosA$$
$$\&\ later\ x = j\omega\ cosA$$

All of which were intended to be the same thing. We had some tremendously diverting times. Then last Saturday Appleton began lecturing. So he said "Professor R has always used p and j so although I prefer ω & i I shall use p & j". (Tremendous roars). "I have good authority for their use" (terrific cheers).

Appleton is now Professor at Kings Coll, London, but still comes back to Cambridge for these lectures. He is one of the greatest living authorities on Wireless. It was he, working up here with C.T.R.Wilson, now Jacksonian Professor, who first found the time of durations of a lightning flash the amount of electricity producing & E.M.F. & the kinds of oscillation on it. He identified the flashes with the atmospherics in wireless. In his experiments he was taking the effects of the flashes in an ordinary aerial & passing it through his apparatus. Incidentally he got once a fifty inch spark to the gas pipe from it. He is only about 25 too.

They produced Handel's opera Semele last week & all the papers Times etc praised the production very much. By the way, don't forget to go to the Merry Widow at the Theatre Royal.

Love from
Maurice

Returning to Maurice's first year, this next letter was posted 13 May 1923

Jes Coll Court
May 6

Dear Mum & Dad

Thanks awfully for sending me so much money but for goodness sake don't go short because I've got money in the bank. I enclose dates for future remittances if you can spare it.

Saturday 12th May 10/-
Saturday 26th May 10/-
Saturday 9th June 20/-

I must tell what happened when the remaining photo was being taken. Dyer, Brown, Field, Warrington, & I were watching the cameraman arranging a suitable spot when Field suddenly turned and said. "Did I ever tell you how I broke a camera?"

"I was taken one day by Stern the photographer & received a polite note saying that as both the negatives were cracked right across would I give another sitting."

Roars, accompanied by observations such as "It's not surprising." He said "I was in Cap & Gown". Renewed applause!

Last Sunday after tea there was about 5 of us in Brown's room which *is at the back of a house in Jesus Lane (Ground Floor). There was a good bit of cushion throwing. One went out of the window. In a rash moment Brown leaned out of the window. Immediately Dyer seized him by his legs & pushed him out so that he was dangling by his legs. There is an area underneath. He caught hold of the railings as they dropped him. He lowered himself into the area, gave us back the cushion & was forced to rush under the porch. Not caring to go through the landlady's private quarters, he was forced to stay there for about 15 mins by means of cushions & jugs of water. It was a great joke.*

Hutchinson told us some interesting stories about beryl gemstones. It is a bright green gemstone & they sometimes set it thus (small diagram) the dark part being the setting, the light part being beryl, & the shaded parts being a piece of green bottle. As beryl has the same refractive index as this glass there is no line of demarcation shown. All the physics tests of the mineralogist on top & bottom will work. As Hutch says "It is a bad thing to acquire among your friends a reputation as a gem expert because you may have to enlighten them on the true character of the long cherished possessions. If you put the stone in alcohol, the Canada balsam that cements them together dissolves quickly away & the stone falls into three pieces."

We had also an interesting lecture on sound by Alec Wood. He said the first two great divisions of sound were notes & noises. There was a great divergence of opinion between the two, (great applause). He then went on to say that a note is always accompanied by a lot of noise, (applause). Thus if you listened for it you could hear the tap of a pianists finger on the keys, and singers, he said, even the best of them, create quite a lot of noise. On the other hand, noise is often accompanied by notes. He took a bit of firewood from a bundle & dropped it. He said you would call that a noise. Then he took eight of them & dropped them & it was a perfect scale of C. Doh ray me fah soh la te doh. (Great applause). The he took them & by dropped them on the bench in turn he played Home Sweet Home (thunders). Then he went to some bottles. "There is, apart from extraneous associations, an extraordinary amount of musical note in the drawing of a cork," (loud applause). He drew out 4 corks in turn & played the common chord.

In light he was showing how light was extinguished by notating perfectly transparent substances in the beam. The arc lamp was not working well. "Now you see we get darkness" & the light went out (applause).

To return to serious matters. We had 4 men in the Freshers Cricket Final & 2 in the Seniors Trial & 4 now in the University Trial. We drew with Pimmer the other day. They got 125, after being 85 runs for 1 wicket. We got 277. Then they went in & got 37 for four wickets. The next two men made 130 before one was caught. Eventually they got 200 for 5 wickets & stumps were drawn. Did I tell you we had a Fair Damsel in our hitherto celibate lab. There is one consolation. Though horribly ugly she has a great friend (a Newnham "Blue" for lacrosse) who drops in to see her (from Heycock's lab) who is quite pretty. We have a wonderful collection of colour in the front two rows of Palmer's Chemistry lecture, but nothing really pretty. The buttery Commons has gone down 8d a week.

With regard to clothes, I have a clean vest & pants on, & a clean pair pants & vest in reserve, 2 clean white shirts & 2 tennis shirts, & a clean shirt on. As its getting so warm, one vest thin will do but you can send two if you like. 1 pair good socks (not black or blue) (Oh! Thanks for watchcase, I meant you to send it in the parcel). One pair grey flannels only.

Can't think of anything else.

I must tell you about the watch. I pushed the regular back about twice as far as it is supposed to go & for three days the watch kept splendid time being 3 mins fast. Then, evidently dissatisfied with the lateness of my getting up it gained 20 mins in one night. Its aim was defeated by my hearing the clocks strike eight. It is now keeping a steady time gaining about 1 minute a day. (Another instalment of this splendid serial will be published next week).

No more today.

Love from Maurice

I am unsure when this was sent other than it was at the end of one term.

Dear Mum & Dad

I am afraid my letter is going to be a short one because I have nothing much to talk about. I shall be home somewhere about the 14th, can't tell the exact day till I get my exeat. Afraid I have got a tremendous lot of dirty clothes to wash. I have several pairs of black socks clean which I shall of course leave up here. I can't use them because I am wearing the brown shoes & you can't wear black socks with brown shoes. The black boots have developed a hole in the first layer of the sole & one is worn at the toe so I can't wear them. To get them repaired up here is too costly. Work is not going too well. Don't seem to get through any but I suppose I do. In Chemistry supervision yesterday there were 2 (out of 10) the week before 3 & before that 3, so you see how hard people work up here.

We had a Latymer meeting last Thursday & Kearsey did some fine conjuring tricks 4 of them being his own invention. Only one of the tricks could I see through. He used a pack like Eric has. Two of the other were particularly good. He has two slates. He comes up close & asks for four words or numbers. He then writes these one on each side of the slates & then a member of the audience signs them. He ties the slates together and gives them to the chairman to look after. He takes a pack of cards & one of the audience takes a knife & slips it in the pack, the top half of the pack is taken by this member of the audience & the bottom four cards given to another member who adds up the number of pips on them & writes the number on a card which is signed & sealed up in an envelope & given to the chairman. Then he phones up old pack with a mock telephone & asks him to write the same number on the slate as is on the card. Then the president opens the envelope, reads out the number on the card & lo! On the slate which still bears the signature originally written there, is the same number in writing; e.g. TWENTY TWO.

In another trick he showed us how to find out a fellow's birthday. About six chaps are given little pads to write their birthdays on. They tear off the sheets & fold them & put them in a hat. A member of the audience picks one out of the hat & gives it to the chairman to sign. It is sealed in an envelope and the envelope signed. Kearsey takes the next & by a process of elimination finds which man has his birthday in the envelope. Then I think he gets him to select a month (from 12 monthly calendars) which is not the month of his birthday & he sticks a piece of paper on any day in it & shows it. The card is signed & sealed in an envelope. After messing about for a little while the two envelopes are opened & the piece of block paper is found shaking on the correct day of the correct month.

I ran in the 600 yds relay last Thursday. (2nd division). We won the final easily in 62 2/5 which is an average of 10 2/5 for the 100 yds & 15 3/5 secs for the 150yds (i.e. for each man four in each team). The best time of the *day. The last Division was done in 63 secs so we would have beaten any college. On Saturday we won the division 2 miles relay & 2 miles team race thus winning all the relay races.*

Cambridge won the Fencing against Oxford but lost the lacrosse. We lost a soccer match against Trinity Hall 5-2. I was playing back & played an awful game. Scored one for them.

With regards to Dower & Brighton I think it a needless expense to go down for one or two days & certainly I can't spare more. In any case I shan't do much work I am sure, & certainly I shan't if I go away. Instead, can you let me have 12/6 extra instead of 10s, then I can pay the grocers bill.

The running business costs 3/- (1/6 a time). Saw the Mikado yesterday. Went in the Gods 8d cheaper than Picture show. Way down East has been here for a fortnight. Haven't been to pictures yet this term.

Love to all from Maurice.

Returning to Maurice's contacts with his parents, at some time in 1923 – I think May - Maurice sent another postcard addressed to Mrs Burwood, the Lodge, Ashburton House, Putney Heath, SW15.

Tuesday

Dear Mum, sorry I put the wind up you. You shouldn't be so nervous. In any case I shan't be going down to the labs till Friday so you need not have worried. So glad Auntie Edie has not been kicked out yet. As regards the extra 10/-. I do not want it thanks. That is to say I should like it Saturday week but it is to count as a week in advance. Twiggez? Will explain more fully in next letter.

Good luck to Eric, Love
from Maurice

This next letter I can clearly date. It is from his Jesus College tutor named Mr E Abbott and gives his exam results for the end of his first year of college. Intriguingly he was the only one doing the Natural Science Tripos that year to take four subjects. Maybe trying four was too much and stopped him getting a first.

Jesus College
Cambridge
16 June 1923

Dear Burwood

You were placed in the second class in the May examinations with a total of 203 out of 400, the details being: -

	Physics	Chem	Numerical	Maths
Paper	34/67	33/67	33/67	26/50
Pract	10/33	23/33	26/33 (paper)	18/50

The other years men of your year took 3 subjects only and their marks and classes were: -

Woolley 202/300 1st class
Benson 163/300 2nd class
Browne 124/300 3rd class
Rudd 122/300 3rd class
Bateman 107/275 3rd class
Brown 58/300 Not classed

I should gather that your place in the second class would be quite high up, but owing to the difficulty of comparing 3-subject to 4-subject men, the Examiners do not assign you a definite place. Your prospects for a first next year seem to be quite good.

Yours sincerely
E Abbott

Edwin Abbott was Senior Tutor from 1912. According to Gray and Brittain he was *"a shy, sensitive man"* who *"nevertheless commanded the affection of graduates of all ages until his retirement in 1933"*. His letters show a very personal concern for a student.

Maurice had enjoyed a successful first year at college, both sportingly and academically. For leisure he had Gilbert & Sullivan and books such as *FIFTY 'BAB' BALLADS by W.S.GILBERT*, subtitled *Much*

Sound and Little Sense. It is composed of very Gilbertian poems or lyrics without music - some really strange. No coincidence that his 21st birthday present from his parents on November 6th 1923 was a 4-volume set of *Original Plays by W S Gilbert*.

Also owned by Maurice at Jesus was *"Pip" A Romance of Youth* by Ian Hay, a schoolmaster turned novelist, dramatist, and historian who found time in the First World War to win the Military Cross. *"Pip"* was a pre-war first novel about a young man who becomes a successful England Test Cricketer.

Also Maurice owned *The Golden Treasury of the best songs and lyrical poems in the English language, selected and arranged with notes by Francis Turner Palgrave, Professor of Poetry in the University of Oxford*. I recognized no titles but several names - such as Byron, Shelley, Wordsworth, Cowper, Milton, Keats, Southey, and Scott.

And perhaps it should not surprise that his library should include *Relativity, The Special and General Theory by Albert Einstein*, second edition 1920.

At this time Maurice moved out of college into digs at 7 Manor Street, but this did not take him far as maps show Manor Street just across Jesus Lane from the Master's Garden of Jesus College.

This letter covers his return to Cambridge in 1923.

Jesus College
Sunday Oct 14th

Dear Mum & Dad

Trunk & bike arrived safely. Things were rather creased but I straightened them out. Haven't room in my chest of drawers to hold everything.

Lecture fees have been put up to 1½ guineas, so in spite of having less lectures to go to they still come to 12.12.0 a term.

The weather was nice the day I arrived, lovely & cold. But it turned warm about 11.30 & started to pour. This rain lasted all night & all the next day (Friday) until 6 at the same rate. It was not pouring hard but it was certainly pouring. I've never seen a more sustained effort. I walked to the Bank & back (about 800 yards) & the rain had got through my mack.

It began to hesitate about 5.30 & stopped at 6. Ever since it has been fine. It has just started raining again.

We didn't have a game of soccer on Saturday. The Rugger people had got the pitch. In the end they did not use it owing to the rain, so we could have had a match. A drier ground is necessary for Rugger than for soccer. Our College Trial match is on Monday. We had a few boots of the ball on Saturday but good shooting was conspicuous by its absence. Old teamers left are as follows. Backs 4 (2 required). Half-backs 4 (3 required). 2 forwards (5 necessary). Of the Freshers 1 is a forward (and probably he is no good) the rest are backs & half-back. There is no goalkeeper anywhere, so I can see myself playing forward again.

I have seen Chilton, Schoenburg, Fann, Burke, Schur as well as Joe, Tommy, and Pars, Taylor, Murphy, Walker, so I have done well. I've ordered the photos. All this I've done since Friday evening because one couldn't stir out of doors until then. I went to the grocers & got some books stamps etc, been to chapel; unpacked & sorted (which took some time); had a kick about Saturday afternoon, went round to visit most of the college people I know (they are nearly all out of college); have arranged my lectures & labs, seen both tutors, helped Taylor distribute some C.I.C.C.U. forms & fixture cards; and incidentally swatted Chemistry for about 4 hours.

My practical chemistry this term takes place 4.30-6.30 Tuesdays, Thursdays, and Saturdays. Football matches finish about 4.10. Get from field home (ten minutes if the match is away) bath, dress & get there in 20 minutes. (if the match starts not too late). Expect I shall do it comfortable. 4 Freshers on my staircase & 1 2nd year man. All are scholars so I am in good company. I had Gandar Dower to tea on Saturday with Dyer. The former said I was the only man he knew except Crosskill in college whom he could cadge a tea from. An amusing account of a night of his will be published in our next edition. I am expecting some men to tea in a minute so I must stop.

Love from
Maurice

Fountain pen's just run out.

Maurice was the first in his family to go to university - a remarkable achievement - but this letter gives a perspective on university life for wealthier students – such as Gandar Dower whose 'amusing night' is described.

Dear Mum & Dad Sun

Thanks for the letter, but I wish you would not keep on chatting about sending that jolly old dinner jacket. I shan't need a dress suit this term & in any case I've got the frock coat. It's a waste of money. I shouldn't bother about the football bag, either, if I were you. It is not essential & essentials are the only thing I bother about. By the way I've found out the address of the people who publish the works of Gilbert & Sullivan, Chatts & Windus 111 St Martin's Lane W.C. This was some years ago. Whether it is so now I couldn't say. I think it was 3/- for each of the two volumes or perhaps for both. Probably its about 10/- each now.

They have now spiked up our back way in over the wall so lowering the status of the college to that of other colleges; which fact reminds me of the story of Gandar Dower. He & Sinclair & several others went out motoring some miles from Cambridge; visited Bedford, I believe. Some of them were tight, some merry & some blotto. As far as I can gather Dower wasn't too steady. However, just about midnight they were 30 miles from Cambridge & supposed to be in by 12. Then coming home one chap took it into his head to ride astride on the bonnet of the car. So after consultation the two soberest Sinclair & Dower decided to let him. Then they drove about 30mph: expecting him to get fed up every minute with being frozen. But he still stuck on, so they decided to let her rip and then suddenly shove the brakes on so as to throw him off. The trouble was, of course, they couldn't see where they were driving. They did it. The back axle immediately expired, but he remained on. Then staggering off, he opened the door & said "Somethingsh happ-pp-ppened, hashintit?" They shoved the car in the ditch & had to walk 4 or 5 miles to a place where they hired a car & got to Gandar Dower's lodgings about quarter-half past three. He, contrary to regulations, has a key with which he let himself in. He stood his companions some more beer or something & they crawled into college the back way just as it was beginning to get light at 4 o'clock. Next day, probably out of bravado, they were salvaging the car at 10 o'clock in the morning.

I have just acquired a book by Pattison Muir, Fellow of Caius, Cambridge with "Dr William Ramsay F.R.S. with the author's compliments" written inside the cover, for 1/-. Georgie will be pleased. There is an amusing story about a classical Tripos some 80 years ago. A man took the exam & much to surprise of the tutor was ploughed. He knew he had done well, too. He then made some enquiries & so the examiners said some of his papers were perfect, which led them to believe he had seen the papers beforehand. He took them to court & won the case & got his degree. Years later he published the true account. He had bribed a printer's boy to sit on the type prepared for the papers. Also, it is very improbable that the boy wore white trousers.

A tragedy has happened at school. Everyone at school omitted to apply for Intermediate County Scholarships on the General Schools; (the School had done it up to two years ago), so none of them got them. Sewel, who should have come up this term, had pneumonia very severely with a relapse so though he's convalescent he is not coming up till next term.

Had an amusing incident in Mineralogy. Hutchinson was telling us good books to get. He mentioned a "manual of Petrology", "The author had been dead a few years." (Great Applause). "His name was Moses". (Thunders) "Still, this book is more up to date that you might suppose." (Applause).

We have a delightful Practical Chemistry Man (by the way he gives us ½ an hour lecture first) Heycock. He is very old, says "Aher, you have to thoroughly shake." (Great Applause). "Aher, aher, to thoroughly shake." (Applause). "You have to thoroughly." (roars) "Oh, I suppose it's over some silly little detail." (Tremendous shouts), then a terrific glare from Heycock.) "Oh, well then, thoroughly to shake." (Terrific applause).

Later on he said "So you filtrate the cyanide against the silver nitrate. Now for goodness sake don't go sucking up cyanide in a pipette or the next thing will be an inquest (great applause).

It was amazing to go into Searle (Practical Physics). He is a big man, a tremendous Beaver with a voice. He immediately rounded on the waiting crowd, picked out those he did not know, asked them if they taking maths. If they were he bullied them, but usually gave them experiments. If they weren't he usually cast them forth into an elementary lab. Woolley & I stood at the back enjoying the sport till after about ¼ of an hour a demonstrator (female) came up & cast us on to experiments. I have practical chemistry from 4.30 to 6.30 Saturdays, Thursdays & Tuesdays.

My programme for Tuesday. 9-1 lectures. 2.15-4 or later football match. Bath, get to labs 4.30-6.30. Rush back to supervision 6.30-7.30. Come out at 8 & expire in armchair. Have had two practice matches. Centre forward in one. Centre half in the other. Drew both. 4-4. Scored the 1 in the 1-1. Had Latymer meeting. Got a man who was at school, in 1915, went into army & they have sent him here with this year's batch of army men. Pars brought him into the meeting. Pars is Tommy's Supervisor.

Had a letter from Eric French. Described Delcy's effort to ruin brass band. They've a Cambridge Musical Society entrance fee 5/- and they need wind instruments badly for orchestra. They seem to be rehearsing the Mikado. There is a second D'Oyly Carte Company going round now. Dyer saw them at Loughborough. Saw Old Boys beat Polytechnic in Middlesex Amateur Cup & Ashford in Amateur F.A. Cup. Replay.

If you want list of Varsity fixtures I can let you have them. Hope you weren't too disappointed because I didn't get a game in Seniors Trial. Probably they saw enough of me last March. The fresher Kenyon who they praised in the papers was the man from Charterhouse I played against there last year. He wasn't bad but he wasn't really much good.

By the way, Gandar Dower got in a trap last night. Constable said he was going 38 m.p.h. He defended his own case & was complimented on getting out without having his licence endorsed.

Sinclair was playing in a cricket match that day so another man Pearce who hadn't been near Gandar Dower on that fatal night gave evidence for him. Gandar Dower admitted he was travelling 38 mph easily. That is how justice miscarries.

Well I must stop now. Excuse this scrawl.

Love from Maurice

This letter sent 25 Nov 1923 mentions the Zev/Papyrus race - a match race between the English Derby winner Papyrus and the Kentucky Derby winner held in November 1923 in America.

Dear Mum & Dad

There's not much to talk about this time. There were one or two rags last week not very exciting. The rugger match on Tuesday in the market square you probably read about. The field was restricted and the play did not last long, otherwise it was fairly successful. On Saturday they had the Zev Papyrus race jockeys the Earle of Sander & Dunnohow. This was, I believe, mostly a dress parade, many characters being represented. Sir Motley Throng was prominent. They had a better one on Saturday night, one grand bonfire in market square. There were lots of police to prevent it. Suddenly there was a terrific commotion in one corner. All the police rushed there in force. Then a terrific fire burst out in the opposite corner. They had filled one of the Queens boats with combustibles & burnt it. An old boat, I suppose.

An amusing thing happened at the Science Club the other day. Baines was reading a paper on earthquakes and there were very complicated explanations involving mathematics. There were present Pars (maths don) Waddams, Schur, Moreton (maths scholars). Everybody was very puzzled over it & Pars had just admitted he couldn't understand it so Baines scratched his head & said, "You have to be a mathematician to understand it". (Great hilarity).

By the by Mascall has got a schol at Pimmer on the results of the Higher Schools Exam. Billie is going to sit at Trinity. Amusing thing in Hutchinson the other day. When you look through a crystal of calcite at a spot on a bit of paper you see two spots. Hutchinson explained that Malus saw this one day (great applause). "It had never been seen before" (Tremendous applause). Perhaps I was wrong there (tremendous applause).

I enclose Soccer Fixtures.

University
Nov 15 Spurs,
17 Cambridge Town
21 Casuals (away)
24 Nunhead
26 Southern Amateur League
27 F.A.

Dec 1 Watford (away)
6 Arsenal (away)
8 Corinthians (away)
12 Oxford (away)

<u>*Jesus Matches*</u>
Nov 12 Trinity Hall
15 Clare
19 Selwyn
23 Caius
24 Wellingborough (at Wellingborough)
27 Trinity Hall
29 Christs
Dec 1 Old Carthusians (Jesus)
5 Fitzbilly
7 Emma
6 Kings Sch Ely

A funny thing occurred in Heycock's Pract Chemistry the other day. (Please excuse the mess I'm making I'm attempting to carry on a conversation at the same time with a silly fool). Eric will appreciate it & may explain it to me. "So you see we oxidise the iron from the stannic to the stannous condition (applause) I mean we oxidise the iron from the stannous to the stannic condition (Tremendous applause) er – er – er – er the ferrous to the ferric condition. (Cheers).

The man I was telling you about who plays goal for us (did I tell you he can throw the ball over the halfway line from the goal) has been in trouble lately. He is married, got a boy & a girl & his little girl has got diabetes. This week-end he had to go home particular because his mother-in-law is very ill, pneumonia I think. However he is very cheerful over it.

The Science Club fee has been changed from 1s entrance fee & no subscription to 1/6 entrance fee & 2s a year subscription so I am getting quickly ruined. I think that is all for today.

Love to all from Maurice

This next letter was posted 29th November 1923, and Maurice combines his enthusiasms for Gilbert & Sullivan and football.

> *Dad*
>
> *A wandering left back I*
> *A thing of shreds & patches*
> *Of stockings, boots, & matches*
> *Which make me pipe my eye*
> *My face is very long*
> *Although the field I'm ranging*
> *And to my humour changing*
> *I sigh my doleful sigh*
> *I sigh my doleful sigh.*

This is absolutely true. The record of our successes is absolutely dismal. They keep playing a silly fool at centre half. Of the matches we've played with him there (omitting Lancing) we've lost 3 drawn 1 & won 1. On Monday we lost against Selwyn. We had 6 men away. I was playing centre forward and the defence was so weak I only saw the ball about twice. I scored 1, Dyer 1, Gandar Dower 1. The defence let 4 through. We were very unlucky only just missing the goal several times. In the last minute Dyer took a corner kick & the ball was just inside the goal when one of our men touched it with his head so it wasn't a goal. In view of the scratch team we have Murphy couldn't gloat because we sat on them in the 2nd half.

On Wednesday we beat Clare 1-0. I was back & I watched the forwards messing it up all the time. Just in the last 3 or 4 minutes they squeezed one in, & we won. Up to this game I could say that in 9 matches at back I had only let 3 goals though while in 3 matches when I wasn't back 8 goals were scored. Friday & Saturdays' matches wrecked it. On Friday we drew 3-3 against Caius. We were winning easily & deservedly 2-0 at half-time. Then they scored one through our goalie studying the moon. It was going so slowly that I and the other back let it go for the goalie. He missed it. Then they got another with a good shot. Then they got another through our goalie. He rushed out to a cross ball, it hit his foot & went in goal. He is a good ball-goalie, a new discovery but he had two lapses. After pressing round their goal for 10 mins we scored the equalizer with the last kick of the game.

On Saturday we played Old Wellingtonians at Wellingborough. They had several blues playing including Sorensen. The match was fairly even but we lost 5-0. Our right half & back kept letting them through so we on the left were helpless. It was a very fast & even game, though. Next Tuesday we play Trinity Hall. If we win & then they lose against someone else we go up. If they draw against someone else we probably go up on goal average. It we draw or lose we stop down.

The Varsity have made some changes. Lowe, last year's outside right, has been dropped. So has Kenyon who replaced him. Now they are playing Taylor of Queens. Piper has been drop. The papers say very great things of Piper at left back but apparently he is teetotal & not in with the nobs. He may get back though.

Wright & Powell got tight with Capel-Slaughter (Sec) & Bell (capt) when they played the Casuals so they will probably get their Blues. Last Saturday Wright came with us but did not get tight, only merry. There were 4 teetotallers present. Gandar Dower is crocked. He & Wright made more noise while watching the match than all the other spectators put together.

We won the relays last Friday by 2 pts. We should have won by more but were unlucky in the draw. Did I tell you Murray also got an £80 at Pimmer. If you are going to send me any money do it this week then I needn't draw any money out of the bank but it doesn't matter. Yesterday was expensive. It is very cold today. Frost is like a fall of snow.

It was jolly funny in Heat the other day. Ellis put an india rubber ball in liquid air & then threw it against the wall. It shattered like a piece of glass (tremendous applause) all over the place. Dyer got a fat nose & a big eye last Saturday from a kick. I have invested in – tell you when I come down. It's a secret. Cost more than £2. Searle suggested I get a stop watch à la Eric, price 3-16-0 (gun metal). Did you think I should cut a soccer match so that I could run as 4th man in a relay team, the time of my running being about 16 secs & the windy period about an hour. Its preposterous. Besides the team would have lost. The relay team same thing.

Well, I think I've missed the post but I'm trying to catch so good-bye

Love from Maurice

Maurice played a lot of football. He even played for Old Latymerians in the same month as for Cambridge: a programme for a Spartan League match between Old Latymerians and Old Lyonians on Saturday 31st March 1923 records M R Burwood on the team sheet as playing right back.

I do not believe he played regularly for Old Latymerians until 1925, but he kept a fixture list for them for the 1922-1923 season with scores input. There are full fixture lists for both 1st & 2nd Elevens, but only four scores recorded for the Reserve Team – three wins and a draw in September and October 1922. The 1st XI list records 32 results between September 1922 and May 1923 - no draws recorded, just 13 wins and 19 losses. Incidentally the Old Lyonians match on March 31st was the Latymerians last win of the season by 5 goals to one.

Oddly the fixture lists for Old Latymerians do not only include long lists of fixtures for the 1st XI and the Reserve Team, but also similarly long fixture lists for "A" Team and "B" Team fixtures – in each of which Maurice has recorded one result as if he had maybe played in those matches – both wins: 6-1 away to West London Catholic on 16th December 1922 for the "A" Team and 9-0 at home against Old Ealonians on 9th December 1922 for the "B" Team.

His interest in his old school did not stop with the Old Latymerians, as this letter from 1923 shows Maurice keeping a close interest in his old school.

Dear Mum & Dad etc.

Thanks for letting me know the result of the school sports. As a matter of fact I could I think fill up many of the gaps in the programme. Jolly good of Bradmore to win. As a matter of fact I worked it out last year & thought that they would win. Did you speak to Blades. I am writing to him. I expect he has gone batchy. I thought I explained that I was told last Tuesday was the date for the Inter-Schools and all the chaps up here said the same thing. If they alter it to a week earlier it isn't my fault. I've got the results & here they are. I've put the names of the schoolfellows.

Under11 100yds 2nd Pascall 1st Wilsons 3rd Haberdashers Time 14secs
Under12 100yds (1) Hampstead Haberdashers (2) St Dunstan's (3) Haberdashers 13 2/5secs

Under13 220yds (1) Haberdashers (2) Strand (3) May (Bradmore) 29 1/5secs

880 Relay race (2) Latymer May (Bradmore) Douet Osborn (Bradmore) Westerland (1ˢᵗ) Haberdashers (3ʳᵈ) St Dunstans *2m 0 2/5secs.

Haberdashers beat record

Under14 220yds (1) Askes Hatcham (2) Porter Cox & (3) Hawkes (both Bradmore) *27secs

Hatcham beat record

Under15 100yds (1) Strand (2) Lovelace E (3) Lovelace F T 11 3/5secs

Strand equalled record in heat

440yds (1) Strand (2) Lovelace F T (3) Debenham R J 60 3/5secs

High Jump (1ˢᵗ) Lovelace F T (3ʳᵈ) Stone 4ft 7ins

Long Jump (1ˢᵗ) Parker Cox of Bradmore (2) Debenham 16ft 1½ins

880yds (1ˢᵗ) Liley (3ʳᵈ) Williams 2m 22 2/5secs

Relay race 880yds (1ˢᵗ) Latymer beat record - Lovelace FT, Lovelace CE, Parker-Cox (Bradmore), Tobias *1m 47secs

Under16 220yds (1ˢᵗ) Heap (2ⁿᵈ) Mountford Beat Record 24 2/5secs

880yds (1ˢᵗ) Gregory (2ⁿᵈ) Harris * 2m 16 2/5secs

Open 100 yds (2ⁿᵈ) Claridge (3ʳᵈ) Faithfull *10 9/10secs

Faithfull equalled record in heat

Inge (Strand) beat record in final

440 yds (1ˢᵗ) Faithfull – Beat record (3ʳᵈ) Claridge *54 3/5secs

Mile (1ˢᵗ) Arnold – Beat Record (2ⁿᵈ) Fenton *4m 46 4/5secs

Mile walk (1ˢᵗ) Parker-Cox *7m 49secs

High Jump (2ⁿᵈ tied) French, Macmillan, Melhuish (Haberdashers) Stubbs (Hatcham) beat record *5ft 4⅜ins

Relay (880) Latymer (1ˢᵗ) Claridge, Kay, Heap, Faithfull - beat record *1min 37 2/5secs

Hurdles Open (1ˢᵗ) Claridge 17 4/5

Long Jump 18ft 2in

Tug - St Dunstans won

Stars indicate records beaten

Points Latymer 135, Strand 60, Haberdashers Hampstead 46, St Dunstans 22, Aske's Hatcham 12, Wilsons 10.

Have heard one or two good things, up here. You know that a preposition is not the thing to end a sentence with. Well, one day a nurse was asked by a soldier to read to him. So she said to him "What book do you want to be read out of from for."

Don't you think it is rather good. By the way it's very old. I heard it at school, but I don't think you've heard it.

People up here do some queer things. A man got a classics scholarship, came up here, and in his first year took the Natural Science Tripos (got first class honours) took to playing bridge & is now studying for a Geography "special". (A special is a very still soft exam. If you can get two (or 3 I'm not sure) one each you get the pass degree).

Another man spent nearly two years on history & then two months before the History Tripos decided he did not know enough & so he switched over to Natural Science with two to get to Tripos standard.

A fellow named Baines did a terrible thing last Sunday night in his sleep. He took a Practical Chemistry exam combined with a theoretical paper & a Geology paper. The peculiar thing was that the exam took place with each man in his own room. For the practical exam to get various reagents he had to go to various rooms in the College. He described carefully how he did his analysis and what a mess he got into, how he got a black precipitate in a group which should only contain white precipitation. Silly ass.

My first exam is Monday week (28th) & the last Thursday fortnight (June 7th) Term ends Monday June 11th i.e. in three weeks' time.

We have three men playing for the Varsity on Saturday against West Indies.

Porter-Cox, I expect won the 100, 220, High Jump, Long Jump, was 2nd in the 2nd team in the under 15 Relay & in the Inter Schools. Was 2nd in the 220 under 14, first in long jump under 15 & in 1st team in the relay under 15. So he gets 7 medals as you heard he had. Claridge gets 9 medals. Aren't you jealous of Claridge! Ha Ha Ha Ha (this is the Venables cackle). When I see him I shall tell him what you said about him. He will be delighted. Personally I don't see why he should <u>not</u> want all the honours & why shouldn't he be in the limelight if he deserves it.

I'm putting in a list of things I should like sent up. My whole heart goes out to Eric in sympathy. I've done it myself. I shall not need drawing instruments, thanks. I've finished or rather borrowed a pair of compasses from the Mineralogy which I can leave there when I take the practical

Mineralogy, the last exam. I've got clean pants & vest on today. I shall therefore need only one vest & thin pants. The clean things I've put on today will last me a fortnight of the three weeks.

<u>List</u> 2 pair socks
1 short pants
1 thin vest
2 shirts

Some camphor balls (Carbons, this is put in because you think they are carbons)

Dutch cheese
Bacon (if you like)
1lb sugar (if you like)
¼ lb tea (or ⅛ lb will do)
Grey flannel trousers?

If there is anything else I've asked for in former letters which is not dealt with in this you had been sent it. I believe there was something but I've forgotten. Anyhow it can't matter much.

It is still cold up here & the idiot of a Bedder has got me some coal in. Its useful, I must admit, but not essential.

Thanks for photo of self. The untidy mess of the clothes was the essence of the whole business. Extract from letter – "Eric don't think he has passed. I think he only done 2 questions – rather bad isn't it? I expect I've done lots of those however in my letters. Another extract – he couldn't think of a thing he said.

Did you mean I couldn't think of a thing he said. Jolly amusing to go through your letter & punctuate same. Enjoy it almost as much as I do the letter.

Must close now with much love.

Your loving
Son (M R Burwood)

I believe that this next letter was sent in 1924 as it refers to an exam on mineralogy which he took in 1924. It mentions his father being in hospital, but could not be for his final illness so Will was probably in hospital in 1924 – possibly in Putney Hospital as in a letter in an earlier chapter.

7 Manor St

Dear Mum & Dad

Just a little scrap to let you know I received parcel. I have had only one letter from Dad addressed by him posted at the hospital. The other is therefore I presume in Penzance or Scotland or somewhere. Anyhow it isn't in the parcel. Hope there wasn't anything compromising in it.

You sent me the most important of the books. Would you have another look for the other. It is a rough book like the mineralogy book you sent me with no cover. It may have deceived you because one end is mathematics I think, & the other end is Physics & Chemistry of Crystals. You may only have looked at the Maths end. It is just possible it has a cover on. If so, it is almost sure to be blue. If I don't get the book I shall either not do the work it contains or else if I do it, it will take me say 5 hours longer. So you see it is not vitally important.

By the way, the time I spent on mineralogy is completely vindicated. It will enable me to answer five questions in the exam I hope with only 2 days revision. We are not allowed to answer more than 12 altogether. I shall be lucky if 3 days work on anything else will give me material for answering one question.

By the way, if Eric knows of any small book on the Vale & its uses (not a popular (broadcasting) book) he might mention same. Will you tell when and if you are going away. I should like to run down by a Wembley Excursion for a day just before the Exam. It begins about the 27th.

If Eric can let me have his slide rule later I shall be pleased. Another thing I want. If he has a broken hack saw blade. The back of it sharpened up forms an excellent glass cutter of a type I may need for a certain experiment. It must be sharp enough to cut glass without having to press it appreciably. And by the way never say less fatter again. The book I want will not say mineralogy on it.

Why shouldn't Dad go to Portsmouth? I hope Old Lady will pay for Working. I am not at the moment in need of money & I think I can pay my Bills. Fountain pen cost 4/-. Now & again when I look at past questions, I think I can't answer any of these. Then I look one up & write it out & feel awfully wise till I look at the questions again. Well bye bye.

Love from Maurice

I shan't write any more letters.
Have not got any more envelopes.

Eric – Appleton says best to have grid leak (&+L.T.) to Earth.
    Amplification factor

$$\overline{d\{ñ\}}\, d´\, k = \frac{pNd´\log e\, d/d´}{\log 1/pNd}$$

N = Distance between grid farms

$$\gamma\gamma\gamma\gamma\gamma\gamma$$
$$\upsilon$$
$$N$$

Anode current = $A \dfrac{\{Va + kVg\}\, 3/2}{\{I + k\}}$

where Va = anode voltage
    Vg = grid voltage

To make a dull emitter – head to 2700 for few secs in vacua with Thorium oxide in bulb. Produces a layer 1 molec thick on the wire of Thorium. Let air in & heat a little. Oxidises Thorium to the) & there you are after exhausting Charcoal for liquid air use requires heating up well at low pressures before use.

If you work an evacuator you might try a dull emitter stand but I doubt it.

I apologize to all mathematicians or electricians reading for not transcribing the electrical equations precisely. It was difficult finding symbols and fonts to match – some above are just best available approximations. I presume they are something to do with electrical engineering and possibly with Will and Eric wiring up Ashburton Lodge or building their own wireless sets. I do not know what the reference about Will going to Portsmouth is about, and I presume that the Old Lady referred to is Mrs Charrington, Will's employer.

I believe this next letter was sent 22 Jan 1924

> *Jesus Coll*
> *Cambridge*
> *Sunday*

Dear Mum

Thanks for letter. I am just sending a little line because I shan't be writing for a week. It's a pity you can't mix the pink & green jumper a bit. Have a peep round for my dress tie. I thought I saw it at home somewhere & I have recollections of taking it down at Christmas. Sorry I've suddenly caught sight of the line in which you say you are going to send it.

By the way I think one of us is mad. I never accused (at least, never intended to accuse) John's of offering to sell us a 4 or 5 valve set for £10. What I did say (or meant to say) was that Tommy's father had bought one for £10. Look at my letter & see what I did say. Did you like Aida & Madame Butterfly. The school drew with Queens 5-5 although Queens had most of the play. I was unable to watch because I was playing in the College trial match. It was a good performance because Queens is one of the best colleges (at the top of the 1st league). They came up by charabanc 7/6 each. They had to pay their own fares. Taylor (the blue) scored the 5th goal in the last minute. Chilton, Tommy & I had lunch at Chilton's with Billy Williams, Arnold (spectator) and Corteen. We 3 shared the expense. For tea the team & 5 supporters & 12 Cambridge Latymerians squashed into Joe's (28 in all). 4 kettles 6 teapots dozens of cakes etc. They left at 6.30.

In my match my team won 3-1. Bill Wright was playing centre forward in the other team & got awfully peeved because he couldn't score so whenever I made a little mistake he sat up & took notice. When the time was up he said play on so we played on. Then after 11 mins he scored a goal and so he said "pack up". However it restored him to a good temper & he condescended to admit I had not played badly.

I wrenched the sole of the boot off from the heel to just past the instep soon after half time & the nails stuck up so I had to hobble about on the toe. It was quite easy though. Sanford the right back was also hobbling because he sprained his ankle a week or two back. However, they had to play extra time to get past the two cripples.

We discovered a new play from Harrow who is quite good. Last Monday Tommy arrived at 12.30 & ran into me in the funnel so I gave him some food. (Tommy isn't a dog).

I can get the Rainbow book for a 1/-. The man said it had been there for a long time & probably would not go. Shall I get it or do you think it is 6d too much. It is in good or passable condition. I think that is all for the present. No schols obtained at Pimmer. Lovejoy sat there, I think. Old Man somewhat peeved. School is not entering the Inter-Schools this year. They have, I believe, arranged a match-cricket-one with Cat's.

Thank Eric for his love. Surely he didn't say he'd write soon.

> *Much love from*
> *Maurice to all*

P.S. I really did air the things but of course I put in to create a good impression. All the latter portion was written on Monday. I put off posting it so that you wouldn't expect a letter.

Chap charged 6d to mend the boot. I'm having the maudlin soccer photo framed.

Oh, by the way, I knocked two men over on Friday in the match. Unfortunately both were on my side, left half & goalie. The latter kindly retaliated on the spot by kicking me on the head & was awfully disappointed because he didn't even raise a bump. It think it was him but there were 4 or 5 bodies on top of us & it may have been one of them. While the 7 of us were all mixed up on the ground Bill Wright scored his goal.

Cambridge Operatic Society is doing Patience this term & another club Pirates of Penzance.

This letter was sent 10th Feb 1924.

> *Sunday*

Dear Mum & Dad

I shouldn't have such a rash promise to write today but I've cut the Ciccu, hence this epistle. Murphy & Kearsey came to tea avec moi today.

At 5.45 Murphy lit lamp & dashed off, came back, said bike pinched from chimney. Kearsey said "Take mine" & we all dashed into chimney. Kearsey's bike gone, so I said "take mine". He took it & I'm still wondering whether he reached the end of Jesus Lane. 6.30 Kearsey and I visited the chimney, found Kearsey's bike. Looked at speedometer. Had seen 12 miles since half past four. Rather funny. Don't know if Murphy's bike has returned. He did not tell us what it was like.

Going to have a big gathering at Latymer Dinner. Over 30 or possibly 40.

Lent commence Wednesday. 1st, 2nd, 3rd, boats bad, 4th passable. Hope for best but will not be surprised at the worst. I'm still in a very bad temper over the football match. Bill Wright was fairly good but missed 4 sitters. Inside left ditto 2 sitters. Complete defence except goalie & I absolutely groggy. Right half & back let the left wing centre every few seconds. Enjoyed myself as far as game went. Ref Fleming (Blue) didn't know what offside was. The last (winning) goal, man (two men) were miles offside & nearly in goal & he didn't give it. Bill Wright told me at half-time that Fleming did not know the rule. Then later on he did give an offside after I had cleared miles up the field.

Caius captain apologised for winning by means of that goal. We were winning 3-1 at one time & they got 2 quick ones while we weren't looking. Bill Wright apologized at half-time (1-1) for missing goals.

Played Emma last Monday with weak team only lost 2-1. I was playing centre-forward. Awful pitch & ball & high wind. Defence was so weak that never hardly saw the ball. Browne played well at left back. I got our goal from difficult place. Fluke.

Kearsey was acting in Pentacle show. Didn't go. Robey is in C.A.O.S. as Bunthorne. Go in gallery 8d. Might go to Shakespeare this week. Came across good joke. Two women talking to one another on opposite sides of street. Decided to cross & looked proper way for traffic. Arrived on opposite side of street & to each one's amazement found themselves still separated by street. I don't think it is true because women don't look the right way for traffic, do they? Hutchinson, our mineralogy man is ill & has not lectured this term. Geule & Farr coming up in a week or two. Pars askes me for examples now & again. I tell him he doesn't want to be bothered with examples from me. He agrees.

O.K. Hope you have all recovered from __Flu__ by now including the lickle picky wickless. Give my sympathy to Mrs Stephens.

Will write off 6 or more letters when I have time – Edmund etc. During Lents perhaps. Please excuse writing. Can't trouble to be careful. Perhaps if you write me a letter quick may feel better tempered. Not being able to swear prevents quick recovery ahem! See if I can collect some jokes for my next bulletin.

If our boats get bumped in Lents will gloat exceedingly. Schur is in 2nd boat so he has done well. Running have tie against Kings on Tuesday. Should win easily. Everything O.K.

> *Much love to all from*
> *Maurice*

The next letter was sent April 1924 and refers to the Rooster Club, which was formed at Jesus College in 1907. Jesus College has a rooster on its coat of arms, and the current college café is called the Roost Café, but I know little more about the Rooster club than in this letter.

Dear Mum & Dad

Thanks for the money & the double letter. I've got ⅓ of the £1 still left today. Your guess about the tow-path was very wrong, for several reasons. (1) the chap has a basket on the front of the bike (2) people who want to use their bikes late don't take them on the towing path, only borrowed bikes & I'm too conscientious to ruin a borrowed or thieved bike (3) Chaps got a hat on & (4) he's standing still (5) Boat is just making a bump. The man on somebody else's bike with a megaphone is a coach, the man on the horse is an umpire.

The other cutting is absolute bilge & Tommy rot. (1) Cambridge is not dropping the Jesus style, Selwyn & Caius are rowing this year in the Jesus style (2) There is no curtailed swing (see cutting) though it may appear short (3) Cambridge have not used the Jesus style against Oxford (4) The Etonians are said by rowing people to be the weakest portions of the boat (5) the crew is possible pretty but __all__ the rowing people are agreed that it is a very bad crew, about the worst Cambridge boat ever seen. Swan the coach has resigned because, it is said, they are putting the light Trinity

(Eton) men in the boat. Playford says it is pitiful to watch them rowing. They may win if Oxford sink.

We beat Pimmer in the semi-final of the running championship last Friday. On Saturday the 2ⁿᵈ eleven beat Downing II 1-0 & so play the bottom team of the 3ʳᵈ Division for the place in that Division next year. Trinity Hall beat Selwyn & they can't lose against Christ's so we shall have to play them a deciding game for promotion to the first league, probably on the Varsity ground. Capel-Slaughter is captain next year & De Koven Secretary of the varsity Soccer.

Did I tell you Dyer had got a job. I'm glad you went to Ruddigore. Eileen Sharp is jolly good as Mad Margaret. For goodness sake don't go to the Gondoliers till I get home. I come down in the middle of it. Princess Ida is a very good very clever & witty. One warning letters about flu. I should like to remind Dad that the Labour Party have to be very careful what they do & every step has to be very constitutional wise because of the minority in the house. No doubt you say how the conservatives saved the Government over the new ships. The Labour Party are practically forced to do as they have been doing which is no doubt very well.

The running people have to compete against Trinity in the final next Tuesday. They should win. Caius soccer team beat Downing & so play Trinity in the final. We should have been there.

Had the Latymer dinner last night. Went off very successfully & nobody was tight. The Old Man imbibed tons of it but he has a strong head. He admitted having a whisky beforehand too, when Walker told a joke about a convict, a clergyman & some whisky. Kearsey, Schur & Ellis did not come but a lot of old boys turned up. Attridge, Baxter, Bennett, Smellie, Ossy Wood of course. Beaky was there as a guest. (Hymn no 25). Russell, the sec of the Latymer Old Boys was present and was very bucked at being asked. Tommy & I had breakfast in his rooms with Baxter & Russell & then we took Russell round Cambridge. On the way we collected Schur, Joe, & Johns & finished in Kearsey's rooms at Christs.

The dinner was a great success. The Old Man was very heavy but cheered up at the end. He talked about 2 years of wracking anxiety & looked worried but now he has reached calm waters. This year is the tercentenary of the Latymer Foundation & he wants to celebrate by building a new front to the school to make it look worthy of the traditional position thereof. He also wants to build a further building at the back so that it will show above the front & give an imposing appearance to it. He wants £10,000.

Beak came up on Friday night & walked to Selwyn, meeting Murphy just outside. They walked all over the colleges looking for Latymerians & they were all out till they came to Jesus when they found the dook in obvious signs of work (tremendous cheers). Schur was in the room so I was not actually working so we all had coffee & Beaky told us some anecdotes. Behind his door is a cupboard on opening the door he is hidden from the gaze of the entering one. A boy came in when he was at the cupboard. "What ho' you chaps. Where's the beak?" Also of a parent who talked to the Old Man of Mr Beak. Beak told us these stories with great glee. At the dinner he said how well the school taught people because no one seemed to need to do work up here & how he drew blanks every time.

I had an interesting talk with Ossy Wood about old signalling corps days. My bike was severely biffed in the bump supper night. I was silly enough to leave it in the chimney. Next day I found the back wheel (fortunately the condemned one with a buckle at least 6 ins out of line). Anyhow I used both feet with my knees under my chin & then half an hour with a hammer & I'm still riding it merrily. The chain comes off now and again but that is a mere detail.

The Roosters decided to present a testimonial of long service. 6d was devoted to Hoppit & 2½d for other charities. An almoner & Philanthropist was appointed to distribute these sums. In reply to this Hoppit sent an 8 line lyric. You have only to see Hoppit to realize the tremendous fun & the wonder of his writing a lyric. "Curly" in return for a ½d sent a long flowery letter of thanks. Wilson, the Almoner, read out a long list of charities on which the 2½ was sent. It was very funny.

Well, I think I've talked enough. It's peculiar but Mum is always in a tremendous hurry hence the shortness of the letters ahem, I mean the sudden abrupt finish thereof. I'm going to make the same excuse. It is now 10 past 9 & if I don't rush down to the post office & post this it will not reach you tomorrow & as there will be tremendous upheavals & cyclonic winds-up & telegrams & inquiries about flu & pneumonia etc.

Did I tell there seem to be some pretty Newnham girls knocking round now. Beaky implored me to get a game of cricket with our place *if it was only our second eleven, so I am dashing round soon. Thanks for money. Did you say Eric had flu. I hope not. Ask him to ask Ward to ask Brier in a quiet way if he had a letter from me. I wrote to him & had no answer.*

Love from Maurice to all

Also in Maurice's second year at Jesus I found a programme for a match on Saturday 5th April 1924: Hertford Town versus Old Latymerians in the Spartan League. The match records Old Latymerians as being at the bottom of the league before the match and Hertford Town five place above them. M W Burwood is recorded as playing inside right this time. Maurice played for Jesus College football 1923-1924, and kept a fixtures card with all scores for both 1st and 2nd XIs.

Returning to Maurice's Academic career it was not without problems as this letter at the end of his second year shows:

Jesus Coll Cam

Dear Mum & Dad

Thanks for letters. Sorry haven't written before, not capable of it. Pretty thin time altogether. Horrible mess up in maths & very poor practical mineralogy. Particulars later. Happy if I get a second. Must go & see landlady. Result comes out Thursday week. You have no idea how absolutely appalling 6 hours practical Min straight off (10-4) are. The professor did treat us to sandwiches & lemonade at 1 & Tea & Scone at 3.30. Came out fairly dead & rushed to Tommy for tea & hit head on bottom corner of door sticking out on stairs. Managed to get in, in time for tea. However, have now reduced the bump to respectable dimensions. I have a lot to say but I have forgotten most of it.

However, very funny on Friday. Essay paper 9 o'clock. Woke up 8.59. Rush. No breakfast. Thieved bike from chimney. Arrived 9.4. Staggered in & tottered up to desk. Knocked man's inkwell off desk with gown. Tremendous crash. Storms of applause. Great chuckles. Essay paper is the only non-serious paper, fortunately. I wrote a fairly good essay, I think. I've come across lots of other funny things, can't bother to think of them. Explanation later. I have got a scheme to go on a walking tour in the Lake

District with a Magdalene man named Atkinson. What do you think of it. Shall be coming down Friday or Saturday. Must stop because post. Love to all

From Maurice

Boat probably going head. Had a riotous evening with Joe Murphy & Lean on Saturday. Will write again soon.

It also records his first plan to visit the Lake District, as does this letter:

Dear Mum

Thanks for letter. With regard to camera what am I doing when I go round lakes. I think Eric will find a tour pretty expensive. Note that our lake tour costs us £6 each excluding railway fare & we are going to stay at farmhouses which are very cheap. Think I'll write to Bert for his job. Should like tennis shoes very quickly.

With regard to G&S on Saturday I think if you turn up at 11.30 you may be given a ticket about 1.30 say. If you like I will write to Dyson & ask him how one gets into last night. I see that the last night is not decided. I think I will come down if I can get Gandar to drive me down. Bring suitcase & save the cost of sending (3s or more I expect). I suppose you saw Daily Mail exposure today. Am now doing a second experiment in physics. Spent two days finding some interference fringes.

Had some games of tennis the other day & today. Only lost 6-1, 6-4 to Tomlinson. Played Pars & Walker at bowls the other days. Pars is good but only lost 11(Pars)-6-2(Walker) & at one time it was 6-6-2, then Pars got 2 points off next throw & 2 off next & then winning point. In the next game we were 4-4-2 & we played one more before Walker went & Pars won it so it was 5-4-2 so I did not do badly.

I have not much to write about, I am afraid. I owe Eric 11/-. Shall I send it or will you pay it him. If I come down on Saturday I shall miss him so no good me bringing it. Botley, the constructor of Tommy's wireless set is up here for 6 days. If Eric likes to come up here for day or two or more he can be put up in the college. That's all now.

Love from Maurice

Maurice fell in love with the Lake District – even taking his bride there for their honeymoon - fortunately a bride happy to trudge up rainy and windswept mountains rather than demand a honeymoon in sunnier climes.

I found this letter from Mr Abbot about his second year exam results.

Cambridge
21 June 1924

Dear Burwood,

I am sorry that the first class did not come off. Mr Madgwick expected it in Physics, but I notice that his expectation of a good second in Physics for Spence was also not fulfilled. You gained second class marks in each of your four subjects. Your Exhibition is renewed at £40 for another year.

In order that you may come up for this Long Vacation if possible, the College has made you a grant of £25 as the grant is for the sole and special purpose of enabling Long Vacation residences. I do not think that the State scholarship is affected.

Will you think it over and let me know whether you will come up for the Long? I probably told you that the normal day for coming up is 7 July, and that the charges are Rooms nil, Tuition nil, College Payment £2, Bed Maker £3.10.0. The fee for the Advanced Demonstrations at the Cavendish Laboratory seems to be £6.6.0.

Yours sincerely
E. Abbott

I think Maurice did go up to Cambridge that summer, as suggested by this extract from a letter with pages missing: *no rules except 10 o'clock rule. Have got 10/- knocked off bill. Have about £3 in the bank now. Have not seen Tutor yet (Elliot). Abbott is not up. Saw Mills the other day. Will Eric let me know when he wants camera? (Exact day & time if poss e.g. Sat morn) & Dad suitcase (by Friday morn). Would like to see Sat week G&S but they don't give exeats in Long Vac term.* In the same letter he adds his own doubts about his academic choice: *Weather is not too hot at present. Horribly hot in Physics lab. In closed up dark room with 5 or 6 Bunsens roaring at full speed. When you first come in you fall over chairs & knock things over etc. I hope you won't say I am making a mistake in taking Physics. I probably am but one has to choose something & it is no good saying its wrong after it is done.*

The Cavendish Laboratory is a very famous Laboratory for Experimental Physics originally created in 1874 under a James Clark Maxwell, the first Cambridge Professor of Experimental Physics, with the help of a donation from University Chancellor William Cavendish. Many discoveries in the field of nuclear research and other fields were made at the Cavendish, including the discovery of the structure of D.N.A. by Francis Crick and James Watson.

Maurice returned In October for his final year, and on 12th October 1924 a card was sent to Maurice at 7 Manor St from C.U.A.F.C. (Cambridge University Association Football Club).

*Dear Sir, Will you act as reserve in Seniors Final on Tues Oct 14th at Varsity Ground. Bring both colours K.O. 2.30. **If unable to play let me know AT ONCE**. R.W. LE R DE KOVEN Hon. Sec. 26, Trumpington Street (Pembroke).*

This next letter mentions Maurice playing in a Seniors Trial.

> 9 Manor St
> Cambridge
> Friday Oct? 1924

Dear Mum & Dad

I am getting on all right. I also hope ditto to you. I had an excellent game today versus Pimmer drew 3-3. Practice game on Monday we played three halves each 25 mins & tried 32 men. Now running three teams. Played in the second half of the Seniors Trial on Tuesday but played fairly badly, back. However, got into photo, but sitting down in front, the only one, too. Have Idris Jones, the Rugger Blue, in the rooms next to mine. Have known him some time. He is researching in Chemistry & used to demonstrate in McCombie's lab. May send chair down about Monday week. Will you give me a list of what you intend to send then I can tell whether I want the articles. I think perhaps I had better have the bike up. I can keep it in the back of the house, so that I shan't have to pay for shed. The saddle does not matter. Give it a soak in ink or blacking or something. All that is needed is to pump the tyres up. The bike is in running order. I think if you send it to the Cambridge station & a card to me I will fetch it.

Congrats about 10/-, what's the Gondoliers? Many who goes in back of gallery in that theatre is a bit of an ass if he wants to see the piece & form an opinion on it. You had better drop a P.C. to A.E.Jones if he is longer than usual. I don't think the prints matter a lot. I enclose envelope addressed to me. Not the correct address. I have, by the way, run out of envelopes. I have a piano in my room. I have bike lamp but no pump or clips. The latter are not important & if you don't send the former I can easily get one for say 1/6. I have had to find a lot of money on writing books, my stock having run out.

I go to lectures by Rutherford. He say er for about ¾ of the hour & is very incoherent. C.T.R.Wilson is perfectly appalling. On the other hand J.J. & Aston are both good lecturers. Rutherford told us of an amusing deduction by Aristotle, showing the fallacious methods of armchair reasoning. It was reasoned that a lump of lead & a feather fell at the same rate in a vacuum. But, said Aristotle, (without trying it) a feather & a piece of lead don't fall at the same rate. Therefore there is no such thing as a vacuum. Well, I don't know if there is anything more to say but I don't think I shall say it if there is.

It was a very exciting match today. Each time they got a goal we got one immediately then right at the end there was a scramble 10 yards in front of the goal. A man headed it in & your humble was standing on the line & interposed his head sending it round the post for a corner, & then the whistle blew, score 3-3. We had a left half playing who is even smaller than I am. His name is Limebeer, but he runs very slowly, poor fellow. However he is not bad. We have nevertheless a shocking team, with a rotten centre & only one good forward at present. Personally I don't mind a bit. All the more for me to do. The boots have turned up a bit at the toes, but have put them in lasts & if they get wet & I do it they will soon straighten out. Photos not important.

Love from Maurice

This letter was written 11 November 1924.

Jesus College
64 Jesus Lane
Cambridge

Dear Mum & Dad

Thanks for the goods. Schur is now playing it. I've thought of two nice cheap things you can get me at Christmas. I have heard from Aunt Clara & Edie. I hope answer look at my letter when you reply because I ask questions which although not important perhaps do come in useful at some time if answered. Usually I have forgotten what I asked.

Some years ago an important formula was developed by Clerk Maxwell in which dp/dt (pronounced deepee, deetee) with accent on pee & tee) was equal to an expression involving T+T' (Tee + Tee dashed) & was also equal to J.C.M. Now J.C.M. equals James Clerk Maxwell, so to his friends he was always known as <u>dp/dt</u>. His best friends were Thomson (T), Tate (T') & books are to be seen in the lab. "To dp/dt from T+T'."

Did you know that teams going to Oxford for matches are not allowed to go through Bletchley. This is because one team found a set of brass band instruments in the waiting room & duly performed on them somewhat to their deterioration.

By the way, let me know the telephone no. at the House. Then if I want to send an urgent message I can phone from our common room & get Garwood to give you a message. Also I should like to bring back some Camphor carbon balls if you have any.

My soccer boots have turned right over & put rather a strain on the ankle. About my suitcase, I had it standing on the platform & a man passing put his foot through the side incidentally falling rather badly. I only recovered the damage later; and he incidentally broke the medicine pot. The sticky stuff fortunately did not come out of the cardboard case & I salved most of it. What is it called, if I want to get any more?

Searle was explaining that air does not follow the ordinary laws of gases because it is a mixture of gases. He said "to take the big things first it contains aeroplanes, then there is also soot & rumours etc." This is a good example of Searle's manner.

I had a triumph in the lab. I got some results & Thurkill worked them out & <u>there was splendid agreement</u>. Of course while he did it I was trembling lest they made awful ones. Searle was also talking about wind pressure & estimated the wind pressure on board a ship's deck under the gun when it is fired. They have to be careful that the deck is not blown in by it. "Of course, they use the deck for dancing so it is pretty strong."

Tomorrow the All Blacks play the varsity & so Sir E Rutherford being a New Zealander has decreed that the Physics lab shall be shut. (Tremendous cheers.) I am going to Ruddigore Thursday. By the way, did you not go to the Mikado?

In the Cavendish Lab we have manuscripts which tell you how to do each experiments and on each manuscript is a specimen of results obtained by Mr "Undergrad" of St Xs. I have the honour of having my name on one.

My valuation comes to 11/1/0. I paid 13/5/6 so have lost 2/4/6 obtained 2 blankets which is not so dusty. Blanket item comes to 11/6 less, so allowing 4/- for depreciation blankets cost 7/6.

When we went to Wellingborough we got part of way & found Payne missing so turned round as a man was coming who did not know where we were going & this great bus went right round him as he wobbled from side to side wondering what to do. We roared. It was the funniest thing I have seen for years. In my next instalment I hope to give some idea of my work in the Cavendish.

Love from
Maurice

Maurice kept a fixtures card recording all scores for Jesus College 1st XI matches in October, November, and December 1924 – 19 matches of which 7 were wins, 3 draws, and 9 losses. Football was his main sporting activity but not his only one. He continued to compete athletically for Jesus College, and possessed a member's ticket for Cambridge University Athletics Club for Lent term 1925. On Friday 20th February 1925 Maurice ran the 100 yards for Jesus against St John's College in the Inter-Collegiate Division 1 Semi-Final. He was not placed in the top three, but Jesus won the match 78 points to 32 and made the final the following Tuesday. Before that final he wrote this letter to his parents mentioning an unfortunate incident in his race.

7 Manor Street
Cambridge

Dear Mum & Dad

I am rather too busy to write much. Thanks for the parcel etc. With regard to money, I don't know how much finances will stand at the end of term but I have enough to get along with. Therefore you need not send any more. The Old Boys Dinner takes place today. Have spent afternoon taking Mr Ayres round. He & Weekes were invited as Guests.

I ran again on Thursday against John's. We won 78-32 & meet Pimmer on Tuesday in the final. I think we shall lose but not by much. In the 100 on Thursday I was rather unlucky. As usual the first start was a false one. On the 2ⁿᵈ start I went off too soon & as the pistol didn't go, went forward on to my hands. Instead of having a third start he fired it once & of course I was nowhere. Rudd was very annoyed about it. My clean clothes will last till March 14. I come down March 16, 17, or 18. So if you send up 1 pr. Pajamas, vest & pants will put them on 4ᵗʰ & so have fairly clean things when coming down.

My purse has gone west so invested in a stray purse 2/11. Am wondering whether to take the London Degree £6/6/0. Forms (which I have got) to be sent in by March 7ᵗʰ. What do you think? Also wondering whether to go to the Soccer Dinner Sat 7ᵗʰ 1/0/0 & drinks. Sorry you did not have longer at Bournemouth. Should be very bracing at this time. The weather has been fairly good all the term & today is a splendid day but cold. I am doing some experiments with Radioactivity on Radium C, D, & E now which are rather interesting.

I did not get any seats for D'Oyly Carte. I had arranged with 5 others. The five started queueing in turns at 7o'clock A.M., got served at 5p.m. & could only get 3 for Ruddigore & 2 for Pirates no others left. One man bought £60 worth. Man queued up at 5 to 6 got served at 3p.m. Queue started at 3A.M. So will have to queue for the Gods if want to go. Well cheerio Pippip.

Love to all from
Maurice R Burwood

On 24th February 1925 Maurice ran the 100 yards for Jesus against Pembroke in the Inter-collegiate final Division 1. He was not placed in the top three and Jesus lost the match, as he predicted, by 62⅔ points to 47⅓ points.

More interesting to learn that he was involved in experiments with Radium and Radioactivity. Did that follow on from a summer visit to Cavendish? In this letter he mentions a lecture by Ernest Rutherford on splitting the atom.

7 Manor St
Camb

Dear Mum & Dad etc

Sorry I have been so long. I have had a lot on. I have finished my 1st experiment this term. One had to bore a hole through glass tubing. You understand it smashes right across on the slightest pressure & cracks along if it doesn't smash. After a day I discovered a method of doing it. File a cross with a sharp-edged file. You have to file without pressing & so must sharpen the file every 5 strokes to be able to cut at all. Then rotate a sharp point in the crack till you go through. The chief trouble is that two holes are to be bores near the ends of a tube 15in long so you have to do two consecutive holes without breaking the tube. Then you seal it into a T-piece by heating it at a point & blowing hard. Then break off the bulge & join another tube to the edges of the hole without melting the tube so that it collapses. All this & the rest of the experiment which I will not describe takes a fortnight.

They wouldn't let me vote. However, it was unnecessary. Rather surprising result. Will attempt to answer your letters – Interval for searching – (1) I always said the chunk of grand opera stuff at the end of Iolanthe is the best part of the opera & probably whacks any grand opera. Many people do not like it, however. They don't know what music is. Sullivan's recitatives are perfectly wonderful. (2) Bad luck not being able to wander round Wembley on your own. I think you want to for one day at least. (3) I have not yet met anyone who could understand why they don't play Patience more. All agree that it gets a better reception than any of the others. (4) In trying to place a play you must consider how often you have seen it before. Remember you are seeing Patience for the 2nd time (which is usually the best) & you have not seen it for a year. You have to consider how you enjoyed the corresponding performance & allow for the time between the 1st & 2nd performances. Of course the vocal is no go to all for the 1st time in a Fortnight's Repertory. (5) You said the other artists were the same as usual. This cannot be true because they changed the cast at Stratford & again at Golders Green. Do you mean same as the latter. Was Goulding the Duke? Who were Ella & Sophia? & Mayor? (6) Hope you went to Mikado.

Interpolation – letter from Chips – complains of ignorance of Welsh kids & how hard he works. (1 boy ear lump of test tube). Very nice rooms up here, very convenient & landlady all right. Cooks breakfast for me. I will try to think if I want anything & let you know, but do not seem to. With regard to birthday haven't thought of anything except perhaps a decent knife – but then of course I have quite a respectable one with 2 good blades which only need sharpening. I expect you have something in mind. I shouldn't mind if nothing more useful can't be discovered having vocal score of Princess Ida – Chappell & Co Bond St.

Team played very badly against Queens lost 4-0, so did I. I scored one next one offside. 3rd goalie missed. 4th offside so partly bad luck. However, they had again played a very bad left half & outside right & inside right so I had G Dower to tea with & spoke lovingly to him. Consequently he selected a better team for yesterday & we played well though I did not & won (Peterhouse) 4-1. Tomorrow we play Pimmer & they have stuck to my suggestions, one or two alterations due to a good back becoming fit. May send chair down soon with other things. I think there is nothing else.

Rutherford explained how to break up the atom by means of heat & get the atomic energy it is necessary to have a temperature of 3,000,000,000° at least & as yet all we can get is to round about 3,000 & each 100 degrees gets increasingly difficult so you can sleep easily.

Ruddigore is on up here Monday week. Have not yet obtained copy of valuation. Must do so. Joe has got a job so all last years men are now fixed up. Our rowing people are frightened. Only ten men wanting to row. Last year was a bad year with only 18.

> Well ta ta
> Love from Maurice.

1925 would be the year Maurice left Cambridge, but upcoming Finals did not diminish his sporting interests and activities.

7 Manor St
Cambridge
Feb 3rd 1925

Dear MDEJ

Thanks for the shoes. I am in them & came fourth by about 6ins, i.e. behind third. However in spite of this we won easily & should get in the final without much bother. The Rugger knockout occurred today & we beat Cato 18-5, this is the hardest tie & we should get into the final easily. In the soccer we play Pathouse next Monday. We are playing the Casuals on Saturday. We drew with Johns 2-2 owing to a surprising & fluky but snappy goal of mine. I am now playing centre forward. In six games I have only obtained 2 goals. Last year & year before I used to get a goal a match. However, playing in better football now.

On Wed at Hall they put something nasty in the food & half the college had "squitters" so I am told. Which explain why I had to get up once in the night. The landlady was worried about it but I managed to reassure her. Most of them had it fairly badly some being affected at least 12 times. The members of the Rugger team in the Cup Tie had to leave at intervals especially at half-time. We accused the Cato men of poisoning our beer. It was all very funny. I put down my comparative comfort to a sterling constitution hey what.

If by chance you should run into Mr Andrews jun. show him the Cambridge Latymerian & ask him for how much he could do the same type of thing. About 200 copies would be the maximum needed. If not perhaps you will send me a Cambridge Latymo & his address & I will write.

Oh, of course, I forgot to mention that I ran in the sports & played soccer v Johns on Tuesday afternoon. Good Work Mess of the Varsity Match Hey What? If you want a good design for a cross here is one containing on 4 & 5 & four 7-letter words.

There is no London match this term & so I should be pleased if you send me back 1 clean vest & pants & pajamas. I think that is all the news,
Love from Maurice.

By early 1925 Maurice was not just concerning himself with his academic and sporting activities – he was also seeking employment.

Granta is a Cambridge University student periodical publication published since the 19th Century.

7 Manor St
Cambridge

Dear Mum & Dad

I shall probably not be able to write a long letter owing to the fact that I have wasted such a lot of time at D'Oyly Carte that my work will get behind. Today we played the Boat Club at Rugger & won about 12-3. They said I played well. I didn't think so. Got a thick lip & black eye again or at least that's rather an exaggeration but I did get a kick on the shin. Last Tuesday we the Lats won a soccer match 4-1. We were playing the 2nd eleven.

I have seen a representative of the Western Electric Co in company with nearly all the Physics part II men. The secretary of the Appointments board thinks I shall get the job. The chap said their works are near Woolwich, they give £200 a year to start & put you through their various departments for 6-9 months & then you start working. Salary is revised upward every year. Average men will get £700 a year in the end but as far as I can make out it rises very slowly. I mean, in 5 yrs he couldn't promise more than £350 as an average. He advised me to find out something about the Co so that if they make me an offer (in about 3 weeks) I could say whether I would take it.

So that's that. He said theirs is the only firm which does that particular work & so experience there is no use for other firms, i.e. it is a life job. I don't altogether believe this.

I have already been to all the D'Oyly Carte more than I intended to or ought to have done. It was like this. Browne sold me a Princess Ida ticket so I was moderately happy, Then I happened to roll along to the box office to see if one could bag 1st choice for the gods (amphitheatre) on Tuesday. I had heard it was poss. It wasn't but I happened as a forlorn hope to ask if they had any odd seats anywhere. They had one for Yeoman & Trial & Pirates & Patience. Well, what could I do. I also secured 2 tickets for Schur & Fann for Ruddigore on Monday next. I can't go then alas. Then I had to see the Gondoliers on Wed aft. & got in front of Gods. Excellent show.

One thing I like about an undergrad audience is that they applaud what is good & not where they should do by tradition. For instance the entrance of the girls in the Pirates is supposed to have a small applause. But they shouted for an encore which was not given. But the action was held up for 5 minutes. The D'OC at used to certain things being encored as tradition says. But this won't do. The result is they give an encore where it is not asked for & there are insistent demands for an encore to something they haven't arranged for. The result is a war between conductor & audience. Of course the conductor nearly always wins. But they could have a 3rd encore to Were I Thy Bride & Poor Wandering One & as I said the Climbing Over the Rocky Mountain duet.

As regards the Company they are in extremely good form as a whole. Elsie Griffin is not & Sydney Granville though good has been rather lifeless. Charles Goulding & Eileen Sharp are in exceptionally good form & the latter was generally agreed to be the best in the Gondoliers. The two girls in the Yeoman were also exceptionally good as you will see in the 'Granta' when I bring it home. Trial by Jury was not as good as I have seen it done. Eleanor Evans was the plaintiff & she was much better than Kathleen Anderson. Which reminds me. One of the biggest hits of the week was made by Irene Hill as Gianetta in place of Kath And who seems to have left. (It is always the female parts which change. The men are the same as at London except for Leo Darnton). Altho' it was only a small part she did it wonderfully well. "Roses, White & Red".

That is about all I have to say, except that I should like reason strong enough to persuade me not to go next week. We lost to Pimmer in the Final of the Rugger & knock out after a good game. I sent in my London BSC form & the 6.6.0 & the odd 1/- etc.

Oh, by the way my bike has wandered away. I think I shall go to the Police station next term & so avoid paying storage for the vac. They only charge 2/6.

> Cheerio
> Love from Maurice

Significantly he also acquired this reference from his ever helpful tutor.

JESUS COLLEGE
CAMBRIDGE
3 March 1925

I have pleasure in stating that Mr M R Burwood, Exhibitioner of this College, has borne an excellent character in every way throughout his residence, which began in October 1922.

Edwin Abbott, M.A.
Tutor of Jesus College

The next letter is from a Mr Madgwick. I am unsure whether it is the same Madgwick referenced by Dr Abbott in an earlier letter which implied that Madgwick was part of Cambridge University, because this letter implies the power to influence employment selections for a private company.

18 Leinster Road
Bays H2O
Wed

My dear Burwood

Many thanks for yours. I shall reply briefly because I'm d—d ill – just recovering from 'flu.

I shouldn't say anything to the Appts Bd. They haven't got full parties yet and in any case I shall be able to do more than they. I believe I shall be able to fix you up provided there is no suitable ex-service candidate.

I should like to have you along fresh from your Pt II course, and I believe you'll like it.

You will be going down for the Easter vac soon I suppose: come along to the station and I will show you round. I will mention the matter to the Director when I return to work.

By the way, you may only get £200 to start. Also the station is to be moved from Acton – probably to Watford.

In the meantime keep your eye open for anything which may appear more attractive, but rest assured that you will be borne in mind and that (except in the unlikely event of my selection being overruled) you will receive first choice from candidates of similar standing.

All this <u>strictly confidential</u>.

> *Best wishes*
> *Yrs*
> *I Madgwick*

The next letter was sent not to Maurice but to his father at Ashburton Lodge and was postmarked Cambridge.

> *Jesus College*
> *Cambridge*
> *21 June 1925*

Dear Mr Burwood,

I am very grateful to you for the kind words about myself that you have sent me from Mrs Burwood and yourself.

Naturally I should have liked to see you son get first classes in his examinations, but the degree that he has got is a very good one and the second examination that he took is particularly stiff. He has, all along, been a most useful member of the College and has conducted himself excellently in every way. I was very glad when he told me that he had been accepted for a definite post and I heartily wish him well at all times.

> *With many thanks*
> *for your letter,*
> *Yours truly*
> *E.Abbott*

This is not the last letter from Mr Abbott to quote in this chapter – two more are to follow, sent in the same envelope as one is another reference.

> *Wellside*
> *Well Walk*
> *N.W.3*
> *7 Sept 1925*

Dear Burwood

I am enclosing the testimonial with best wishes for your success in your application. You had I think a post in view when you went down, so I rather suppose that the post at Acton is one which you would prefer perhaps as involving more in the way of research. The London list must have escaped my notice in the papers.

> *With kind regards*
> *Yours Sincerely*
> *E. Abbott*

The second one is the testimonial.

> *Jesus College*
> *Cambridge*
> *7 Sept 1925*

I beg leave to support heartily the application of Mr M.R. Burwood for a post involving research. I have known him since he came into residence in October 1922 as an Exhibitioner of this College. He has borne throughout a most excellent character, both in general and for industry and the interest he displayed in his work. He has good brains, and obtained second class honours in both parts of the Natural Sciences Tripos, specializing in Physics for the second part.

He has borne his share in the general life of the College being among other things a good Association footballer. His bearing is modest and he is a pleasant man with whom to have dealings. He is trustworthy and fully capable of taking responsibility, and will carry out his duties with the utmost thoroughness.

> *Edwin Abbott M.A.*
> *Fellow and tutor of Jesus*
> *College, Cambridge.*

Maurice started work with the engineering department of Standard Telephones and Cables in September 1925, but that is another tale.

Time to return to Marjorie and her sister growing up in Portsmouth.

Maurice at Jesus Oct 1924 - with a study partner called Pickles

Maurice & his parents in Fellows Garden at Cambridge June 1925

Cambridge Graduate

CHAPTER NINE

Growing Up Tanner

Olive and Marjorie Tanner attended the same schools before going into Teacher Training, but to different colleges – resulting in Marjorie also going to college in Cambridge – in a way.

I refer to the memories of Marjorie and her elder sister Olive as published in *Memories from Ninety Years – the lives of the Tanner sisters of Portsmouth,* and to Marjorie's school reports from the Southern Secondary School for Girls, where she was a pupil from 1931 to 1938.

The Tanners lived at 88 Alverstone Road in Milton, very close to Portsmouth Football Club's Fratton Park Stadium, and to St Mary's Hospital and to Milton Cemetery. Milton had been an entirely separate village until the latter part of the nineteenth century when house-building expanded the old Portsmouth city across Portsea Island from west to east and Milton was swallowed up, but residents still referred to it as 'The Village' when Olive and Marjorie were children. Marjorie provided these memories of the area:

"Opposite Alverstone Road, Velder Avenue led off to the shore. Milton Cemetery was on the left and a row of houses on the right. We could walk along the small stretch of shore, and I delighted to see the people in their houseboats. The Eastern Road led off following along the railings of Milton Cemetery - it was later to become a very busy main road.

"Alverstone Road consisted of a short road followed by a longer road which turned off at the end. This led to Carisbrooke Road on the corner house of which my aunt and cousin lived. I never knew my uncle, Dad's brother, who had died."

That Aunt and Cousin were Caroline and Nene Tanner. The uncle was William Herbert Tanner – known as Bert - a Dockyard shipwright like his brother.

"Entering the short Alverstone Road from Milton Road, there was a stonemason's on the corner, a hedge (later to become garages), and a block of three terraced houses. We lived in the corner house, and the back gate in our garden opened onto Vernon Avenue. Then there was another block of about eight houses. Across this longer road was Mrs Tagg's sweet shop. Behind her shop was a lane, bordering Pompey football ground, which led over the railway to Fratton Road. This was convenient if one needed to shop there."

Fratton Railway Station was a short walk to the west - as was the Sea Front at Eastney to the south beyond the Royal Marine Barracks. Wally Tanner cycled to work at the Dockyard – a comfortable distance by bike though a long walk. War enforced a much longer commute when the blitz drove the family to take overnight refuge in his mother's home north of Portsdown Hill.

Wimborne Road School, the Southern Secondary, and Portsmouth Teacher Training College were all within walking or easy cycling distance of their house in Alverstone Road.

As Olive was the elder, I start with Olive's memories of childhood, and her first memories of school.

"A little school for young children was run by Miss Anne, in the room attached to the old building of Milton Congregational Chapel on the corner of Edgeware Rd.

"I caught chicken pox, then a cold while at Wimborne Road School, & was away a lot in the first few months, & then was sent to Miss Anne's. I don't remember learning much, but we wrote with slate pencils, or chalk, on slates."

Slates were traditionally used in English schools before paper was readily and cheaply available. A 'slate' was normally a board made of slate in a wooden frame. A slate pencil was then used to form letters on the slate. The advantage of slates was that they could be wiped clean and used again and again - hence the phrase 'wiping the slate clean'.

It also saved the extra expense of using more paper every time.

237

"Later, when this school closed, I went to a class run by Mrs Ray, in the back room of her house in Edgeware Road. I seem to remember there were 4 girls & 3 or 4 boys - aged 5-7 years. It must have been a proficient school.

At 7 years old, I went to Wimborne Road School, & after 2 days there I was promoted up to the top class of 8-9 year olds."

Wimborne Road School still exists, though now divided into Wimborne Infant School and Wimborne Junior School, and its catchment area still includes Alverstone Road, but back to Olive's memories of her education.

"I was taught to read by phonetic method. I clearly remember one day when we were going along Goldsmith Avenue where there were big billboards, advertising, I read the letters by sounds c, e, g, g, & so on until I was told by my mother not to make silly noises."

Phonetic teaching associates sounds with letters and combinations of letters so that children memorize pronunciation rules, then learn to repeat and combine sounds to produce words.

"I probably learned to read a lot from the weekly comic "The Rainbow", which I had every week - the antics of Mrs Brown's school - Tiger Tim & the other animals, & this, I suppose helped the reading."

Olive also went to Sunday School at the Congregational Church as the family were churchgoers.

As Olive remembers:

"I also went to the 'Band of Hope' held at the chapel. I remember singing:-

> *"The little stockings, boots, & shoes,*
> *The try, the top, the ball*
> *With every little dress & hat*
> *The drunkard swallows all.*
> *Oh mothers stop & think*
> *Oh fathers stop & think*
> *What do you love the best on Earth?*
> *The children or the drink?*

& there was Sunday School opposite a couple of old country cottages up on a low bank."

The Band of Hope started in the mid-19ᵗʰ century as a series of children's meetings by Presbyterians and Baptists wanting to warn children about the dangers of alcoholic drinks. At one time it had a very large membership of both children and adults, and it was still going when Olive was young.

Unsurprisingly, the girls were also brought up to be prudent with money. Among old papers I found a Post Office Savings Book opened for Marjorie on 13 December 1921 (2 days after her second birthday) with an initial deposit of £1. Additional deposits were made either by Marjorie or her parents or grandparents until 27 July 1935 when over £27 was in the account and a first withdrawal of £3 was made by a 15-year old Marjorie.

The family found other ways to be thrifty, as Olive remembers.

"My mother left school when she was 13, and went into tailoring.

"Looking back I think how lucky we were having mother & aunt so able to deal with clothing costs. Money must have been saved, when our clothes were so often made from remnants bought at sales, or from clothing cut down - to make something from the best of some old coat."

The Aunt referred to here is Aunt Nell, and Olive goes on to remember that thrift was even taught at school.

"This was often done in those days. In fact, at training college, for the Needlework course we had to produce an economy garment, made from someone's "cast-offs". My first navy school coat, when I went to secondary school, was Grandma's, washed, dyed, & turned & re-cut for me. At college I had a skirt made from my school gym tunic. I can remember that as a child I had two dresses made from the robes that I, then my sister, had worn when in long clothes when babies. My first school uniform for the Portsmouth Girls' Secondary School was home-made - tunic, blouses, blazer."

Marjorie had a more straightforward start to her school career, probably because the school system was getting more organized.

As she describes it: *"When I was five, I followed my sister to Wimborne Road School. The Infants' School Head was a Miss Grant. When I reached the top class, I used to share a desk with Fred Thornton.*

"The bigger school was across the playground. The boys worked in the bottom half, and we girls in the top half. One day as I entered the

playground for school I saw Fred Thornton at an open window. I naturally waved. Fred, however, coloured up and hastily shut the window. Thus I learnt that boys and girls did not mix.

"The girls' section had a corridor with classrooms on each side. After the first year in Miss Wright's class, some girls went up to the next form. A fair group of us passed over this and went to the one above with Miss Muriel Fawcett. She belonged to the Portsmouth Teachers' Dramatic Society and she used to tell us about acting. In the Winter's Tale, she was the queen, Hermione, and she told us how difficult it was to stand still enough to be taken for a statue. She also told us about the difficulty of falling to the floor in a faint."

I remember Marjorie describing herself getting repeatedly told off by a gym teacher for not fully relaxing when letting herself fall. She could not let her head hit the floor without tensing herself up to brace against impact however harshly the teacher scolded her. I cannot imagine that happening now.

"While at the Junior School there was a campaign to get children to 'Eat More Milk!' 'Eat' so that we would realize that milk was a food. Of course we went home, all eager, to tell Mum that we must have milk. Mum said that she could not afford it, but would get it if we paid her out of our pocket money that Dad's parents gave us. I was very proud to think that I could pay for my milk. Our milkman served our milk from a can, but Mother heard that there was a new milkman, Street, who was providing milk in bottles. So she got our milk in bottles for us to drink."

That indicates how poor they were – girls spending their own pocket money to buy milk. It shows the value of free school milk when they were young – compared to the1960's when free school milk at my secondary school was mostly wasted because everybody there could afford milk and most preferred other drinks. It explains why people still remembering the past were outraged when free school milk was withdrawn. Marjorie was teaching by then, so the withdrawal had her whole-hearted approval because she knew how it was being wasted.

Staying with milk but returning to Olive's memories:

"Until the late twenties, milk was delivered early morning, in cans, by a man with a milk float that was triangular shaped, more or less, with milk cans hanging around, & a big churn on the middle. Cans were left in the

early morning, & a milkman came to collect them later in the day, & fill jugs from the churn if one wanted a second pint, (or half-pint). Half-pints could be bought.

"The baker - all horse-drawn - called daily, & if one was out, the bread was left - uncovered - sitting on the window sill. I vaguely remember that it once got very wet, & was dried in the oven.

"Also a greengrocer - also horse-drawn - called, & a man with a handcart sold fish."

Bread, fruit and vegetables, and even fish – delivered separately by traders. When I was young home deliveries from anyone other than the milkman or the Post Office were a disappearing service. Now home deliveries are back.

"There was the call of 'Co-o-ol' from the man on the horse-drawn truck with 1 cwt sacks of coal, & "Rags & Bones" from the Rag & Bone man with his truck.

"Sadly, one, at times, heard someone walking in the road, singing, hoping to get some pennies.

"There was a morning post, & one that came to us about 5p.m. On dark evenings the postman had a little torch strapped on to read the addresses. The postmen wore navy blue uniforms, I seem to remember. It was taped with red on collars & cuffs. Telegram boys, also in uniform, had red bicycles. The postman's hat was a bit different from the usual peaked cap - flat, with a longer, downward peak in front. Postman always gave a good rap at the door when they dropped the post in. One could usually recognize the postman's knock."

Olive and Marjorie grew up with a resident grandmother – as Marjorie remembers.

"I was very proud when I was nearly nine, to be told that I could take my Grandma round each week to get her Pension. This meant taking her round to the Milton Road and round Priory Crescent and back by Vernon Avenue. The Post Office had one counter where she got her 10/- pension each week, and a counter at right angles that sold sweets. She always got white striped mints."

Ten shillings a week pension – fifty pence in decimal currency - presumably the state pension for over seventies.

On a side note – in her final years Marjorie displayed a regular taste for black and white striped mints called Everton mints – very much like the mints her much loved Grandmother used to eat.

That grandmother was Grandmother Hale – Ethel's mother, who lived with them - but Wally's parents, William and Emma Tanner, lived elsewhere.

"Our grandparents moved from Orchard Road to Drayton, just past the Drayton shops, and we used to go up to visit them. At first we took the Portsmouth Corporation buses to the New Inn, Drayton. Later, for some reason, they had to stop at Cosham. Rather than change to the Southdown buses, we walked on. We went by Court Lane School which was being built there in the 1930s. Little did I know that my children would start their school life there."

The twenties and thirties saw a massive programme of building new houses on the southern slopes of Portsdown Hill, and around the old villages or hamlets of Wymering, Cosham, Drayton and Farlington. It was mostly farmland before being swallowed up by the expanding city of Portsmouth.

"We used to get loads of small fallen apples from our grandparents' Drayton garden. We were very grateful because Mum used to make apple pies for us. However, it was a mighty chore. Mum, Gran, Olive and I peeled apples - they were maggoty, and the pile of rejected apple was larger than the good fruit."

"A great treat was at Easter time. Dad used to take us both for a bicycle run on Good Friday. We went all along the Sea Front, and returned with Hot Cross Buns.

"Dad's father & mother gave us pocket money. We always put some into our Post Office books, bought presents for friends' birthday parties, paid our tram (later trolley bus) fares down Goldsmith Ave on occasion when we did not do our usual walk, bought our own hankies etc, & any sweets if we could afford them. Until the sweet shops, in Fawcett Rd, where the Sec was, objected, chocolate was sold in the Sec. Playground at recreation time."

One small health note I came across – in 1935 Marjorie was diagnosed with slight pleurisy – had some sort of radiography and spent three weeks under observation – but she was recovered by July 1936 and went on a school trip to Paris, from whence came a postcard and two letters to her family.

The postcard was dated 13 July 1936 and read, *"We have been round churches today, Notre Dame this morning, where we saw a marvellous service – Sacre Coeur & St Sulpice this afternoon – Tuesday night we go to the opera to see The Magic Flute. Olive's letter will be arriving next – please keep all cards.*

Yours Meme.

'Meme' was the family diminutive for Marjorie. 'Meme' mentions other postcards, but I only found two letters - one in French to her sister, the other in plain English to all her family.

This is the family letter.

> Hotel Vaneau
> Rue Vaneau
> Paris VII

Dear All,

We arrived at last at Hotel Vaneau, but discovered that we were not to sleep there. We nearly got turned away but later went in for supper? (1-2 A.M. morning – is it supper?) Then we went to a road leading off from this road, & here at 'Hotel des Colonies' we stopped – we go to Hotel Vaneau, however, for all meals & all letters are to be addressed there.

In the postcard, which I presume you have received, I said we were going to Versailles to-day – instead, however, the time-table is turned upside down & we had a civic reception at the Hotel de Ville – mayor gave a talk in French (translated mostly by our head leader) & we were told meanings etc. of various of the more important pictures & statues – also had our own photos taken plenty of times – came back to lunch – went to Hotel des Invalides & there saw various old flags taken in battle – uniforms etc. etc. - & Napoleon's tomb with its surroundings & relics of Napoleon e.g. cahir, table, ….. Then we went to Eiffel Tower – you go the whole way up in a lift, & scarcely know that you are in one – all whole (nearly) of Paris beneath you – then came back to Hotel V--- had dinner – returned here – half past eight – go to Versailles tomorrow – get up, breakfast & leave at 8a.m.!!!!

> Well, goodbye
> for present
> Yours, Meme

P.S. please steam off both stamps if possible for me to save them anyhow – Nora & I are sharing our room & bed. We are just going to bed now – tell Olive I have not forgotten her French letter.

Here is the letter in French to her sister Olive – presumably promised. I will not attempt to translate.

Hotel des Colonies,
Rue
Paris VII

Ma Chère soeur

Je vous donnerai l'histoire do no vacances. Mercredi, le huit mars, nous sommes arrives à Folkestone où nous avons rencontré Miss Gregory, et sa niece, Margaret Knight, une jeune fille, très amiable, de dix-neuf ans. Elle est venue avec nous. Nous sommes arrives à Boulogne sans mal-de-mer pour moi, quoi que vers quatres filles de notre école l'eussent. Nous avons passé le sofficiers de (customs) sans aucune mesaventure. Puis nous sommes allés à Paris dans un des trains les plus inconfortables. D'aboid, nous avons cru que nous n'avions pas de chambres à coucher, mais bientôt nous les avons trouvées.

Le lendemain nous somme allés à L'Hôtel de Ville pour (a civic reception). Puis nous sommes rentrées pour le second déjeuner. Alors, nous sommes allés aux Invalides où nous avons vu le Tombeau de Napoléon, et au Tour d'Eiffel que nous avons monté par un ascenseur toute la journée – à la cime nous avons aux Paris autour de nous. Après celà, nous sommes rentrée par omnibus pour diner. Vendredi, bonus sommes allées à Fontainebleau, où nous avons marché dans les bois. Le soir, nous sommes allées aux Boulevards, dans les Champs-Elysées vens L'arc de Triomphe où nous avons v le tombeau du soldat inconnu.

Excuse this writing, won't you – I have just been out shopping – got to get ready for dinner – go to the Opera – get packed & sleep – so goodbye – no more time.

Meme

Besides going on school trips, the sisters were also winning prizes.

Olive got a School prize in Secondary School for School Year 1927-1928 for getting Second Position (and satisfactory conduct) in Form IVB. Amazingly it was a later edition of a book possessed by Maurice at Jesus College - *The Golden Treasury* by F T Palgrave.

Marjorie got a school prize for the school year 1932-1933 for Latin in form IVA – the book is *Ivanhoe*, by Sir Walter Scott, then got two prizes for the school year 1933-1934 for 'General Subjects' in form Upper IVA. They are *Rob Roy* and *Woodstock*, both also by Scott – but both inscriptions for these two prizes spelt her name as *Margery* instead of *Marjorie* – that error would always irritate her.

At some point she acquired the book *Anthology of English Prose from Bede to R L Stevenson* arranged by S L Edwards for Everyman's Library, and edited by Ernest Rhys. Everyman's Library is a book publishing company founded in 1904, and this Anthology contains extracts of writings in English starting with the Venerable Bede (673-735) describing the conversion of King Edwin somewhen before 625, and including prose by Alfred the Great, John Wycliffe, Thomas More, John Milton, Samuel Pepys, Walter Scott, Jane Austen, Charles Dickens, Lewis Carroll, Thomas Hardy, and Robert Louis Stevenson – among many others.

Also she had a book entitled *Selected English Essays* from the Oxford University Press containing writings from men like Francis Bacon, Daniel Defoe, Alexander Pope, Charles Lamb, Percy Shelley, William Thackeray, and Robert Louis Stevenson.

Another book inscribed with M.Tanner is an edition of the *Canterbury Tales* by Geoffrey Chaucer – known as the father of English Literature and born in 1343. She pencilled multiple notes on every page, and also owned a small book called *the Links of the Canterbury Tales* edited by A.J.Wyatt, which concentrated on analysing the links and preambles of *the Canterbury Tales*.

She also had copies of Edmund Spenser's *Faerie Queene Books 1&2*, an epic poem first published in 1590. She kept these very old poetry books, so she must have appreciated them. I remember her recommending the *Canterbury Tales* to me, and accompanied me to a riotous theatrical version.

Returning to the tale about Olive and Marjorie Tanner growing up and going to school – starting at Wimborne Road School. Portsmouth was an expanding town which officially became a city in 1926. Wimborne Road School was opened in 1916 as a two floor building with boys on the ground floor and girls on the first floor. It expanded, as Marjorie remembers in this section describing her school years.

"Our school went from 7-14 years, but half way through my schooling, a new school was built in Francis Avenue for Seniors. Therefore, by the time I got to the Scholarship Class, we were top of the school."

"Three of us at school were moved up to the scholarship ahead of the rest of our year. This meant that I was two years in that class. In my second year I went, each morning, round the classrooms and obtained the total of children present from their teachers, and wrote the total up in the hall."

Marjorie did well at Wimborne Road School, and started collecting signatures in two autograph books - not of famous people but of her friends and family and neighbours. The first book became more of an improvised poetry book than an autograph book. It is labelled on page 1 *Marjorie Burwood 1927* – so she was only 7 when she began it. The first entry on the first page is her 12 year old sister Olive who on 30th September 1927 wrote on page 3 *"By hook or by crook I'll be first in your book"*. However a friend of Marjorie's called May Phillips got round that by writing on the inside of the front cover *"By pen or by quill, I'll be earlier still"*.

I suppose the modern equivalent would be a social media page with likes, friending, etc, but Marjorie clearly started it as an autograph book, because on page 4 she created a *"Wall of Friendship"* – where she covered the page with spaces shaped like bricks, and got 15 friends to sign their names – Hilda Steel, Mary Pearce, Betty Kingston, M Thomson, J Hoare, M French, D Salter, J Brooks, M Norman, H Stubbs, K Bone, D Betteridge, R Jones, Eileen Goss, and S Roberts - all when she was only seven years old, but maybe the rhyming couplets of her sister Olive and May Phillips started something for Marjorie or her friends, because page 5 sees an M Hyslop – who I think was a neighbour and possibly another Marjorie – writing a fun little poem on 26th October 1927.

I stood on the bridge at midnight.
And the thought came into my head.

How silly of me to be standing here.
When I ought to be home in bed.

May Phillips then chips in with another poem on page 7.

If you have a laugh to spare,
Always let it go,
In this world of ware and tare
Laughter's wanted so,
Troubles coming on your way
All divide in half,
If you lift your chin and say
"It do make I "<u>larf</u>."

May added a little sketch of a boy and a girl to her poetic effort.
The autograph book somehow turned into a poetry competition, because on 3rd March 1928 a J Dicks joined the fray with this effort on page 9.

A wise old owl sat in an oak.
The more he heard the less he spoke.
The less he spoke the more he heard,
Why can't we be like that bird.

On 20th October 1927 T E Grant had contributed a more modest

"Not what we get,
But what we give,
Makes up our treasure
While we live."

But added a wonderful sketch of a small boy and *"With every good wish"*.
On 6th May 1928 E A Edwards contributed

Be good, sweet maid, and let all those who can be clever.
Do noble things and dream them all day long.

On 4th May 1929, Marjorie's mother Ethel Tanner chimed in with what reads like a limerick.

> *It is hard to lose a friend*
> *When you heart is full of hope,*
> *But it is harder still*
> *To lose a towel*
> *When your eyes are full of soap.*

Surely something only a mother would write?

On 9th July 1929 a Marjorie Hind contributed two poems – the first a rather downbeat effort.

> *Can't think,*
> *Brain dumb,*
> *Inspiration, won't come,*
> *Can't write,*
> *Bad pen,*
> *Best Wishes,*
> *Amen.*

Inspiration clearly did come the same day – with this result.

> *A thousand years ago today,*
> *A wilderness was here,*
> *A man with powder in his gun,*
> *Went forth to hunt the deer,*
> *But now the times have changed somewhat,*
> *And on a different plan,*
> *A dear with powder on her nose,*
> *Goes forth to hunt the man.*

Marjorie kept the book on transferring from Wimborne Road School to the Southern Secondary School for Girls in 1931, and entries kept being made.

On 31st July 1931 E Ray wrote

When you see this remember me
And bear me in your mind
Let all the world say what they will
Speak of me as you find.

The same day F Kelly provided

"Better late than never"
Is a saying to refrain
But when you arrive at the station
Just too late to catch the train.

And M Berryman provided

Good better best
May you never rest
Till your good is better
And your better best.

In February 1932 Muriel Norman wished Marjorie the best with

In the parlour there were three,
The parlour lamp & he & she
Two's company without a doubt,
And so the parlour lamp went out.

Marjorie was only twelve years old, and so probably was Muriel Norman.

On 24th February 1932 M French was even more succinct with

Nib bad
Pen worse
So I'll just sign
My autograph.

Marjorie's lifelong best friend Kathleen Bone contributed an upside down verse on 1st March 1932.

When in this book you look,
And on this page you frown,
Think of the one who spoilt it,
By writing upside down.

On 14th March 1932 Hazel Stubbs wrote in very neat handwriting

If wishes could paint a picture,
What then without more ado,
What a picture of livelong happiness,
My wishes would paint for you.

On 23rd March 1932 Mary Pearce provided one that I cannot transcribe exactly as she wrote.

Two in a hammock
Attempted to kiss
In less than a minute
They landed like this

But the last two words *like this* were written upside down.
M Thomas contributed this oddity without making the date legible.

My heart is like a cabbage
The centre cut in two
The leaves I give to others
The heart I give to you.

Surely the 1930's equivalent of social media messages - the young then were just as inventive as today's young. To bolster that theory I present I.E.Burge on 29th July 1932 proving that texting abbreviations are not a modern invention!

Y Y you are
Y Y you B
I C U R Y Y for me.

Chris Britton, son-in-law of Marjorie's cousin Nene Sansom (née Tanner) pointed out that 'Y Y' must mean "Too wise". Meanwhile, 'I C U R' clearly stood for 'I see you are'. *Too wise you are, too wise you be, I see you are too wise for me* – and that was 1932.

On 28ᵗʰ July 1937 Stella Dyer wrote:

> *In a promise, what you thought, and not what*
> *you said, is always to be considered.*

An undated contribution was provided by S Roberts:

> *When the Great Scorer comes to write your name,*
> *He writes – not that you won or lost,*
> *But how <u>you played the game</u>*

One game that Marjorie played differently was her second autograph book, which was filled almost exclusively with autographs. Prominent are those of her parents on 24ᵗʰ September 1933, but on 28ᵗʰ July 1933 – probably the end of term and her second year at secondary school, she obtained nearly 30 signatures from her schoolmates. There is a small surge of signatures in December 1934, and another in July 1938 – which is when Marjorie left secondary school to start at Teacher Training College that September.

I am jumping ahead again. Time to return to the Tanner sister's education, and after Wimborne Road School, both sisters went on to the same secondary school – starting with Olive.

"The exam for Secondary was taken at 11 or 12, but I was one of those who took it the first time it was for 11 years old only - 1926. The Girl's Secondary had some classes at St Peters in Somers Rd, until the Annexe was opened in 1927."

Southern Secondary School for Girls transferred from Francis Avenue, Southsea, to a new building next to a boys' school in Fawcett Road, Southsea in 1907. It became overcrowded when the school leaving age was raised to 14 in 1918, which would explain the Annexe.

"I remember some of the rules at the Secondary. Gloves had to be worn to school. Order marks were given if a desk was opened during a

lesson - or anything lost. Homework required 3 subjects a night, & 4 at the weekend."

Marjorie would follow Olive to the Southern Sec, as she called it, but not before trying to gain entry into the top school in the city for girls - Portsmouth High School, founded by the Girls Public Day School Trust. For a long time it would be a direct grant grammar school, but became independent when comprehensive schools were created to undermine the country's education system. It still records high exam pass rates, and even then was tough to get in - as Marjorie found.

"Mother wanted me entered for the Girl's High School in Southsea. When I did not pass she said I could not have tried. However we were rather unsettled when we arrived. We were waiting in a hall, on benches, but every time another school arrived we were moved along to another bench. Of course we dropped our pens, pencils, and rulers on the way - very disconcerting. When we eventually sat at our desks ready to start the exam, there were girls from another school in the other half of the room. On a level with me, two girls in different rows whispered now and then. When I looked up I saw the teacher's disapproving eye scanning the room to find the culprits. It did not help my concentration."

Next best choice for Marjorie was the Southern Secondary School for Girls.

"Entering the Southern Sec in Fawcett Road, for their exam, was very different. We went in a throng through the playroom and across the playground to the annexe, were seated, and started writing quickly. I was lucky to pass 3rd, tied with another girl from our school who went on to the High School."

The letter notifying her parents that Marjorie had passed the entrance examination for the Southern Secondary School for Girls was issued on 6 July 1931. Her parents were 'instructed' that Marjorie must *be in attendance at 10a.m. on Tuesday September 15th, the date on which school duties will commence.* It added that places were much in demand and asked to be informed at once should Marjorie for any reason be unable to attend. The next paragraph explained that it was a fee-paying school.

The fees are £6 6s per annum, payable in instalments of £2 2s at the commencement of each term. Payment should be made at the school on the first day of the term, and only in exceptional circumstances will the pupil be retained at the school if payment is not made before the close of the first week.

The letter was issued by the Portsmouth Education Committee, and payments could have been made at the Offices of the Portsmouth Corporation, so this was a state school. The letter does go on to mention that a limited number of scholarships are available covering the whole of the fees *subject to report as to regular attendance, ability, attainments, and conduct.* I do not believe that Wally and Ethel applied for scholarships for either daughter.

The letter next required a signed undertaking to keep the pupil at the school at least until the end of the school year in which the pupil became 16. The school leaving age had only become 14 in 1918, and was not raised to 15 until the Education act of 1944. Pupils were not admitted without this signed undertaking. At that time the financial problems of working class parents usually forced them to take children out of school to start working as soon as legally possible.

The next paragraph stated that all pupils must be examined by *the Committee's Medical Adviser for Gymnastics, as soon as possible after entry*, and instructed the parents to refrain from providing a gymnastic outfit prior to this examination - reflecting official concern about the health and fitness of pupils – Portsmouth was a city where poverty was still widespread, although reducing.

I remember many houses which would now be classed as slums when I was a child in the 1960s – including a small street of houses near the top of Cosham High Street from which came a girl in my own class whose clothing clearly betrayed a lack of family money – though I was too obtuse to understand that at the time. I just noticed that she was always an outsider who did not fit in. It was poverty right in front of me, and I did not realise it. Yet, when that street was being demolished and I welcomed it, my mother commented on the pride with which some of the residents looked after their homes and kept them neat and tidy, and how sad it was that they should be losing their homes. She understood people as I did not.

Returning to the Portsmouth Education Committee letter, the final paragraph instructs parents to provide a case for the pupil to carry books to and from school, and reminds the reader that books are only on loan, and to be returned - with any loss or damage to be paid for by parents.

Returning to Marjorie's memories:

"In September 1931 I started my 7 years at the school. Miss Hitchcock was Headmistress, but we hardly saw her as she was ill. She retired in December, and her place was taken by Miss Knight."

Marjorie's school reports demonstrate that she started in form 3A for the Autumn term of 1931, and finished 9th out of 33 in the form and 12th out of 130 in the 'set of forms' – which I suppose would mean the whole school year. By the time of her school report in the summer 1932 she had risen to 8th out of 33 and earned a succinct teacher's note: *Marjorie has improved this term.*

The school report lists the subjects in which Marjorie was marked as Arithmetic, Algebra, Geometry, Nature Study, English History, Geography, English Grammar, English Literature, French, and Drawing. The report listed other subjects with no marks given – presumably not taught to Marjorie that year - Elementary Physics, Chemistry, Botany (i.e. science subjects) plus Verse Speaking, Composition, Oral French, and Needlework.

The first report of her next school year is for the Autumn Term of 1932. Marjorie had moved up to form Lower 4A, and this year science subjects were added to the curriculum – specifically Natural Science and Physics plus Latin. Needlework was also added, and there are notes about Music and Gymnastics as well as the standard marked subjects of English Language, English Literature, Arithmetic, Algebra, Geometry, History Geography, French, and Art. There is no mention of any position in the class but her report states that her progress was *very satisfactory* and her conduct again was *good*.

She was not only doing schoolwork at this time, as these extracts from *Memories from Ninety Years* record.

"We played netball for our sport. There was voluntary hockey on Saturday mornings at Alexandra Park. I joined this and preferred dribbling a ball with a stick to having to leap for a ball in netball."

This was a very important choice, because after the Second World War Marjorie would join the Civil Service Hockey Club where she would meet Maurice playing the last regular sporting activity of his life. I remember her mentioning that he would give her lifts home from away matches on the back of his motorbike.

"Later, under Miss Knight, we had afternoons on the timetable for sport. Tennis was held in courts in Milton Park which was very convenient for me - a very short walk home.

"At the end of our year in the Upper Fourth we were able to make a choice of a subject to take. I chose Latin. It was very interesting to see how this knowledge helps in understanding many longer words. Our language has so many words meaning much the same, e.g. start, begin, commence. The longer ones usually comes from Latin."

I remember her enthusing to me on the linguistic importance of Latin.

Her spring 1933 reports simply said *Marjorie has worked very well* and her conduct was *good.* In summer 1933 the report changed to *Satisfactory throughout the term.* Marjorie was too quietly good a pupil to merit more than brief comments. In Autumn 1935 she was in form Lower V(1) and she earned *A satisfactory term's work* while Trigonometry and Domestic Science were added to the curriculum and Physics dropped and the teacher was so unoriginal that she used exactly the same words for the Spring and Summer 1934 and Autumn 1934 reports.

Oddly Marjorie seems to have stayed in form Lower V(1) for the 1934 to 1935 year – but presumably that was just how the school operated.

The first school report to give any more details is, for some unknown reason, the Spring 1935 report where each subject gets a one line report initialled by the teacher in question. It is a fascinating list – summed up by the Form Mistress as *A good term's work except in English.* Some of the comments seem nitpicking. The music teacher said Marjorie should be more vigorous in use of her voice – which can only mean sing louder. *Must take a more active part in classwork* for Mathematics means become extrovert and outspoken – meaning change her basic personality – I got similarly impossible injunctions from my teachers – and Marjorie scored percentages in the 80's for the subject, the best on her report. Nastiest of all was the gymnastics one which simply said *Marjorie must make more effort to improve her carriage.*

Most reports were good – *works well, painstaking, good thoughtful work, good term's work, interested*, so what went wrong in English? In 1970 Marjorie would take and pass an 'A' Level in English Literature by correspondence course, despite running a household, working part-time, and coping with widowhood during her period of study, so I do not know why her English teacher called her work disappointing. The Summer 1935 report drops all individual reports and returns to the one overall report *Marjorie has done a good term's work*, and the English % had shot up to 75% for the term's classwork. Possibly there had been an essay the teacher did not like the previous term, or homework turned in late.

Autumn 1935 shows Marjorie in form Upper V(1) and varied the mantra to *a steady term's work*, but Spring 1936 once again supplies a list of individual teacher reports, and none were as critical. *Steady* and *works quite well* appear more than once, as does *tries hard*. The only two negative comments are for History and Maths which report *disappointing* exam results after *steady* or *hard* work during the term.

The Summer 1936 report does, however, produce a step change in the report. No individual teacher reports again, but the main comment is *Marjorie has done a very good term's work* – and there is a major addendum in another line which says that *Marjorie has done good work as a prefect*. So both Maurice and Marjorie were prefects. Apparently Marjorie's school could make Upper Fifth pupils prefects instead of only Sixth Formers.

Autumn 1936 and Marjorie is in the sixth form, and now individual reports are coming, but Marjorie was to find A levels a struggle, as she wrote herself.

"After gaining my Oxford School Certificate, I went into the Lower Sixth and Upper Sixth where we studied for A Levels. Here we had to take turns in joining the Head on the platform in the morning and reading an extract from the Bible - very nerve wracking. At A level I am afraid that I only passed in French. I was told by Miss Webster, who was Head by then, that I was so near in History and English that had I passed one I would certainly be considered for the other."

In Marjorie's time passing exams was much harder. A newspaper cutting I found recorded that only 358 out of 635 local candidates were successful in gaining the Higher School Certificate that year – since replaced by A levels. That same year the School Certificate (taken two years before the Higher) had only 67.7% gaining certificates out of 11555 local candidates. It shows how few pupils did well enough to even enter the sixth form. Judging by those figures I calculate that in even taking her equivalent to A levels Marjorie was therefore probably in the top ten per cent or so of local pupils in her year and passing them would probably have put her in the top five percent or so.

The system then worked against her, because the Higher School Certificate system required students to study and pass a wider range of subjects regardless of which subjects suited their strengths. A levels would permit them to study a narrower range of subjects better suited to them, increasing their chances of passing said examinations.

Marjorie's sixth form studies were therefore very tough by modern standards, as her first sixth form report in Autumn 1936 implies. The overall assessment is *Marjorie is working steadily*. *Working well* or *working steadily* appear on nearly all individual assessments, but the history teacher provides the following discouraging line *Marjorie's work is not up to sixth form standard.*

The Spring 1937 report highlights another type of teacher criticism. In Marjorie's case the words used were *Marjorie's work will be good when she shows more self-confidence* and *wants more confidence in class discussion*. If a child lacking in self-confidence is criticized for lacking self-confidence that is surely only going to undermine their self-confidence more?

Come the Summer 1937 report and *works well* and *works steadily* are recurring themes, but so is *she seems afraid of discussing what she reads* and *she needs to work with greater vigour* – the latter comment coming rather strangely from the history teacher.

In her Autumn 1937 the injunctions to have more self-confidence continued, along with injunctions to speak out more, and euphemisms for that injunction such as *needs to think more for herself* and *must strive harder to develop mental alertness* and *be more forceful*. More meaningful criticism related to her needing to work faster, and her essays and examination results being too variable in quality – the latter would naturally result from being unable to work fast enough.

The general progress report instructed her to *strive to discipline herself against daydreaming*. Maybe just a teacher making an assumption as to why she was working too slowly.

The Spring 1938 report was much the same. *Works steadily – must try to work more quickly and with more confidence,* and *her essays lack force* – whatever that means. On the plus side the main conduct report confirms that *Marjorie is a reliable prefect and has developed greater firmness*. What she was never going to become was forceful or assertive.

I remember decades later seeing her working for or chairing committees. She did not chair the meetings by being forceful or asserting herself but by quietly and steadily getting on with the hard background work with no interest in gaining power or fame or applause for herself. Even decades later she showed no interest whatsoever in seeking limelight or power or authority.

She worked in local politics for years without ever attending or wanting to attend any civic ceremony or function. That was her nature, and all the criticism from teachers could never change it. Others would get involved in politics seeking to win elections and attend civic events and get involved in public meetings and be applauded and rewarded. Marjorie's way was always to stay in the background working steadily without any expectation of acclaim or interest in reward.

Digressing for a moment, doing that background work would stimulate her to remember some of her schooldays, as she wrote.

"At the Southern Secondary School I used to play with Hilda Stubbington & Muriel Combes in Vernon Avenue as a child. We were not disturbed by cars. They both lived in the road. The third house, on the other side of the Hyslops, was taken over by Muriel Ribbon & her father. He had been transferred from Pembroke Dockyard to Portsmouth Dockyard. I got to know her a little. Years later, when married, I knocked at a door in Highbury while canvassing for the Conservatives. The former Muriel Combes opened the door. While chatting she said she wanted a postal vote for her husband who had heart trouble. I was able to supply that. I also found that, living opposite, was the former Muriel Ribbon.

"I also canvassed at former Mavis Cadd at Highbury. She had come to the Secondary from school at Plymouth where they started a year earlier than us. Despite the year's difference she coped in 3A with us except in Algebra which they had not started. Both of us walked back via Goldsmith Ave to Milton, & I took it upon myself to coach her in Algebra. She would therefore spend an evening occasionally at my home with Algebra homework."

That she should have coached a friend on her own initiative was typical. Working in the background helping people out was very in character. In later years she gave a lot of her time helping out elderly and frail neighbours – neighbours with dementia or Parkinson's - without any fuss or any expectation of recognition or reward. She and her sister would volunteer for activities like literacy projects and charity collections.

Marjorie was a good friend as well as a good neighbour. Marjorie did not only remember old friends from her schooldays but even stayed friends with some all her life, but I digress again.

Her final report at Southern Secondary School for Girls was for Summer 1938. Reading the comments it is impossible not to notice the continuity from previous years. *Marjorie has worked steadily, Marjorie has worked well, Marjorie has continued to work steadily and with interest, Marjorie has always worked well & with interest, Marjorie has worked well this term,* and *Marjorie has worked carefully and well*; but there are still the classic criticisms *she still lacks power to think quickly & to adapt her knowledge to answering questions* and still needs to have more self-confidence.

The final line of the report could be said to sum up not only her school career but her nature: *Marjorie is quiet & reliable.*

From school, Marjorie went straight into teacher training – that she did not need the equivalent of A levels to become a teacher is a comment on both the standard of that exam and the general attitude to teachers. She went into teacher training as her sister had done five years earlier, which is why it is time to return to Olive's memories of her school and school career.

"There was no Sixth Form at the Girls Secondary School, but while I was there, a Post Certificate Form was started for girls waiting to *enter Teacher Training. Those wishing to study for a degree went to the Municipal College. The P.C. as we called it was a useful year, & interesting, & there were new subjects such as Zoology, & German & Hygiene & First Aid. Also, a commercial class had started, in 1930.*

"When the new Northern Secondary Schools opened in 1931, & in 1932 it took pupils living in the north of the city, our Southern School gained a Sixth Form. I spent one year in the P.C. & one year in the Sixth.

"I walked to school from Milton, & often while I was on my way sheep or cattle were being driven from Fratton station to the slaughter houses - one foggy day I could hear the cows coming from behind me, & could not see them, which was a bit scary. One day a flock of sheep tried to get into the school gates, & quite blocked entry."

That is a reminder that Milton had been a village surrounded by farmland only a few decades earlier - it is now an inner-city district of Portsmouth.

"Everyone, except a few from Cosham, went home to lunch. No lunches were provided at the school. Hours were 9-12.30 and 2.15-4.15. Sports were held at Alexandra Park. Apart from netball in the playground, sport was an extra on Saturday morning for those who wished to go."

All this education and reading was producing career options – and both sisters chose teaching for their career. Olive chose first.

"In 1933, I went to Bishop Otter Training College. It was then a college for women teachers. This college had been one of the first training colleges, & had been a men's Church College. This closed down, & the college was started again for women, in 1873."

Bishop Otter College was at Chichester in West Sussex. William Otter was the first Principal of King's College London who became Bishop of Chichester in 1836. After his death, a college for training schoolmasters was established as his memorial in April 1840, and in 1873 became a teacher training college for women. It is now part of the University of Chichester.

When Olive went there the facilities were just starting to modernise.

"The main buildings were quite Victorian. We had dormitories with cubicles, an old kitchen with an ancient stone sink, & rails across the ceiling for the washing - for 50 students. One gas ring, penny in the slot in the kitchen - However, two years before I arrived, a new building had been

added, & in my 2nd year everything was modern, up-to-date & one had one's own study bedroom."

But not modernise that much.

"*Rules and Regulations were quite free for those days, though one could only be out in the evenings on Saturdays & Sundays, & we were locked out if not in by 9.40p.m. Lights out at 10p.m. strictly.*"

As if they were still children at school instead of young adults who would go out into real classrooms as trainee teachers – which Olive goes on to describe:

"*The practising school had been closed - & students went to schools in Chichester, in Portsmouth, & to various schools to the East of the college. I went to Lancing & to Southwick & to a Chichester School. History field work took us to various little churches in the villages. I remember Boxgrove, West Dean, particularly, & there was much of historical interest in Chichester.*

"*The college chaplain was Canon Campbell, & Mrs Campbell invited groups of students to tea at the Chantry - once a chantry chapel. The bathroom had once been a small chapel, & the bath probably where an altar had been. "Cleanliness next to Godliness" they said.*

"*College food, I suppose, was adequate, but not exactly plentiful, or particularly tasty, or filling! The joy of being in the new building was to have a room in which to have the Sunday tea that you had bought during Saturday afternoon shopping, & a kitchen with a gas ring (penny in the slot) for cooking.*"

It was a two year teacher training course, and then followed the challenge of finding schools to employ them. In the thirties jobs for teachers were not plentiful, as Olive describes:

"*There had been an educational report, & it was expected, in about 1930, that more teachers would be wanted. However, the crisis of 1931 changed things, & financial troubles led to cutting of government salaries by 10%, later changed to 5% & back to normal in 1935, or 36? Cuts all round, & education included. Jobs were hard to get.*

"*The Principal of the Art School kindly allowed teachers who could not get a post to attend the Art School in Portsmouth, & I was able to do some pottery & embroidery.*

"*Later I got supply work in Hampshire. This was, at least, interesting. I would receive a telegram, usually on Saturday morning, to "assist" at* some school in the country, often having never heard of that village. A rush to the Southdown bus office to find out where the village was, & how to get there. I went to Ropley, North Waltham, Rowledge, Totton, Hartley Wintney, Purbrook, Droxford, Twyford, Whitchurch, amongst others, sometimes staying from Sunday until Friday, sometimes travelling daily.

"One example - leave Milton to Fratton station, by train to Liss, run to bus stop, & take bus to the lane to Rowledge (2½ or 3 miles from Farnham), & run down the long lane arriving at school just after 9. Public transport was good.

"At North Waltham the buses only ran on Sundays, & 3 weekdays. On Friday the Head would send two senior boys, on their bikes, to the bus stop to see it waited for me to get there - as there were few services each day.

"One Sunday night I arrived there at 8p.m. by a bus which had gone around the little villages on its way there, to find that I could not get in the house. This was in November, so I went to the cottage opposite where the lady's mother lived. When I knocked at the front door there was a sudden quiet from within, & a scuffling. Then a face peered warily out the door. It appears this cottage was haunted. People would see an old lady walking up to the door, apparently they thought a ghostly apparition as she just disappeared - never went in - Always village people used the back entrance.

"At my first supply post, I had the class of 8-10, with a few older ones. It was a village school - boys and girls and ages up to 14. A certificated teacher had the infant room. I was replacing an uncertificated teacher - under 30 in the class. The large room had a partition, and on the other side 8-12 years - a certificated post.

"It was not an easy job - mixed ages, & most certainly all abilities, and included one boy who would now most certainly be labelled Attention Deficit. The teacher had only been there a few terms, straight from College. The Head was going to another school, & this teacher was shocked to be told that the managers did not want her any more. It was a C E school.

"I was moved up to take this class. It was not easy, but the new Head was most supportive. Someone from the NUT turned up, & after a talk with the new Head I was told by him that jobs were so hard to get that I should apply. I was a bit doubtful, but then got a surprise letter from the Authority on Saturday to move to Farnham on Monday.

"When I got there on Monday morning I was not wanted - so I returned to my school, and found the Head most annoyed. They had moved the wrong person. I was then told to go to Whitchurch next day. Luckily the lady at whose cottage I had been staying was able to give me a bed for the night. I often had to find accommodation when I arrived at a village on Monday morning, but the Head or school manager had usually found somewhere for me - a country cottage with its own well in the front garden, a newly built Council house, a house on a big country estate where the estate worker was the chauffeur.

"The day I received a notice to go to Tadley, the News Chronicle, which then showed pictures of villages on Saturday, showed "Tadley - God help us!!"

"Actually Tadley had some village aspect but quite a modern part as well. The story was that in the distant years a balloon had come down there. Villagers were scared at this apparition, and asked by the travellers where it was, were told "Tadley - God Help Us!!" There one often heard electric saws working, where brushes of wood were made for use in industries in the North.

"Then I got a permanent job in Chichester, & within a few weeks I also got an offer of a job in Portsmouth - but stayed at Chichester."

Olive went to College in Chichester in West Sussex, and got her first permanent posting at Chichester. This left one person with decidedly mixed feelings – Olive's mother, Ethel Tanner. Ethel had been born in the nineteenth century, and married before the War. She was not happy to see her daughter go so far away as Chichester. Nowadays a moderate commute by car, but this is a family for whom the much closer village of Hambledon was chosen as a destination for a week's holiday as recently as 1925. To Ethel it was a long way – so long that Olive went to live in college instead of at home.

Nowadays children expect to 'fly the nest', but Ethel grew up at a time when children mostly lived with the parents until they got married, and nobody in her family had ever gone to college. As a result, she would ask her younger daughter, Marjorie, to go to the local Portsmouth Teacher Training College instead – within cycling or walking distance of home – and Marjorie willingly did just that – as she explained herself.

"I decided to enter for teaching and was accepted for a two year course by Portsmouth Training College. My sister had chosen to go to Bishop Otter College which meant that she would live away in term time. My mother said "You don't want to go away like Olive, do you?" I said, quite honestly, that I had no wish to do so. Little did we know what would happen.

"For the first term of my two year course we had to go to the Municipal College behind the Guildhall. Here the seats were arranged in tier. At Christmas time, however, our new lecture rooms were opened - Foster Hall at Eastney, named after Alderman Foster. We had a grand opening ceremony with us parading round in a procession with the tools of our trade - sport, art, etc. I was in the needlework group as I had opted for Embroidery and basketry.

"So, for two terms, we went to Eastney. Here I used to cycle as it meant only a short distance along the Milton Road.

"Towards the end of the summer holidays, with two friends, Kathleen Bone and Edna Shaw, I took a railway ticket for a week to go east towards Lewes. It was very cheap, only £5 I believe. We could get out anywhere to explore. One day we paid extra to go to Eastbourne, where we climbed a little way on the hills. However, we were not able to finish our week. On 3 September 1939 we were huddled around the radio to hear Prime Minister Chamberlain speak. He said that Hitler had not answered his message and so we were at WAR."

War would bring Marjorie Tanner to living only a short walk from where Maurice Burwood was living – which brings me back to Maurice's story and how his life and career brought him to Cosham.

Marjorie & Olive on a beach with friends

Ethel's mother Sarah Ann Hale

Marjorie & her parents & possibly Lil Hutty behind them

Back Row l to r: Bert Holton, Ethel Tanner, Marjorie Tanner, and Walter Tanner. Front Row l tor Sarah Ann Hale, Minnie Holton, Emma Tanner, and Bob Holton. The child is Joyce Holton.

CHAPTER TEN

Maurice & Ada

Will Burwood died in October 1926, after Maurice finished college and started work in September 1925. Eric was married and expecting a child, so it was Maurice who promised his father that he would look after his mother.

They found a new home at 52 Rosslyn Crescent in Wembley. Maurice purchased it, signing the purchase contract on 17th February 1927, witnessed by his first cousin Bert Sparshatt. Maurice and Ada had moved in on 15th January after Maurice wired it on 8th January – previously they had been living at 6 Harcourt Terrace in Mill Hill (opposite gasworks so significantly less salubrious than the newbuild at Rosslyn Crescent), and paying £1 a week in rent there. Eric and Dolly joined them 22nd January paying £1 a week rent including light and gas.

Intriguingly, I found a book inscribed as being owned by Eric on February 1st 1927, but presumably passed on to Maurice. The book is *Debits and Credits* by Rudyard Kipling – a collection of short stories including *The Janeites*. Its spine featured a Hindu good luck symbol. Kipling had spent years in India and used the symbol for years before Hitler stole it for National Socialism. The name of the symbol is the swastika – it was never Hitler's property.

Maurice was continuing with his active life, and finding entertainment. Before signing the purchase agreement on 17th February, Maurice had already in 1927 seen Shakespeare's *Twelfth Night* at the Old Vic theatre on 6th January, the silent movies *Nell Gwyn* at Finchley on 11th, *Ypres* at Golders Green on 13th, and *Black Pirate* on the 25th. He went to a Cambridge Latymerians dinner on 29th January before attending the Lyric Theatre in Hammersmith on 1st February to see a performance of *Beaux Stratagem* by George Farquhur. On the 9th Maurice went back to the Old Vic to see Shakespeare's *Richard II.*

Maurice was working for Standard Telephones and Cables – a period of employment which he would, in 1938, describe in a job application as follows:

"I joined the engineering department of Standard Telephones & Cables Ltd in September 1925. For some years I was engaged in problems connected with the development of the automatic telephone system for London, including probability research in connection with telephone traffic, & current drain to switchgear. Later I handled problems involved in the installation of automatic telephones in Egypt including design work, preparation of maintenance information & instruction of Egyptian State Engineers. Following this I was one of five circuit designers engaged on the development of the "bypath" system of automatic telephony. In recent years I have been engaged in the design of circuits & equipments for remote control & indication of power station equipment for the Central Electricity Board & other supply authorities. Among small equipments I have designed & tested are remote control circuits for broadcasters in Norway & South Africa, radio transmitters, long & medium wave, in the "Queen Mary", & automatic lifts for the L.P.T.B."

L.P.T.B. meant the London Passenger Transport Board which operated between 1933 and 1948. The *Queen Mary* was the famous ocean-going passenger liner which was launched in 1934. Standard Telephones and Cables was a prominent British manufacturer not only of telephones and cables but also of radio and telecommunications generally. It began life in 1883, according to www.gracesguide.co.uk, but did not adopt the name Standard Telephones and Cables until 1925 when taken over by a company called International Telephone and Telegraph Corporation. Before that it had been involved in military communications during the First World War and was one of the companies involved in setting up the British Broadcasting Company. It would go on to set up the entire radio systems for both the *Queen Mary* and her sister ship the *Queen Elizabeth*. Maurice would work for them until 1938 when he went to work for the Admiralty and moved with Ada to Portsmouth. I do not know why he changed his job, but it is obvious why the Admiralty were recruiting.

His diary gives other mentions of some interest concerning his work. On 1st June 1928 he writes that he *'Demonstrated Artificial Traffic Machine at Royal Institution'* – or did he mean that he watched it demonstrated? It was what he was working on at the time.

Eric's family seem to have remained living with them until 7th May 1930 when they moved to 23 Kathleen Avenue in Wembley. They clearly managed, but not without problems. On 4th March 1927 Maurice records the words *"Black Pirate" trouble with Dolly* – whatever that means – and on 12th February 1928 he records that *Mum & Dolly had words.*

Nothing unique about mother-in-law and daughter-in-law having disagreements, and I remember my mother saying she had to be careful what she said as Ada could take offence rather easily.

Meanwhile Maurice was living an active social life. For entertainment he was going to both theatre and cinema, meeting friends – like on 13th March 1927 when he had his friend Phil Farina and 'bros' (presumably Phil Farina's brothers) to tea – and continuing active participation in sport. He also worked on wireless sets, selling one to 'Chips' – a friend from Cambridge - on 22nd February, then on 8th March 1927 erecting a wireless set for Mrs Glass who lived next door at 54 Rosslyn Crescent. On 7th October he 'mended' Chips' wireless set.

The diary also shows day trips, such as taking a steamer to Sandown on the Isle of Wight on 21st July 1927, or going for a ride with cousin Pearl Tyler (daughter of his mother's sister Edie) on 23rd July 1927. The diary does not say that the ride was on Maurice's motorbike, but the diary records that on 3rd June 1927 he bought a 250cc BSA bike, registration number MH7487, from a Mr Knight for £22. He also acquired a driving licence on 2 June 1927 from the County Council of Middlesex licensing him under the Motor Car Act of 1903 to drive a motor car or motor cycle – so I assume that was when Maurice started driving. No driving tests existed before 1930 and driving tests were not made compulsory for new drivers until 1934, so Maurice never took a driving test.

On 7th June he went to work by bike and on 16th July he went to Brighton by bike. He was a 24 year old man with a new motorbike taking his pretty 23 year old cousin out to show it off. He took Pearl on another ride on 27 August, having fetched her from Brighton on 21st, then took her home on 28th. On 3rd September he records going on a ride with Alma – another cousin, the teenage daughter of his father's sister Edie Sparshatt, and younger sister of Bert.

In future years, Maurice would carry many others on the back of his bike – including two women more important to him than Pearl and Alma. He would take his mother with him on holiday to Scotland in 1935, and in 1947 would take his bride on honeymoon to the Lake District. No crash helmets then – but traffic was sparse. Accidents did still happen, and Maurice would have two accidents.

The first involved a cyclist, and produced the following responses from witnesses concerning the incident on 10th December 1929. The first is in response to a questionnaire sent by a Mr Stunt – presumably a solicitor or a representative of an insurance company.

Mrs. J.R. Hardwick 215,
STRAND
LONDON W.C.2.

Madam,

As I understand you witnessed an accident in Colindale Avenue N.W.9 on the 10th December 1929, whereby a cyclist, H.Walker, was knocked down by a motor cycle ridden by Mr. M.R. Burwood, I shall be glad it you will kindly answer the following questions, and send this sheet by return of post to me

Yours truly
(sgd) F.B. Stunt

1. *Was Mr. Burwood on his near side? Yes*
2. *What pace was he going? About 10 miles per hour.*
3. *Do you consider the injured party was sober? Yes*
4. *Who in your opinion was to blame? Mr. H. Walker*

5. *How was the accident caused? Mr. H. Walker came out of a fried fish shop, mounted his bicycle, with one arm loaded with fish parcels, and he pedalled straight out into the middle of the road, which was clear enough except for Mr. Burwood. Mr. Burwood swerved as much as he could, in view of the fact that he had very little time, falling off his own motor-cycle in his efforts to avoid Mr. Walker. In my opinion Mr. Burwood did all he possibly could to avert the accident, which was entirely caused by Mr. H. Walker cycling out into the middle of the road, with the object of reversing his direction, having only one hand available for steering his cycle (owing to the parcels he carried) and apparently also misjudging the distance between himself and Mr. Burwood*

> *Signature GLADYS B.*
> *HARDWICK*

The second response is only to question 5 of the above questionnaire, but from another witness by the name of Miss Brunt. It confirms Ms Hardwick's statement exonerating Maurice of blame for the accident.

> *3rd May 1930*

Miss Brunt's reply to Question 5

H.Walker, after leaving a fried fish shop in Colindale Av. with one arm loaded with fried fish parcels, mounted his bicycle after first glancing both ways to see what traffic was about. After pedalling some few yards in a northerly direction, he swerved round to the right with the object of travelling in a southerly direction, and owing to the right arm being loaded he was therefore unable to give any warning whatsoever of his intention to oncoming traffic.

H.Walker should have turned the machine round to the southerly direction before mounting the machine, and could have thus saved the accident in question. The sudden turning gave Mr.B. very little chance to avoid the accident very little chance to avoid the accident, which caused both men to fall off their machines.

The second accident referred to an incident in 1932 which I remember him mentioning once. He was approaching a Zebra crossing which had a centre island, and when a group crossing from his left reached the island he started to move his bike across the crossing when a woman abruptly turned round instead of continuing across the road and stepped right back into his path. That is all I remember, but this witness statement confirms the basic outline - referring to an incident on Thursday 13th October 1932 when he knocked down a Mrs Gilbert.

29th Oct. 1932

Dear Sir

I am sorry I did not answer your letter earlier, as I slipped it in my wallet one morning before going to work, & completely forgot about it until I received your second letter, I hope you will accept my apologies.

I cannot say exactly how far you were when the lady stopped, but I should say very roughly about 7 or 8 yards away. The lady turned from you. When the lady stepped forward you were about a couple of yards away & it was just the 2 or 3 steps that resulted in the accident.

I hope the lady is recovering and all will soon be right again.

Yours truly

R. Cullum

That must have been a really ugly experience. I know of no other consequences and it did not put him off motorbiking. Nor would other minor accidents such as crashing his bike on Monday 13th August 1928, after doing ten thousand miles on it. The crash might have caused Maurice to buy a new bike on 25th August: a 493BSA registration number TW8587 from Godfrey's Ltd. He did not get rid of his previous bike, mending the 250cc bike on 11th September, but does not say in his diary which bike he was riding when on 14th November he fell off his bike and broke his kickstart.

Maurice did not only change motor bikes because of crashes. On 20th July 1931 he bought a new bike in the form of a 350cc GAV BSA for £42 19s, and on 23rd April 1933 be bought a 250cc Rudge – which he crashed on 9th June 1934, then sold on 4th August and bought a 350cc Velocette – which had to go back to someone called Stevens for repair on 29th December and which Maurice did not get back until 19th January.

Clearly he liked Velocette bikes, however, because on 15th November 1935 he bought a 500cc M.S.S. Velocette registration number CGN 857. He would keep CGN857, and keep insuring it, until he died in 1969 – though rarely using it in later years.

He clearly did not just ride motorbikes but serviced them, and he was not the only family member to ride one, as this extract from a 1962 letter from his cousin Bert Sparshatt illustrates:

I wonder if we are ever going to meet again. I believe the last time was our Wedding Day in June 1933. I often think back to the Motor Cycle days when you used to have the kitchen floor at Rosslyn Crescent strewn with engine parts and on the occasional rides together when invariably after a few miles you disappeared in a cloud of smoke & we met back home.

I think the best ever when you showed me the road back from Southsea via Aldershot but I didn't see much of you after Petersfield, darkness overtook me at Staines and along the Staines Road well outside the town my gas lamps failed when I did reach London I hadn't a clue where I was until I recognized the name of a customer of Meltonian over a shop in Chiswick.

There is no doubt that it was a grand feeling sitting over a tank on a motor cycle – a feeling of exhilaration that I don't get sitting in a car (or is that old age creeping on).

Maurice's interest in motorbikes included visiting the Isle of Man for the famous TT (Tourist Trophy) races in 1932 and 1936. In 1935 he acquired a National Rally Badge from the Auto Cycle Union, the body responsible for organizing the TT races among many other motor cycle affairs.

He took regular holidays in the twenties and thirties - most if not all on his motorbike. Some were solo, others with friends (or mother). From 1919-1923 he just recorded going to *'camp'* – presumably scout camp.

In 1924 he toured the Lake District, and in 1925, presumably between graduating from Cambridge and starting work, Maurice records his holiday as '*Camp. Thames. Farina.*' This might mean scout camp again, or maybe he just went camping by the Thames with his lifelong friend Phil Farina.

In 1926 Maurice did a solo cycle tour – not motor cycle – and reached Bournemouth. In 1927 he only mentioned going to Brighton with 'Dorothy & Mum' – maybe just visiting relatives with his newly widowed mother & what I assume was Ada's friend as Maurice's diary for 1927 does mention a Dorothy Deer visiting them on 23rd February.

I have referred to Maurice taking young female relatives on rides on his new bike, but he records going on rides with other relatives and friends in 1927 – though not necessarily with them on his bike. On 24th July he went with Eric to Brighton for a walk with Alf Tyler - and on 28th July he went for a ride with Vic Tyler, youngest sibling of Pearl and Alf.

The Tylers lived at Brighton and Maurice was close with his Tyler cousins as well as his Sparshatt cousins – coincidentally both sets of cousins were children of Maurice's two Aunts named Edie. Also at Brighton was his cousin Edie, daughter of his Aunt Clara Brown.

Maurice, and probably Ada, spent Christmas 1927 at Brighton, though I am not sure with which relatives. His diary records him going to Brighton on Christmas Eve and going to the pictures with Alf, Vic, and Edie (probably his cousin) the same day, then laying wreaths on family graves (presumably including Will's grave) on Christmas Day, and returning home on his bike on 27th December through heavy snow drifts after heavy snow on Boxing Day.

In 1928 he returned to the Lake District on holiday, but this time with his friend Phil Farina. On 27th August they stayed at Wall End Farm in the Langdale Valley, and then on to Burnthwaite in the Wasdale Valley on 31st August – both places where Maurice would take his bride on honeymoon. In 1928 they walked up fells such as Pike of Blisco, Gable, and Pillar – but Phil Farina went one better and climbed Pillar Rock.

Climbing Pillar Rock means actual rock climbing. Maurice fell walked a lot, but never went rock climbing – and Pillar Rock was a dangerous climb. Among his papers I found a letter to Maurice, dated

10th July 1933, from Andrew Claude de le Cherois Crommelin, a former President of the Royal Astronomical Society, thanking Maurice for a condolence letter on the death of his son Claude and daughter Philomena who fell 600 feet to their deaths at the foot of Pillar Rock. Claude was an electrical engineer in Blackheath so probably worked with Maurice at some point.

In 1929 Maurice went to North Devon with Ada and 'Gertie' – presumably Gertie Speakman. In 1930 he went to Scotland on his own, and in 1931 he went again to Scotland, but with a 'Herr Kleffel', who was German - literally all I know about the man. Maurice reached the top of Ben Nevis on 3rd September 1931.

In 1932 Maurice went to the Isle of Man for the TT races, then in 1933 he went to Scotland again but with Anderson and Zurcher – abbreviated to initials FFA and WZ in his diary - and spent a few days in the Lake District on the way back. Frank Anderson would be a long lasting contact – for unhappy reasons. On 11th April 1934 Maurice writes in his diary that *Anderson had fit.*

He did not mean an epileptic fit. I have vague memories of my mother explaining that Frank Anderson was a brilliant man who had spells of 'brain fever'. Maurice's diary records that Frank Anderson (or FFA) was a friend whom he met regularly before that date, and contact continued after Frank's admission to Wellhouse Hospital Barnet – a site which began as a workhouse, had additional infirmary blocks later built, and became a military hospital during the First World War. It is now the site of Barnet NHS Hospital.

Maurice would visit Frank frequently over the next months – including going on walks with him and fixing his wireless set but on 22nd July records *FFA not good.* Maurice would keep meeting and talking and walking and playing bowls with Frank Anderson. Frank was discharged from hospital on 9th September that year, but his recovery was clearly not permanent because on 20th January 1936 – the day that George V died – Frank Anderson was sacked by his employer. On 3 January 1937 Maurice records meeting Frank at Hadley Wood – possibly at a hospital – but Frank did not become a resident of mental hospitals until later, because this letter was sent to Maurice by Frank's sister Barbara at the end of 1937.

John Burwood

4 Surrey Drive N2
27.12.37

My dear Maurice

Very many thanks for the lovely box of chocolates & pretty Christmas card, which I found on Friday morning. Marjorie also wishes me to thank you for her nice box of sweets which she has been sharing with us.

I feel so distressed to think I did not send you a card. As a matter of fact I lost my first Christmas card list and made out another hurried one on Wednesday evening and I forgot several people that I would not have missed for anything. It's strange how one forgets the most important people, and I did not want to send a card that would arrive late. I try to pack in so much at the last minute much as I try to get forward beforehand. And I was sorry not to say goodbye to you on Thursday, it was because Leonard was so long-winded telling us a story.

Please will you thank your mother for her card, I have only put upon the mantelpiece the most artistic ones and both of yours are there, they are both so pretty.

How very lucky I have been this Christmas with regard to gifts, cards, and a really happy season. On Tuesday we saw a lovely nativity play that Marjorie produces, on Thursday when you came we entertained the carollers and I've thoroughly enjoyed the four days holiday although it's been quite quiet.

Frank has not joined us very much but is in a good obliging mood and that is always a comfort. And I am so thankful that he has you to come round & see him & play a game with him sometimes. Nobody else comes to see him. You are a real friend to us, and that is why I am so very sorry to have forgotten you.

Good bye for now.
Barbara

It is wonderful to read that Maurice was the only friend to come to see him in his distressed circumstances. That friendship would not end, though it would retreat to letters when war and marriage combined with Frank's indefinite residence in hospital rendered regular visits impractical.

The result of that friendship is a long series of letters from Frank Anderson to Maurice – and later to Marjorie after Maurice's death. The first I found was sent in January 1943 in reply to a Christmas letter from Maurice. Frank is writing from a mental hospital in Bedfordshire, and describes himself as still officially declared insane so clearly has been in hospital for some time, and would remain a resident of mental hospitals until after Maurice's death.

The two would continue to correspond until that date, and the letter Frank wrote to Marjorie on hearing of Maurice's death included this quotation. *"It is sad for me to lose an old friend. At a time when I was rather lonely, Maurice invited me to accompany him on holiday to Scotland. Later we made day excursions into Buckinghamshire and he remained loyal when medical practitioners took a dim view of my state of mind."*

Maurice had the ability to make good friends and remain in contact with them for the rest of his life. Another very close friend was Phil Farina, with whom he went on holiday again in 1934, but this time either on or by the Thames.

Not all his friendships were so continuous. Edward Schur was a friend at Jesus, and for some reason Maurice re-established contact with him in 1967 after several decades – and found that Schur was living at an address on Burwood Avenue in Middlesex.

In 1935 Maurice went back to Scotland – only this time he took his 60-year old mother Ada with him all the way on the back of his motor bike. It was not the first time she had ridden on his pillion, but this time they travelled up via the Lake District and back via York. Her courage in making the trip must have been amply rewarded by the wonderful views he would have proudly shown her.

In 1936 Maurice went to the TT races again, but this time with his cousin Vic Tyler, and then they went to Wales with the Holiday Fellowship.

In 1937 Maurice went on holiday with Vic again, but this time to Glencoe and Ben Nevis and, inevitably, the Lake District. In 1938 Maurice went to a Glasgow Exhibition, then to the Lake District, and in 1939 he went even further and visited the Hebrides.

He even managed to get 40 miles out into Atlantic on 8th August to St Kilda, from where he sent a postcard to his mother describing it as the *edge of the world.*

Amazingly, he did not visit the Lake District – probably in order to take the night train straight home for the funeral of his uncle Joe Brown, husband of Ada's sister Clara. Joe Brown was just a postman when he married in 1898, but his death certificate recorded him as a retired Head Postman.

The Second World War broke out three weeks later and put an end to Maurice's holidays.

It also heavily reduced his time for his other favourite activity other than work and family – namely sport. Maurice had not stopped being active in sport. Prior to his father's death, he kept playing football regularly, as confirmed by these two letters received the August just before Will died.

> *Hampstead Football Club*
> *8 Sandringham Road*
> *Golders Green N.W.11*
> *23rd August 1926*

Dear Sir, Athenian League

> *You are selected to play v SOUTHALL next Saturday at Western Road, Southall at 3.30. Meet on ground at 3p.m.*
>
> *If coming from Town the best way is by train from Paddington (G.W.R.) to Southall. Trains 1.33 and 2.03.*
>
> *Please advise me by return if you cannot play.*
>
> *Return train from Southall 6.06p.m.*
>
> > *Yours sincerely,*
> > *W. J. Styles*

> *P.S. We play Botwell Mission on the same ground on Wed 1st Sept at 6p.m. in Final of Middx. Charity Cup and shall be glad to know next Sat' if you can play in this game.*

Not only was Maurice playing football, but he was clearly good enough a left back for there to be competition to recruit him, judging by this desperately appealing letter sent a few days later. It is headed 'Sutton Court Football Club' but according to its rule book its official name was *"Old Latymerians (Sutton Court) Football Club"*. On the Spartan League's tables on Wikipedia there is a record of Old Latymerians being in the last three of Spartan League's Division One for the three seasons ending 1925-1926.

> *Sutton Court Football Club*
> *Hon Secretary*
> *W P Reed*
> *22 Rylett Crescent*
> *Ravenscourt Park*
> *W12*
> *31ˢᵗ August 1926*

Dear Burwood

Many thanks for your letter from which I am sorry to learn that your father has been so ill. Ere long I hope he will have fully recovered and relieve you of your anxiety.

We all quite realise the circumstances you are in, but speaking of actual football matters, it would be a great blow to us if you had to leave us. We all thought you a "find", and evidently Hampstead must think you a tremendous acquisition, or else they would not ask you.

But the point I want to stress is that we want our best players to get us out of the last two places. It is essential for us to be higher up this year, as we have been re-elected three times to the Spartan League, and I doubt whether we could get back a fourth year. This would mean that in time our club would become a junior Club and gradually fade away into obscurity.

It was the considered opinion of our selection committee that you were the best left back, even if not right back as well, since 1921, the days of Hoyle and Macdonald.

I think you will see that we actually require you in a far more degree than Hampstead, and even if you could only help us until we are out of the mire we should all much appreciate. We hope that not only will you help us to keep out of the mire, but that you will stay with us and help when we are on our feet again.

Although we do not wish to stand in anyone's way, we have a greater moral claim than Hampstead as we are really an Old Boy's side, and you are an Old Latymerian, but apart from that we have much more need of a fellow like you than Hampstead. It is people like you who can help us to get higher up the table, after being at the bottom for three years.

Yours very sincerely
W.P. Reed

P.S. You will be wanted for Thursday evening 9th Sept v G_____ and Saturday afternoon, 11th v Wealdstone.

The writer was clearly anxious for the future of his club, and ready to use any means of persuasion. He did play for Old Latymerians for the 1926/1927 season but they finished bottom of the League and got relegated to Division 2B. Maurice played for them for part of the 1927/1928 season when they finished second from bottom again and left the Spartan League altogether.

Maybe the experience of playing for a constantly losing team put Maurice off football because he stopped playing football regularly, though he played for his brother Eric's team on 18th February 1928. He kept doing athletics once a year at Standard Telephones and Cables Sports days up until 1937 running 100 yards, 220 yards, and long jumps, but after 1928 he took up rugby union and, from 1931, hockey. He pulled a muscle at STC Sports on 7th July 1928, but the 1931 STC Sports day was a better experience because the Hendon team won what was called the "Honours" Cup.

Probably he changed sports because his rugby team was the first XV of STC's Hendon club. He records playing for them in the 1927-1928 and 1928-1929 seasons, and becoming their secretary in 1929. He was injured in the last match of the 1929-1930 season, dislocating his collarbone on 26th April 1930 while playing against Harrow Welsh and had an X-Ray on 28th.

It was no minor injury. He had another X-ray on 10th May, 'Plastering' on 16th May, and a visit to a specialist at University College Hospital on 20th May before returning to work on 22nd May.

This injury might explain why he records not playing rugby in the

1931-1932 season but remaining as secretary for that extra season. A picture taken of Hendon Rugby XV for the 1931-1932 season shows all but three of the nineteen men in the picture in rugby kit. Three are in normal clothing, the President, the Chairman, and the Hon. Match Sec. M R Burwood.

It might also explain why he took up playing hockey instead for STC's second XI. His debut season with them was the 1933-1934 season when he made 26 appearances (only the 1st team captain made more). In the 1934-1935 season he became captain of the second XI making 23 appearances and scoring 5 goals, and in 1935-1936 he was also 'acting match secretary' while making 22 appearances – more than any other player – and scoring 5 goals. In 1936-1937 he describes himself as 'acting' second XI captain and in that season he made 16 appearances and scored four goals.

After that he changed employers and address – then began to play hockey for the civil service – a very important choice of his after the war, because it introduced him to his future wife.

Back at home with Ada family life was also continuing. Besides his friends and colleagues Maurice was meeting and visiting and being visited by many relatives. They were in contact with extensive family one way or another, and there are many mentions in his diary of such – not only with the Tylers and Sparshatts already mentioned.

The diaries I have begin in 1927. I already mentioned his interactions with the Tylers at Brighton in July 1927, but on the 27th of that month he recorded Aunt Bertha arriving to see him. I believe that Maurice meant Bertha Cook, mother of the Rex who went to scout camp with Maurice. Rex was married to a Pat, and Maurice's diary records that on 30th July he went to Portsmouth and saw Rex and Pat and on 31st July he went for a ride in a car with Rex – presumably called Rex instead of Arthur because his father was also Arthur Cook - so the list of cousins with whom Maurice was in contact extends from the Tylers, the Sparshatts and Edie Brown to the Cooks.

This was not Maurice's first visit to the Cooks. Maurice sent this card to his mother on 12 August 1918, when 15 year old Maurice and his brother went on a visit to Portsmouth – it also provides a bizarre nickname for his mother.

Dear Macgum Monday morning

Arrived 12.5 Fratton & Cosham train left 12.4. Rode on back of Eric's bike 4 miles Stony broke nearly. 3 in a bed sardine wise I in middle & Eric's feet on my head Rex's in my face mine kicking Eric & Rex alternately. Fine weather. Plenty (1)birds (2)sailors (3)air (fresh) (4)fun (5)sun & tons & tons of food. Mutton (lamb). Land w.off. Excess clothes collars not needed. Slips good enough. Afternoon bathing. Fine "romps" all well. With plenty of love etc.

Maurice

On 30th August 1921 Maurice was sent a telegram from Putney by Will or Ada congratulating him on winning his State Scholarship, and it was sent to the Cooks' address at 35 Windsor Road, Cosham – although Bertha, at least, was living at Waterlooville when the Second World War began.

Maurice returned home on 2nd August, and Pearl Tyler came from Brighton to visit them from 21st to 28th August – taken there and back by Maurice, and on the 29th Maurice went for an early morning bike ride and his silencer fell off. Fortunately it waited until he was riding alone and not taking Pearl back to Brighton.

At 5.34pm on Saturday 3rd September the Burwood family of Rosslyn Crescent had a very important addition to their numbers in the birth of another William John Burwood – to be known as Bill or Billy - to Eric and Dolly. I doubt there is any significance to Maurice taking his teenage cousin Alma Sparshatt for a ride the following day.

The following weekend 10th to 11th September Maurice went to Portsmouth again to visit Auntie Annie – Will's elder sister who married a Charles Williams, so Maurice had family connections in Portsmouth to two families – the Williams and the Cooks – a decade before moving to Portsmouth.

On 9th October there was another birth – Maurice's Uncle Warwick and his wife Lu acquired a daughter whom they named Greta Myfanwy. Lu was forty and her previous child was born nine years earlier, but Lu (born Harriet Louisa Hamer) would live another forty years while Greta would go on to marry a Roger Ivens in 1946, have two boys and a girl in the next five years, and live abroad in places like Sierra Leone and British Guiana because her husband was an architect on building projects for the Colonial Office.

Greta would not be the only one of Warwick's children to be well travelled because of work. Nellie & family would spend time in Abadan in Persia because of her husband's work, and would have travelled elsewhere had not her husband deserted her for a woman he met on a ship, while Max's musical career would take him on tours to Europe and North America.

On 11th December Billy was christened at St Cuthbert's Church in London. The family was growing, and Maurice was keeping up with the Sparshatts again as on 19th February 1928 he took Bert and Alma's 19 year old sister Winnie Sparshatt for a ride. Then he was back to the Tylers at Brighton in April and going on rides with Alf and Vic Tyler.

Aunt Bertha came to visit again on 24th April followed by her son Rex on 28th April, and on the 29th Maurice's cousin Bert Sparshatt introduced his future wife Lillie Florence Toten – or Lily. Bert and Lily got married in 1933, and had one son Derek Edwin born on 9th July 1935.

Derek lived until 2014, but never married. He looked after his parents until they died, taking early retirement from his career working for a railway company to do so, then moved down from Sutton in Surrey to Gosport for the rest of his life.

My mother Marjorie told me that his life had been difficult and she was sorry for him. She invited him to stay for a few days after his mother died, and after his move to Gosport she invited him several times for Christmas - until he had a minor stroke, crashed his car, and spent several weeks in hospital. The rest of his life was not happy, as he suffered what I think was vascular dementia.

At the same time Olive was herself ill and moved into Marjorie's spare bedroom to be looked after, while Marjorie's own health was declining. My brother Geoffrey did a lot to help him, but Derek's main help came from a care package arranged by social services, and the last couple of years were spent in a dementia care home – where he established himself as a real character – solitary, cantankerous, and prone to confusion. After Olive and Marjorie died I started visiting

Derek, and arrived one Saturday to see an ambulance in the car park, and discover that Derek had just been found dead in his room.

Sadly there was just myself, my brother, and two women from the care home to attend his funeral. Nobody else came - his other relatives who were still alive were either too old or lived too far away or both.

Returning to 1928 Maurice's entry for 16th May consists of one single word *'Maud'*. On 15th July the entry is *'to Mauds'*. At the end of the year is the line *'At Mauds Boxing Day'*. In 1929 Maud *arrived* on 18th February and left on 25th February when 'Etty' arrived to stay until 28th (having previously been there from 22nd January to 15th February). On 22nd December they once again went *to Mauds*. I have no idea who Maud was, but visits at Christmas suggests family.

'Etty' was family - Ada's cousin Ethel Marian, born 1879 so only three years younger than Ada and the youngest daughter of Ada's father Richard Hollingdale's sister Ellen Stepney. Ada recorded that 'Ettie' sent this to her when Will died.

(I have underlined spaces where I could not decipher some words.)

The Home Life

In the Christian home death is the fulfilment of the highest and most eager of the heart's application; the hand of God, adding to the beloved the touch of divine completeness, and lifting them to the home when the whole family will at length be one.

Very benign too, very precious in the reflex action of this ministry of death on our home life here.

That he may bring heaven nearer to the following he separates the two hands, Life never becomes earnest and sacred, as it was meant to be, until the shadow of death _____ the face of the beloved dead know what is meant by life. A family lives but a half-life, until it has sent some whom it has clasped in its embrace to join the forerunners, whose life it inherits, until those whose work is still in this world, in spirit can cross the river, and fold beloved but transfigured forms to their hearts. Some shadow on earth's sunlight there must be, and the darkest of all shadows on a home is the shadow of death.

No agony known to mortals can surpass and little can match, the anguish of Eve, of Jacob, of David, of Mary when their dearest lay dead. But behind it, within it let us say, if we fear not to enter the cloud lies the glory. "Said I not unto thee, that if thou wouldst believe thou should see the glory of God.

And those who have been permitted to stand by the deathbed of a noble Christian disciple, who have seen him sustained and possessed by the powers of the world to come. The dying eye ranging on through the bounds of the world of sense, and lit by a gleam from some sphere which was beyond our sight – and then the light fading from the eye, and the face setting into the awful but beautiful serenity of death, till it put on the aspect of a warrior _____ have known a moment of sublime joy which was hardly fallen short of transport, and have gone down to the common world again like Moses, with the lustre still on them, and with a sacred power to penetrate the inner sanctuaries of the hearts of their fellow men.

Those most familiar with the higher aspects of death know most of the higher aspects of life. To them the common ground becomes sacred, for saints who are at rest with God have trodden it, the common duties become holy for they mingle with the earthly, the thoughts, and the energies of the heavenly sphere. And if God makes breaches in your home circle, understand the loving reason it is that they may separate the <u>one</u> into two bands awhile, still declaring their oneness, and so may marry the two spheres. The little home that has sheltered you in its sunny nook has expanded. There is now but one home everywhere. Those who are bone of your bone and flesh of your flesh are treading the heavenly pathways.

How often as you gaze longingly on your fair stars do they cross the line of your sight. How lovingly will they welcome you, and efface all strangeness when you join them. Dear hands will one day lead you through the unaccustomed paths. The bringing you into _____ whole family, will be one of their most intense delights. They wait they share the expectant attitude of the universe God has prepared some better things for all of us, they, without us, will not be made perfect.

The image of Rachel came back to Jacob as he stood on the shore of the dark rolling stream. It is very touching to not how the memoires of

285

her moral sickness shaped themselves into clear images before his failing sight. "There I buried Rachel" were among the last words on his dying lips. His eyes were dim, the forms around him were fading – his hands drooped wearily, as he left us his last patriarchal blessing to his sons, but the inner eye was lighting with strange lustre, was flashing with a glorious joy, as he saw his living Rachel, sunlit beyond the shadows and his arms strained forth with no faltering motion to clasp her transformed form and gather it to his heart of hearts.

So clearly Etty - or Ettie – matched Ada in religious mindset. I do not know much about Ettie other than from a letter sent by Ada in 1952 referring to a Lily about whom Ada says *Ettie left her the house & so much money they took her old-age pension away.* I surmise that Lily was Ettie's sister actually named Emily Eliza but known as 'Lil'.

Definitely from the Hollingdale side of the family came Mr & Mrs Marchant who visited on 16th February 1929, and the Marchant who visited on 19th January 1930, because Ada's mother's maiden name was Clara Marchant.

Maurice's friend Phil Farina married his own Edie on 11th July 1929, and Maurice went on holiday to Devon from 12th July to about the 28th. Ada seemingly went down by train from Waterloo while he rode down. I surmise that Ada visited 'Gertie', while Maurice rode around.

Maurice visited many places – among them Combeinteignhead, Ivybridge, Totness, Dartmoor (twice - the second time with Ada), Plymouth (with Ada), Teignmouth, Wiveliscombe, Minehead, Porlock, Dart, Hay Tor, Exeter, Combe Martin, Ilfracombe, Crediton, Tavistock, Cheddar and many others.

Maurice would repeat the pattern of travelling around the British Isles for his other holidays – mostly to the Lake District and Scotland or on the way to and from them. He never holidayed abroad.

They were home on 29th July, when Maurice's cousin Edie Mclees née Brown visited.

On 1st August Maurice experienced a historic moment – his first talking picture at the cinema.

On 24th August Maurice's uncle Alfred Tyler had appendicitis – probably why Maurice went to Brighton County Hospital on 1st September.

During the rest of September he spent time with Pearl & Vic Tyler, Edie Brown, and Alma Sparshatt. Cousins getting together to enjoy life – enjoyment stilled on 17th November when Cyril Tyler, brother to Pearl and Vic, died at the age of only 21.

A final note of interest for 1929 – on 29th December they were visited by a 'Nobby' who was presumably Alma Sparshatt's first husband Thomas "Nobby" Steer. They would marry in 1936 but get divorced. Alma would remarry a Patrick Bates and emigrate to Australia about 1951. Maurice recorded that she was living in Sydney in 1969, and I believe that she had a son called Peter who gave her four granddaughters, named Vanessa, Amanda, Toni, and Kerri.

Alma would be followed to Australia ten years later by another cousin - Vic Tyler and his family – but only Vic would remain in regular correspondence with Maurice until Maurice's death. Vic would take his two children Jennifer and Christopher with him. Jennifer would tragically die suddenly in her first year at college, but Christopher would marry an American called Nancy Potter and provide Vic with granddaughters Alison, Vanessa, and Jacqueline.

As the years went on Maurice (and Ada) continued to visit or be visited by or go for rides with cousins Bert, Alma and Winnie Sparshatt, cousins Bertha and Nellie Burwood, cousins Pearl, Vic, and Alf Tyler, uncle and aunt Alf and Edie Tyler, cousin Edie Mclees and her husband Jim, Aunt Edie Sparshatt .and friend Phil Farina and *his* wife Edie.

No less than four Edies. Not as many Ediths in the Burwood family tree as Williams, but all at the same time and all *called* Edie. That might have caused some confusion.

Also there were more contacts with the Cooks - Bertha, Arthur, Rex, and Pat. Meanwhile one family contact moved away but increased, because on the 7th May 1930 Eric and his family moved to 23 Kathleen Ave. Wembley, and on 12th August Dolly gave birth to their daughter Marianne Frances – future top model and the celebrity of the family.

On 14 March 1932 another cousin arrived in the form of Bertha Burwood, daughter of Will's youngest brother Warwick. Just over a month later this fascinating letter arrived from Warwick himself.

5 Circular Road
Betteshangar
Nr Deal
18/4/32

My dearest Ada

Just received your letter. We are thankful that you can have Bertha a little longer. We realise she is in the best of hands, and that she is trying her best. We should all love her to stay with you until she is settled. The reason why I thought she had better come home is that I was worried in case it was too much expense for you, and our hands is tied for a few weeks to send to you what is due for you for being so kind to have her. There is nothing about here, and I am sure if Bertha does come back she will be very upset to think she has been to London & then had to come back here, so dear if you can possibly have her until she gets a post. We should be so thankful to you and Maurice we will see you get every penny.

It has just happened in a most awkward time the expenses with Max. It's all going out for him, as soon as he gets it. Festival has exam fees, 5/- for one book this week for his organ, and two weeks ago 10/6 worth of music for his violin. But as you can understand dear we have to go right on with it now, no going back else his career will be thrown away and he doesn't care how hard he works to make good. He very often says never mind, Mum, it won't be long before I make it up to you tenfold, poor old chap he is still very young it is a shame but we poor parents have to push them on isn't dear, where as some flops with plenty of money, take about two years to go out for an exam. We have to rush them through in half the time.

Max is doing his final exam in November at only eighteen, and hope to go in for his letters next year. His teacher which is a professor of music at Folkestone was thirty five when he went for his letters. It is 55/- to go in for his final and 5 pounds 5 shillings for his letters & after that he will be able to take a school or college as Professor of Music.

He also wants to go in for his C.R.C.O. for the Organ they want him at a very large church, how, but he cannot leave this one for a year or two as they are so fond of him, and he cannot leave them just yet it would be mean. There was a choir made of men and woman when Max went there but now he has twelve choir boys who he is training properly for choir work apart for the grown-ups. He was invited last year to Canterbury Cathedral to have instruction for the training of choir boys from Dr Palmer the Choir Master and Organist at the Cathedral.

You must see Max this year. You only have to glance at him (so everyone tells me) to see he is a musician. Now dear enough of that. About Bertha, can you really have her a little longer. She would be so thankful to you I am sure, so should we, you will never regret it dear for your great kindness. I think it is wonderful of you & Maurice to do this for Bertha. I am sure she appreciates it, and will never forget you. Now dear I must close as I want to catch the post

Much love to you all from us all

Your loving brother & sister Warwick & Lu

Have enclosed one or two cuttings out of papers of Max. I cannot remember if I sent them to you or not. Send them back won't you dear as I like to keep them & make more somewhen or other

C.R.C.O. stands for Colleague of the Royal College of Organists, and according to the Royal College of Organists website it is a qualification *aimed at the amateur player with some experience of playing in public and at the developing student* – which would definitely fit Max Burwood.

Max was born in 1914 and clearly seeking a musical career. A Christmas letter from Warwick in the 1950s would amplify his career with these words: *Max is very busy still with the London Symphony Orchestra. He not only plays viola but is also the official Librarian. It keeps him very busy indeed.* An internet search found a reference to him as a 'principal' viola player and member of the LSO's Board of Directors.

I found another reference on www.kitchenercamp.co.uk referring to a Max Burwood as conductor of the Sandwich String Orchestra way back in 1939 – Sandwich being a town near the village of Betteshangar in the area of a Kent coalfield – which would fit a son of Warwick Burwood. The viola is a stringed instrument so it could be the same Max Burwood.

Kitchener Camp was a camp for refugees from the Nazis, and the website recorded that Mr Max Burwood spent some time training and conducting the Kitchener Camp Orchestra.

Returning to Max's sister Bertha, she clearly came to London looking for employment. Good of Ada and Maurice to give her the opportunity, and it seems to have worked out because on 14th May she finally found a job – though not before going for a ride with Maurice on his motor bike on 30th April where the diary succinctly notes *'Fell off'*. But employment was not all she found. On 20th March 1932 – just 6 days after Bertha's arrival, Maurice's diary records *F. Patching* here. On 22nd April 1935 Bertha L Burwood would marry Frederic Patching from Barking in Essex at St Augustine's Church, Northbourne, near Deal in Kent – presumably the local church for Warwick's family.

Bertha and Freddie Patching would have a son named Roger in 1936.

Before that marriage things would not go entirely smoothly with Bertha Burwood – especially between Bertha and Ada, as this subsequent letter from Warwick reveals.

5 Circular Road
Betteshangar
Deal

My darling old Sister Ada & Nephews

This is a time when short letters are the custom & also a suitable time for me to practice the art. However it is just to wish you all the very best and a most happy & prosperous new year. We understand that Nellie has been to see you. I am so pleased to hear that and hope she will see you as often as she can. How are you all. (This long time) We are all keeping fairly well so far and are expecting to have them all together for Christmas. About Bertha we are not sure if she is coming or not, naturally we hope so. We are very sorry how she has treated you, Ada, she has been the same to us. But she loves you very much, and she cannot help it. It was as I was when a youngster. But since she has become engaged it may mean she will try & be better.

I know she is trying very hard just at present she has to fight herself. She came home last month for a week-end, and I believe she is coming again for Xmas. Well my darling Ada, I do not forget and you have my best love & all good wishes for a happy & bright Xmas & New Year. We all join in the wishes to Maurice, Eric, Dolly & the dear little lambs.

Warwick & all

Clearly Bertha and Ada had fallen out – maybe just the generation gap - Bertha being barely 20 and Ada nearing 60.

The Nellie mentioned was Bertha's elder sister Nellie, who married John Haynes in 1936 and would later have three children Jill, John, and Janie. Jill would become a fashion model like Maurice's niece Marianne.

Maurice, meanwhile, was keeping busy even when not at work or visiting relatives or going on holiday or to cinemas and theaters or the Proms (first visit 28th September 1931) or participating in a variety of sports. He also got stuck into some serious D.I.Y. in house and garden.

In July 1930 he made a hall cupboard on 20th, a bedroom cupboard on 26th, and a wireless on 29th, then on 2nd August he made an arch in the garden at Rosslyn Crescent and on 11th August he varnished doors and on 5th September he mended the porch. In August 1932 he painted, plastered, whitewashed, and papered. He continued with D.I.Y. all his life – valuable when the economic depression caused his salary to be reduced on 8th October 1931 by 7/6 (seven shillings and sixpence).

But Maurice and Ada did not stay in London to enjoy the fruits of his D.I.Y., as Maurice changed his job and moved to Portsmouth – where he would, after the war, meet Marjorie.

A letter dated 24th December 1937, from the Civil Service Commission at Burlington Gardens London W1, states *I am directed by the Civil Service Commissioners to state that they have reported to the Secretary, Admiralty that you are qualified as Temporary Asst II in the Technical Pool of the Scientific Research and Experiment Department of the Admiralty. You should at once communicate with the Authorities of that Department with a view to entering upon your duties. I am, Sir, Your obedient Servant, GG Mennell Secretary.*

I do not know why Maurice changed his job, but it was 1937, so the Admiralty would have been recruiting. Whatever the reason, Maurice gave his month's notice and left his employment with Standard Telephones and Cables on 28th January 1938 to start at the Signal School Portsmouth on 31st January, attending what he called AC lectures at a Technical College. He had a care of address at a place called 'Woodlands' at Hambledon Road Waterlooville – possibly his

Aunt Bertha Cook's address of 88 Hambledon Road - but went home to Wembley for weekends.

However – typically – he soon started playing hockey for the Civil Service.

He did this despite being only at the Signal School on a temporary contract, as this letter states.

> *Lendorber Avenue*
> *Cosham*
> *Hants*
> *Your ref CE10970/38*

Dear Sir

May I make an application for a permanent post as Assistant II in the Admiralty Technical Pool. I have held a temporary post as Assistant II at the Signal School, Portsmouth for one year. I was born on Nov 6th 1902 at Talywain, Monmouthshire, of English parents. I was educated at Latymer Upper School. I left Standard Telephones on January 1938 to join the Signal School Staff. I enclose my tutor's testimonial at Cambridge, a testimonial supplied by Standard Telephones for another application in 1934, & another more recent one.

> *I am*
> *Yours faithfully*
> *M R Burwood*

The application was accepted. He recorded 20th March 1939 as his Date of Establishment as a Civil Servant.

Ada's view on her son's plans to move to Portsmouth are displayed in this moving and loving letter sent a month after his move. Clearly she had loved the house at Rosslyn Crescent, and many pictures were taken of her with relatives and friends in its garden. She described it as twelve years of happiness, yet she left it without protest when Maurice's career took him to Portsmouth instead, and was insistent on him looking out for himself and finding his own way and his own happiness and not worrying about her because she could look after herself.

She meant every word, no doubt, and yet he could never do it. He could never give up wanting to do everything he could to look after her, nor stop feeling frustrated that he could not look after her better because she was determinedly not letting him for his sake – telling him not to let her welfare hinder him from finding his own happiness.

Maurice could never stop trying to look after his mother whatever she might say or want. That conundrum – that tension – would cause problems for the last fifteen years of Ada's life – the first fifteen years of Maurice's marriage.

52 Rosslyn Crescent
Wembley
Feb 22nd/38

My Dearest Maurice, I enclose papers for you to fill up from the Agent, he is coming to look over the house some time. He closes at 5:30 on Saturdays so you will have to let me do the business – I asked him some questions, he tells me his fee is 5 per cent the first £300, 2½ the remainder of his fee so the same as sole agent, only that he will endeavour to get you a better price & take an especial interest in other way in getting a buyer – he didn't actually say but implied it was easier to sell a house with garages or at <u>least,</u> garage space isn't there, he said, just sufficient space for garage – so I think my dearest we had better sell it, as you say, about the 2 movings if you do get on the permanent staff later, your position being assured - you would be in a position to marry.

It's my dearest wish for your happiness, get the right partner – one who is a sincere Christian & loves God she will mould her home on truly Christian principles. If troubles come there is another to hold on, believe me my beloved in all my ups & downs in my life it's the knowledge I have had God's guiding presence & help that has sustained & helped me & enabled me to take up life again - & you dear above all I love. I want to see you happy in a home of your own, I feel now at the parting of the ways you must not let my welfare hinder anything you may have in your heart. I could always make a living with my pension & a little job of work. I can be content in a little room or flat, you deserve a fuller, richer life. The last twelve years have been so happy for me - & now I feel it's your turn. I have often said before, it's too expensive as you & I are situated to keep on this expensive house – it's so different with husband & wife.

I hope you will fill in this paper, this agent seems rather an old fashioned one, I mean he struck me as being too English – I can't quite explain – I saw Mr Gibbs & he seemed sorry you couldn't let the house to him. I gave him your message.

I am glad your cold is better. Look after your dear self. Whatever we arrange to do, there will be sure to be something unsuitable to our plans – if we moved to Portsmouth say for the 2 years & then you married I could always go to Brighton. I have had too many moves to regard any other place as home as far as locality was concerned. I should have peace of mind & contentment knowing you were happy & settled – besides dear. I've not too many years in course of nature to live, I have lived too long in the sunshine of God's love to dread leaving this life, for it's only passing from one room to another.

Don't think me too sentimental, there is always so much to do when we meet, there seems little time for heart to heart talks –

I think, with you about the Labour Government may upset all property affairs – buying a house too ties one down, if the money we put in the house to invest in Government securities that should be safe but would it be under a Labour Government –

I must close now with my love. God bless you your loving mother
A Burwood

The agent hasn't put the name down officially in his books until you sign the agreement, but will send anyone if they happen to call.

Ada is very loving and generous to her son in urging him to marry and assuring him that she can manage and that he should not worry about her, but maybe she is not being entirely realistic about her ability to manage as she aged, or about Maurice being able to not worry about her.

After Maurice's was married and with children Ada insisted on moving out and into lodgings of her own in Brighton, but could never settle for long, and sent letters about her struggles to find new digs which are distressing to read, as in this extract from a letter written by

Ada just after attending the funeral of Alf Tyler, husband of her sister Edie – Alfie being Alf & Edie's eldest son.

I wonder why I am always called to so many times to others, & when I need some help I can get none. It was trying that I had 3 places to view of unfurnished rooms. I really do not know what to do; am in as much a fix as ever. Alfie is at his wits end to know what to do, no-one on Earth could ever put up with Edie, you understand, but Alf's wonders if I had their front room on my own if I could come here rent free, he says that would be the ideal thing if I could manage it, but dear me, at my age I surely must have a more peaceful life.

This was 1951 so Ada was 76 or 77 years old. It is distressing to read now. How much must it have distressed Maurice! Ada moved around a string of different lodgings until 1953 when Maurice made an arrangement with two of Marjorie's relatives – Marjorie's Aunt Min's adopted daughter Joyce and her new Husband Richard Welch – bringing Ada back to Portsmouth.

The arrangement was for Maurice & Marjorie to lend Richard & Joyce £400 to buy 68 Balfour Road, Portsmouth in return for Ada being allowed to reside on the first floor with agreed arrangements for access to garden and other facilities – the loan to be interest free as long as Ada remained in residence. Richard and Joyce had one son at the time – Roger, born in 1952. Their second son Ian, would be born 1959. I remember Ian as being very tall, and I believe that he went into the church so may by now be the Reverend Ian Welch.

Ada had left Balfour Road in 1957 when her health required her to avoid stairs and receive more care, so Maurice borrowed to purchase the house next door to his new address and move her into the ground floor – with Marjorie fully sharing the burden of caring for Ada for her remaining years.

Maurice's new address was Lendorber Avenue in Cosham. Maurice agreed to sell 52 Rosslyn Crescent on 1st April 1938, chose his new home on 15th, signed the agreement for selling Rosslyn on 20th and moved to Cosham on 22nd as a tenant and no longer a home owner. Rosslyn Crescent was finally sold on 30th May for £815, but was rented out for a few weeks first according to a receipt dated 31 May 1938 for one week's rent received from Mrs L F Rance for the week to 28/5/38 – total £1:5shillings.

Visitors soon started coming to their new home in Cosham – the earliest being Maurice's brother Eric and Aunt Edie Sparshatt. In October Maurice's nephew and niece Billy and Marianne would visit and get taken to see H.M.S. Victory. There was also a week-long visit from Barbara from 10th July while Maurice and Ada were at home, and Maurice spent a week at 'B's' from 3rd August.

The first mention of 'Barbara' dates back to 1934 when his entry for 26th April records *saw Barbara & heard news*. This was shortly after Frank Anderson had his first fit and was first admitted to hospital, so must mean Frank's sister Barbara, born 15th August 1903. There are other entries in 1934 referring to a 'B' – often at the same time as 'F' of FFA & Mrs A – so presumably referring to Barbara and Frank Anderson and their mother, but not all entries involve Frank Anderson. There are days when the only entry is 'B' for the rest of 1934 and similar entries in intervening years, so he was clearly meeting Barbara Anderson on a number of occasions – if only to talk about Frank.

Or possibly more. Or possibly Ada hoped for more – or maybe it is only coincidence that his mother's letter back in February mentioned the possibility of Maurice marrying. The diary does quote Maurice meeting B at Glasgow on 14th August – the day before Barbara's birthday – and going to a Glasgow exhibition, and the entry on 19th August goes *Borrowed Barbara's boots to Burnthwaite*. Burnthwaite is in the Lake District. That same day, according to the diary, Maurice knocked down a cyclist named John Brown damaging his bike, and climbed Great Gable near Burnthwaite.

I make that two cyclists and one pedestrian knocked down since he started biking.

The next entry referring to B is 3rd September, and states *B friction – midnight journey home*. There are no mentions of meetings with B after that, and only this letter the following January, which tells me nothing about the 'friction', but something significant about Frank's state of mind – so maybe Frank was the source of the 'friction'.

120 Falloden Way
NW11
15.1.39

My dear Maurice

I have picked an evening away from Church in order to do some of my Christmas correspondence. You are not the last to get a letter. Thank you very much for the very delicious chocolates. They are the only ones I had & were most acceptable & enjoyable.

I spent Saturday, Sunday, Monday & Tuesday with different friends & had a happy time – I hope you did too

Since then I have been pretty busy and realise that I've not been to a film for months – I was sorry to miss "Pygmalion". All my spare time & money seems to have gone on the house. I am enjoying being here – I like the cottage effect, and like making everything look as nice as possible.

If you look like paying a lightning visit please stay to a meal another time. I wish the rain would stop as I want to go to Winifred's to supper.

Frank has hacked down the front hedge – to my great dismay. It was after he had not slept for 4 nights & did it to relieve his feelings.

I talked to him very seriously and told him that if he could not live without mutilating property he could not live here at all. I have suggested to him before that he obtain some kind of sleeping draught.

Please give my love to your mother. I hope you are occupying yourself with congenial occupations.

With love
Barbara

I have no further reference to Barbara Anderson until ten years later when she writes to Maurice and Marjorie about her brother and exchanging Christmas cards. All seems perfectly amicable – the connection between the two seems to be her brother, and maybe that is all it was.

Returning to Maurice, he was now moved to Portsmouth, and his application for a permanent post resulted in an entry in capital letters in his diary for 20th April 1939: - *DATE OF ESTABLISHMENT as CIVIL SERVANT.* No doubt a good day for Maurice, but I doubt that he danced with joy at the news because his entry on 6th April described him cracking a bone in his foot playing hockey, and ending up in plaster.

Maurice moved to Cosham, and here a startling coincidence happens – considering that Maurice was to be living there when he met his future wife Marjorie Tanner. The coincidence is that Maurice rented the house from Miss Annie Couzens and Miss Ellen Couzens, whose address was 'Westmorland', Havant Road, Drayton, Portsmouth. 'Westmorland' was the very same house where Marjorie's grandparents William Richard Tanner and Emma Jane Tanner had been living up until William Richard Tanner died on 28th December 1936. The house was left to his widow, who moved to North End in Portsmouth 'a year or two before the war' as Olive remembered before moving out to Purbrook.

Clearly after Emma Jane Tanner moved out the two Miss Couzens moved in - just in time to rent another house to Maurice.

A decade later Marjorie would be very surprised when, as a newlywed, she went along to pay the rent to their landladies, to find that she was paying it at what had been her grandparents' house.

Proof positive that coincidences do happen, but further events were needed to produce this coincidence. Maurice was living in Cosham on the northern edge of Portsmouth and not on Portsea Island. Marjorie was still living down in Milton in the south east corner of Portsea Island several miles away. An event would be needed to bring them to living a short walk from each other.

That event would be the Second World War.

Rosslyn Crescent Wembley

Ada sitting under the arch built by Maurice in the
garden of their house in Rosslyn Crescent

Ada with Maurice & cousin Winnie Sparshatt

Burwood family gathering. Eric & Dolly at back. Ada, Nell Burwood & Edie Sparshatt in the middle line. Closer are Bill, Lu & another woman & either Max or Glyndwr - then Maurice & Warwick with the two girls in front being Greta Burwood & Marianne

Ada & Maurice ten miles from Ben Nevis

Ada in Rosslyn garden with grandchildren Billy and Marianne

CHAPTER ELEVEN

The Blitz

On 25th August 1939 Timothy White's and Taylor's Ltd sold an air raid shelter to Mrs Burwood of Lendorber Avenue in Cosham.

It was two days after the Molotov-Ribbentrop pact between two Socialist tyrannies – the Union of Soviet Socialist Republics and National Socialist Germany. Their conspiracy to destroy Poland triggered the Second World War, and the purchase of air-raid shelters - important to Ada because on 7th May 1941 a delayed action bomb fell into Lendorber Avenue, and exploded at 3.45 pm demolishing 3 houses.

The bomb exploded directly opposite the house where Ada lived – as confirmed by this letter from Pearl Tyler – a very sweet letter, though unfortunately with a page missing.

58 Cobden Rd
Brighton 7

My Dearest Auntie

I hardly know how to begin to thank you for your lovely letter & gift. I can only say thank you very much. There never has been anyone so understanding as you. I owe you such a lot.

I am very sorry that I did not send you my new address, it was constantly in my mind that I must write to you, but I was feeling so homesick, it hurt too much to talk about it. Even now, comfortable as I am I would be home like a shot if I felt that Mum really loved me & wanted me. Parents & home ties are too deeply rooted to be broken away without hurt. All the time something in me is longing to be home again.

It would have been different if I had come to live with you, because I have a love for you that goes right back to my childhood. You have always been my very special Auntie, & I have such wonderful memories of holidays & week-ends spent with you, that I shall never forget. You are such a homemaker, there is always comfort & happiness where you are. If I could only at this moment sit down in one of your comfortable armchairs, by the side of the bookcase, & just laze & read. One of the joys of staying with you was that one could relax. Dearest Auntie, I have such a longing for you at this moment. I am sorry that you have been feeling poorly, do take care of yourself. I couldn't bear it if anything happened to you. It was such a shock to hear about the bomb dropping so close. What a blessing you had the Morrison Shelter. I feel quite safe in ours, & there is one advantage about an indoor shelter, it is warmer you can lie down in it & go to sleep if necessary.

What a blessing it will be when you can go home again, I don't like to think of you uprooted from your garden & your flowers. I shall never forget the lovely flowers you used to put in my room when I came for a holiday.

I will write and tell you how I feel about it here in my next letter, I am feeling tired tonight & I want my own people, & though I know that I am much better in health & nerves since I came here, at the moment it doesn't seem important.

That last paragraph does sound miserable, doesn't it, but you told me to open out my heart to you.

You are right about Mrs Baker being a sweet lady, she is. She also has your love of flowers. You should see how she treasures any flowers she has given her, & can she cook. She cooks as well as my Auntie, & that is saying something. I wish you could come & stay here for a holiday, wouldn't I be happy to have you all to myself.

Well dearest Auntie, I will say good-bye for now. May God bless you & Maurice & keep you safely.

I will write again very soon & I will tell you more about it here.

I feel sorrier than ever for our poor men & women in the forces, as well as feeling homesick, they are in most cases worse off as far as comfort is concerned. I have no right to complain, but thank goodness. I can feel you will understand, & won't be fed up with me.

(Here there was a page missing)

find yourself joining in & enjoying it.

I find that I haven't got your address so I will have to post this letter when I get back to Brighton.

Well dearest Auntie I will say Good-bye for now. I *will* write again soon. With fondest love to you & Maurice

Your loving niece

Pearl

PS thank you very much for that lovely little booklet, that is two now that I carry about with me, & I assure you they are much the worse for wear. Good-bye, God Bless You.

The Morrison Shelter was an indoor shelter – a caged box designed to be strong enough to withstand the upper story of a two story house collapsing on top of it. Their house was not demolished, but Pearl's letter implies that Maurice's home was damaged by the blitz.

Pearl Tyler was a regular visitor to Ada and Maurice. She came to visit on 26th August 1939 – and went home on 3rd September when war was declared. She clearly had a very special relationship with Ada.

As to Pearl going straight home, Portsmouth was an inevitable target for air raids, and Maurice had already reacted by becoming an Air Raid Warden. He records in his diary that he manned Air Raid Post T1 on 28th August 1939 – presumably training for what everyone could see coming.

There was a lot of training for ARP Wardens. Maurice filled a notebook with 60 odd pages of notes on a multitude of relevant subjects – the first page being about options to protect food. The second page covered bombs including angles of descent, velocities, types of bombs, and protection thicknesses for walls or other defences needed to guard against bombs. Further pages had sections entitled *Danger Area, Overhead Protection, Blast Pressure,* and *Incendiaries.* There were also many pages on gases and chemical warfare and first aid and refuges.

In addition he had 21 pages of printed advice on dealing with gas attacks. Gas was never used in the Blitz but it was seriously anticipated.

It was not until mid-1940 that air raids began on the British Isles. The next mention in Maurice's diary of ARP duties was of attending an ARP lecture at Portsmouth Dockyard on 3rd April 1940. He recorded the first night raid warning on 21st June, and the first bombs on Portsmouth on 11th July – landing in North End but not Cosham.

It was not only as an ARP warden that Maurice was contributing to the war effort – he was working for the Admiralty as an electrical engineer. In March 1943 he became an Associate Member of the Institute of Electrical Engineers, and among the work he would be doing for the Admiralty would be working on the electrical systems of warships – working with great concentration according to some verses written by his colleagues when he eventually retired from the Admiralty in 1966.

And then again - whilst hard at work
In "Vanguard" it was said
Some "boffin" had received a mark
Upon his balding head.
No cry of anguish came from him
Though he shouted "something's burning"
For soldering iron had burned his skin
The colour of which was turning.
So deep in thought he'd felt no pain
For mind surpasses matter
He surely used throughout his reign
More former than the latter.

He would be very busy for the next few years, changing address on several occasions – for work purposes both as his job required and because of the bombing. The threat of bombing and war got many moving, not only those who joined the services as did Warwick's two sons - and I have no idea why he signs himself as BOOVOO.

160 Middle Deal Road
Deal
21/12/39

My dear Ada & Maurice,

We received your letter tonight, and I may add very pleased you remembered us. I often think of you both, and Eric & family and to think we were at Cosham last April & did not know where you lived. We went to Southampton to see Glyn go to Singapore, where he is still. Max ran us down there the day he sailed only for 1½ precious hours we lost time looking for Annie & she was out when we found her place. I told her we were calling for her too, but she did not get the letter in time.

Max is at Farnborough in the RAF and is coming home for Xmas thank God, it has hit us fairly hard to lose him, I can assure you, it was bad enough when Glyn went, but the parting of the ways is inevitable. We can only trust in God for the secession.

Well, Glyn has not been very lucky out there. He is very keen on soccer or any sort of sport and plays for the RAF and has twice broken his collarbone & has been plastered up for 16 weeks but is now on the mend. He does not write very much. Max is a jolly good lad. He writes regularly & loves to come home. He has been home 3 or 4 times & likes the RAF fairly well, of course it is a great change to him but he has taken to it like a duck to water. I hope you Ada are fairly well & you are apparently very busy knitting well done, some poor fellow of someone's anxious thoughts will be comforted by your effort. Give my love to Eric & family when you write to them would you.

Maurice I am pleased you both are fixed where you are. I only wish our two boys were in a similar position & maybe it is a selfish way of looking at it. But it is a terrible job so far, and it is well we know not what is in store for us. It however seems to me it is going to last a long time and the nation will be sorely tried. This blackguard's principles must not be understated & they know not any international law. All I hope is that we do not relax too much & they do not catch us in an unprepared state. So far it is a Naval & Air war, but probably may turn to land fighting later.

Anyhow we must not look on the gloomy side & Thank God we were not foolish enough to scrap the Navy as Ramsay Mc would have us do. They are top hole and reliable, steadfast & unbeatable thank you. I don't think we can have any doubt as to the issue. But it is going to take some time as we are bound to declare on Russia if not Italy when this inhuman crowd has been finished off.

Well now God bless you both & protect you & may your years be long & peaceful are the wishes of all here at 160.

> *Your loving brother*
> *& uncle*
> *BOOVOO*

Sadly Glyn would die of malaria in Singapore the very next year, so Warwick and his family would never see him again.

Another long move was of Eric's wife Dolly and their children Bill and Marianne who were evacuated to Canada in July 1940, while Eric remained and was kept busy maintaining lighting, heating, and air-conditioning at – among other government facilities – Churchill's Cabinet War Rooms (now a museum). According to his daughter Marianne, Winston Churchill sometimes talked to Eric when Eric was on night shift.

Possibly connected with Eric living alone is the fact that Maurice took leave from 19th to 24th August with Eric at his house at 21 Kenton Gardens in Harrow, and took Ada there to stay with her elder son. Maurice had already been taking precautions in the light of anticipated dangers. The same day that Eric's family left the country, Maurice records storing a 'box' at Haslemere for fourpence a week. Maurice returned to work on 24th, leaving Ada with Eric, but, possibly because of the bombing of nearby Wymering on 26th August, Maurice records going to his Aunt Bertha Cook's house at Waterlooville – north of Portsdown Hill – on 27th August.

Many residents of Portsmouth moved over the hill to spend their nights away from the Blitz at this time. Maurice recorded in his diary that he paid his aunt two shillings and sixpence a week to sleep there. Not that he always slept there – on the night of 7th September his diary records *Invasion night at Cosham - duty 8 p.m. to 5 a.m.*

Ada returned to Portsmouth on 7th September - the day that the Luftwaffe commenced its all-out Blitz on London, which had until then been spared the bombing that the Naval City of Portsmouth had endured.

It should not be thought that Ada was simply trying to stay safe. She was in her mid-sixties but still wanted to do her bit for the war effort. A letter was written to Ada dated 18th January 1940 from Margaret Daley, the Lady Mayoress of Portsmouth, which went as follows: -

Dear Madam

With reference to your very kind offer to undertake needlework for the Hospital Supplies which has been organized, I am writing to inform you that the material has now been received and I should therefore be very grateful for any help you can give.

The working party meets every day at the Southern Secondary School for Girls, Fawcett Road, Southsea, from 10a.m. to 4p.m., with the exception of Saturday.

It would be of the very greatest possible assistance if you could help in this work as it is very probable that regular requests will now be received for Hospital Supplies, and in addition demands for clothing of all descriptions steadily increases.

May I add that I should esteem it a personal favour if you could assist me in this way, and you will, I am sure, appreciate that your services in this direction will be of immense value to those for whom the clothing is intended.

Another coincidence: Ada was invited to work in school buildings where her future daughter-in-law had been a pupil only two years earlier.

Needlework would not be the only way in which Ada would try to aid the war effort. As Maurice would later join the Home Guard, so Ada would recall her First World War training in First Aid – as this next letter proves.

First Aid Post, No. 10.
Futchers School, Drayton.
1st August 1942

Dear Madam,

I wish to thank you for your offer of assistance at the 1st Aid Post in the event of an emergency. Will you kindly arrange to call at the Post any afternoon at 2.30, or any evening at 6.0 P.M. in order to be shown all over the buildings and to discuss the nature and times of duties which you could perform.

Yours faithfully
H.M.JEHAN
Superintendant

At some point, possibly when they were living in Petersfield, Ada befriended someone named Lowdell, but all I know about them is this intriguing letter.

7 Sussex Road
Petersfield
Sept 18th 44

Dear Mrs Burwood

Just a line to say I found the books & your treasured one included. To say that I was touched by your kindness is but a poor description of my feelings. I know that you know your little book will continue to be a treasure. The reading is beautiful & just what I love. The tiny illustrations are delightful to say the least. Many, many thanks also for the lovely flowers. They will always serve to remind me of you & the pleasant hours we spent together.

Yours sincerely
A Lowdell

While on the subject of interesting letters – this exchange is definitely a sign of the times.

John Burwood

Lendorber Avenue
Cosham, Portsmouth
Hants
30/1/40

Dear Mr Tanzer

I was glad to receive your card at Christmas & to hear (by presumption) that you were "safe" in England. I should be glad to hear how you have been getting on & whether I can help you at all. You must have had a bad time. I do not know what your impression of England at this time are, but I can assure you that we are very much alive. You probably know already that we are a very misleading race. We always seem to be bigger fools than we are (as the saying goes), & we always rise to the occasion. I have not much spare time, owing to overtime & ARP duties.

I am
Yours faithfully
M R Burwood

Tanzer in Czechoslovakia was probably a Jewish name – hence the bad time and need to escape the Nazi subjugation of Czechoslovakia in March 1939 – and concern for relatives still in Prague.

56 Manchester Street,
London, W.1.
5th February, 1940.

Dear Mr. Burwood.

I was really extremely pleased with your letter, which, in a proper English style, expressed in a few lines what other people would have tried in vain to press in many pages.

You are quite right, I had a very bad time, many ups and downs, many disappointments, awful worries, yet fortunately enough, I have been busy all the time and that is still the chief thing. Since a few months I have been on the BBC, yet it is rather funny that in summer we did not stay very far from each other, since I spent August in Havant-Warblington, doing harvesting work and my wife has been all the time in Emsworth. Up to

*now all was so uncertain as far as my job was concerned, but I am glad
to say that now, after one year's gipsy life, we are going to live together
again, even if we are far from settling down.*

*Well, that's our present position and if it were not for all our relatives
still being in Prague and all the other common trouble, we could perhaps
heave for breath a bit. Yet, at any rate, I thank God that I can stay in this
country and do my small share to help her to win a cause which is our
cause not less than yours.*

*I should be glad if change would bring us together again. Please do
come to see me, if you should happen to be in London.*

Meanwhile, all the best!

Yours
W Tanzer

This letter implies that Mr Tanzer was working for the BBC, probably
for their Czech Service, but all I know about him is from an old address
book which stated that his first name was Willi and that at one time he
lived in Emsworth. Probably Maurice met him at work.

Returning to the Blitz and Maurice's ARP duties - he records that
on 29th September there was a search for an unexploded bomb at
Cosham. The nights on watch no doubt took their toll on his health
because he records being sick with a cold from 14th to 19th October
at Cosham not at Waterlooville. Maybe he was letting Ada look after
him – whatever the case he records leaving Aunt Bertha's Waterlooville
address on 27th October and getting his 'boxes' back from Waterlooville
on 1st November, but then moving to 35 Lovedean Lane in Lovedean
on 2nd November.

From 1941 Maurice's diary gets somewhat confusing as to exactly
where he and Ada were living, possibly because of the house in
Lendorber Avenue being damaged by that bomb on 7th May - there
is a possibly significant entry for 24th October of *Drains mended at
Cosham*, but in Maurice's case it could have been because of his job.
As would be the case for his post-war career – he was sent around the
country for different assignments.

Post-war he would stay in hotels or B&B's before returning home
to mother, wife, and children, but during the war he found lodgings.

His diary for 1941 has the following entries – 24th April (before the bomb) *Moved to Stroud* – 27th May *Moved to Haslemere*.

His diary entry for 7th May – the day of the bomb across the road – just says *firewatching* so he clearly was not at home and may not even have been in the Portsmouth area. His work for the Admiralty had him travelling – in 1941 alone he mentions visits to Whitehall, to Farnborough, to Inverness, and to Scapa Flow. Clearly he was in the Haslemere area for some time, because he resumed playing football for the Admiralty Surface Establishment Haslemere in the 1941/1942 season. While playing for them his performance was assessed this way, and it should be remembered that he became 39 years old in November 1941.

It should also be remembered that he was bald.

<u>M R Burwood</u> *who, according to one wit, delayed the taking of the photograph while he borrowed a comb. A remarkably consistent player, who has never had an off game throughout the season. A left back who rarely misses a tackle and who places the ball when clearing.*

Maurice would return to the Portsmouth area in 1942, while his future wife had returned to Portsmouth in 1940 from her year at Cambridge and was seeking work as a teacher - but would also see her family home damaged by bombing.

Marjorie spent the school year 1938 to 1939 at Portsmouth Teacher Training College – an easy bike ride from her home – but there were family holidays, as well, as Olive remembers.

My parents married at the end of May 1914, so 1939 was their Silver Wedding. For this we went for a week-end to Sundridge (in Kent), to stay with mother's sister Lil. It was lovely weather. I do not remember much where we went, but it was by car. Uncle had one of the little Austin Sevens, & my cousin was on leave from the army, & had his small old car. I mostly remember the country walk on the Saturday evening, - & the hawthorns in flower.

Lil was Lil Hutty, and her eldest son was Vic Hutty, a sergeant in the Royal Signals, and a regular correspondent with his cousins, especially Marjorie.

Not to be confused with Maurice's cousin Vic Tyler, who visited Maurice on 3rd July 1941 before joining the RAF.

But it was not only weekends with family that the Tanners took as holidays in 1939 – They took a family holiday in South Devon, going to

Torquay on 5th August, Plymouth on the 8th, Widecombe on the 10th, and Dartmouth on the 11th. Regular holidays were not in their budget, as the most recent previous family holiday that I know about was in 1935 to Combe Martin in North Devon – they clearly liked Devon. Marjorie was also planning a series of excursions with her close friends Kathleen Bone and Edna Shaw.

They started the excursions, and definitely reached the Seven Sisters - white chalk cliffs on the East Sussex coast at the end of the South Downs Way. Marjorie's diary mentions starting trips on 21st and a last trip on 25th to which Edna did not come, and all holiday plans were forgotten as the threat of war emerged. On 27th August Marjorie's diary simply says: *Expecting war every min. Agonising week.*

Hitler invaded Poland on 1st September, and war began. Portsmouth Teacher Training College was evacuated to Homerton College in Cambridge for the second year of Marjorie's two year course. Portsmouth was an obvious target for German bombing, but Marjorie's year in Cambridge coincided with the 'Phoney War' before any bombing began. It meant that Marjorie was not at home while her sister had to cope with the pressures of wartime teaching at her school in Chichester – as Olive remembered in *Memories from Ninety Years*:

Evacuation of the children had started. We were too small a building to be used as a centre. Any messages for us from the centres to us were brought by Boy Scouts on bikes. We had the job of finding places for the staffs of the schools - not an easy job! People were willing to take children - not adults. Finally the Rectory opposite took in some, & some staff were at the Bishop's Palace.

By Saturday afternoon all was quiet, & I went home to Portsmouth.

The Dockyard was, of course, very busy. Father was working all day Saturdays & all day Sundays. It seems that the Air Road alarm that sounded in London started a hurried major evacuation. Children arrived at Chichester & were settled in homes - unfortunately some of them in the sort of home they were not used to. I heard that, later, some girls were found at the station trying to get home. Their billet was too posh!

On Monday morning, a worried elderly lady came to the school - she had taken two boys. She lived on the outskirts of the city, and apparently had a good garden. The boys enjoyed themselves - racing around, sliding down the banisters, & picking up the chickens - they had learned that chickens laid eggs. We could only point her to the billeting centre.

When the schools started, in the early days of war, with so many evacuees at Chichester, schools worked ½ day local, & half day evacuees. More rooms were required, & some lessons were taken in a room in the pub next door - invariably some children were sitting under the billiard table.

The evacuees had one session in the classroom, & one in the two rooms we had managed to get set up in the Guide Hut on our field & the billiard room in the pub next door. We had the classrooms in the morning on alternate weeks - Children carried their gas masks with them. We had no air raid shelters. Arrangements were made to split the classes into groups & rush them to houses nearby in the event of an air raid. By the time the raids did start, in the next year, we had proper air raid shelters on the little school field, & each child had their gas mask, & cushion to take with them.

Luckily the worst of the raid warnings when they came, the next year, were in a warm summer.

There were difficulties with the billeting. One mother came to me in tears. The children that she took in had head lice - her children caught them. She got them all clean and free, and then the evacuees' mother came to visit them, stayed a day or two, & the trouble started all over again. Our caretaker found that the boy she took in had hardly any clothes, & she had to fit him out with clothing.

While Olive was struggling through all this, Marjorie was settled in at Cambridge – as evinced by a couple of postcards she sent home in November 1939 with pictures of Homerton College on them.

Dear All,

I couldn't get this before, so am sending it on now. There are more views I am told, which I will send on later. I will send one to Aunt Lil, only I can't remember her address (please let me know it). Received letter from uncle this morning. My cold <u>much</u> better.

Love
Meme

P.S. this is front of building, overlooking hockey pitches etc. Dining hall has the spire – pride of place – built for men originally.

She sent a similar postcard to her grandmother in November, but addressed to her parent's address, so maybe Emma Jane Tanner was staying with her son for a while, and this is a second postcard addressed specifically to her mother.

Dear Mums,

Show you here 1/ Fire-escape by which we descended from top floor to air-raid shelter in practice. 2/ is room I occupied on 1st arrival. The room I have now is on other side of building, directly opposite room marked no. 3. You see we are right up in the gables – 62 steps down each time. Thank Olive for the letter – tell her I'll answer soon.

Love
Meme

They only practised for air-raids as the anticipated air-raids were not happening, with consequences which Olive remembered.

Gradually the evacuees returned to their homes, & things got back to normal. A few children remained, & these - with those who had come with their families from other areas put up our numbers. After the new intake of 5-year olds at Xmas I had 55 on roll, though measles, mumps, chicken pox, and German measles kept the numbers down. I sometimes had to take the children & get them somehow fitted into another room - as mine was too smoky.

Life was not easy, but it was carrying on regardless, and these letters to Marjorie from her parents illustrate that:

88 Alverstone Rd
Milton
Southsea

My Dear Marjorie

Just a line to let you know that I am still in the land of the living. Well how are you getting on have you found that there is no place like home even with the fire out. I am working only 5 hours overtime a week & am very pleased to say that there is no Saturday afternoon and also no decent football matches.

Mum & I went for a walk along the front on Sunday afternoon & it was glorious the sun actually shone as soon as we got out of the bus at the Pier. We saw Bert & he was seated in the motor with his tin hat & rubber boots on & my word he looked exactly like a real soldier.

We have got your Ration book home here. Have you had any information as to whether to have it sent on to you at Homerton if so let us know & we will forward it on.

Well I have sent you at last the One letter that I may write so I suppose that you will have to have a frame made. I have got your allowance but will keep it till you come home so I will you send now only my best love.

Dad

This from Ethel was part of the same letter as Wally's 'few lines' above. The Bert referred to was Robert Arthur Holton, son of Ethel's sister Minnie Gertrude Holton. Bert spent the war working and travelling with barrage balloons.

Dearest. At last, I have teased Dad until he has written you a few lines, isn't it wonderful? So pleased to hear you received cake, alright, was it broken through the post? Did it taste O.K.? Have you had any bad effects? Olive started this morning, Monday, her throat still is a trouble, tonsils, you know. I am very glad your cold is better, continue with Owbridges & you will eventually lose it. Take every care of yourself Meme & fancy 16th Dec will soon be here. How long do you have? How is Kathleen & Edna, do they get parcels from home. Have you made tea in your teapot yet? Should be enough for two. Bye bye will write soon, love from your loving Mum.

That was obviously written before Christmas, when times were still reasonably pleasant, but the first bad time of 1940 actually began in 1939, because the winter of 1939-1940 was one of the severest on record. In particular there was a severe frost from 27th December to 18th February. How it hit the family was described in this letter:

88 Alverstone Rd
Jan 29th 1940

Dear Marjorie

Many thanks for your letter received this afternoon 4 o'clock. I was surprised to hear you did not receive your parcel until Monday morning, as I posted it on Thursday morning before 1 o'clock. Your first parcel I sent Wed: before 1 o'clock & you received it by the next day. I wonder the pudding was good all that time. I hear you have had plenty of snow, well we had some on the same Tuesday as you said 16th, since then we have had frosts every day. Yesterday the streets were just like glass you could not walk & to-day if anything they were worse. Dad had to walk to work as it was so dangerous to ride, having fell off his bike five times the day before.

When the Baker Hicks called to-day, three men were pulling the cart along, one pulled the shafts, whilst one pushed the back, & one pushed the wheels round, the horse had to be kept in the stable. I watched a man trying to ride his Bike along this road & he fell off four times just along this piece of Alverstone Road. Our upstairs water has been shut off for about three weeks, & downstairs the scullery door is so frozen that it won't shut & the lavatory door won't open because the latch has frozen in & the back gate we can't open at all it has froze as firm as a rock.

People who are walking here are wearing socks over their shoes, or else stockings over their shoes to keep them from slipping. Olive says my letter sounds like a chapter of woes what price hers. Well, it is now Tuesday, will try to finish your letter, the snow is very thick in places. I went to Winter Rd this afternoon but was obliged to wear Russian boots with galoshes over them. Everyone you meet out looks queer either their head & ears are all bound up or else their feet. I saw a piece in the paper about opening your college again, also more schools in Portsmouth.

Have you made up your mind about half term yet? I fancy you will soon become a strong Methodist by the sound of it. I made some bake to-day, hope you will receive it before next Monday or else it will be a week old before you get it. Have you heard from Vic since he returned, we have not. Olive has asked Winnie here this week, so am expecting some weather. Well I am stumped for news now, so must close with love from Mums.

P.S. There is plenty to do feeding the birds here, I found a loverly starling frozen to death in the garden, it is now Wed: morning & Olive has just set off once more, also Dad walking all the way to the Dckyd main gate, it is thawing a bit now & I can really shut the scullery door now & feel a bit warmer about the legs. Oh, have got the Electric Stove.

The Winnie referred to in the letter was Winnie Ashworth, daughter of Gertrude Ashworth née Gibbs, Ethel's cousin and friend.

The Vic referred to was Marjorie's cousin Victor Hutty, son of the Aunt Lil she mentioned in the first postcard.

As Olive remembers:

Aunt Lil married William Hutty. He had been in World War 1, & had been employed driving to & fro with equipment, I believe. My father was exempt as he worked on the ships in Portsmouth Dockyard. Will, when back in England, was engaged with vegetable production & selling I believe. When I got to know them more they lived at Durley Ave, Cowplain. My father laughingly said 'Dirty Ave', as it was not made up & got very muddy in wet weather. They had 2 sons, Vic & Ed. Vic went into the army & Ed into Portsmouth Dockyard. Will & Lil moved to Sundridge, Near Sevenoaks Kent, & kept a shop there. Ed went into lodgings with Mr & Mrs Dummer, a pleasant elderly couple. He married Dorothy, & they had children, twins & 1 other, I think. I have never met them. They all went, later, to Kent.

Ed and Dorothy's children were named John, Patricia, and William. Vic married Rita Smith and had three sons named Richard Vernon, Roger Vincent and Robert Victor. Vic's widow Rita continued exchanging Christmas cards with Marjorie's children until she died in 2018.

But Vic's marriage to Rita would not have happened if he had proved less resourceful in surviving the Fall of France.

The German offensive in the West began on 10th May 1940 – and immediately disrupted Tanner family plans. As Olive remembered it:

For Whitsun, my parents & I had arranged to visit my sister - as the Training College where she was a student had been evacuated from Portsmouth to Cambridge.

Whit Sunday in 1940 was on 12th May.

I did not hear the news on the morning of Friday 10 May, but at the station, when calling the London train, to my puzzlement the porter called "Don't worry. Hitler's not got there." Then I heard about the entry into Holland and Belgium.

Unfortunately, I was on bus duty, & was having to wait after school to put some children on the bus to Hunston. A boy scout arrived with a note for the Head, who had left.

As the certificated teacher I was in charge so I had to sign it.

'No teachers to leave the area this weekend'. Possibly a sudden evacuation from London was expected. I don't know the reason. It meant that I could not go to Cambridge. My parents were all ready to go, but under the circumstances decided not to. I suppose that transport might have been held up by the forces transport.

Marjorie was still shielded from the storm at Homerton – enough for a day trip to Ely on 18 May in glorious weather, but she never got the opportunity to show her parents and sister around Cambridge that Whitsun as this letter to Marjorie from her father explains:

> *88 Alverstone Rd*
> *Milton*
> *Southsea*

My dear Meme 12/6/40

Just a line to thank you for the cigarettes & soap which you sent to me for the glorious 12th of June.

Please do not have a shock when you see the handwriting as it is now 11.15pm and I have just had supper (English tomatoes & lettuce) don't it make your mouth water? and am just feeling tired. Mum & I have just had a walk along the front but it was rather blowy.

Well you have made a record. A second note from me. Me. Me. So you will have something to talk about now won't you.

I hope that you are getting along nicely with your exams & shall be glad to see you home again but I am afraid that holiday week for me on July 15th we will not get as all leave has been cancelled for the time being & we are working at top pressure now Sundays as well as Saturday evenings.

Mum has gone to bed now so I must close with best love from
> *Dad*

Walter Tanner was in his early fifties at this time, so having to work such long hours must have been a strain – and the strains were going to get greater. Marjorie must have been under strain herself by this time, as she was still away at college and having to take exams while the German offensive was sweeping all before it - while France was falling and the Dunkirk evacuation taking place, and while her cousin Vic was trying to escape from the advancing German forces having been unable to reach Dunkirk to be evacuated.

As Marjorie remembered it:

Vic was in N. France (a wireless unit) with the French. When the French line broke, his unit had to burn their equipment & hurry south. At a port, they were lucky to meet a sailor who told them to go on board the last ship for England which was about to sail. He reported in, & was told to go home & await further directions. Lil was very thankful because he had been reported missing.

Olive went into more details in her memories:

With the fighting in France, the advance of Germany, & the reports of the bombing there, the war so very near to us - One night there was a notice given out on the BBC asking for reports of small boats & ships.

My father said "Now, what are they wanting that for?"

Then came Dunkirk, & we wondered what had happened to my cousin, in the Royal Signal Corps, somewhere in France. A birthday parcel sent to him was returned - "missing".

My aunt & uncle had a small shop in a village, in Kent. It must have been upsetting, I suppose, if people were asking if she had any news when they were shopping, & awful when he had not come in the Dunkirk evacuation. My aunt came down to us, in Portsmouth in mid-week, so worried, & fearful of bad news. Then, late on the Friday night, a telegram arrived from my uncle - just 2 words "Vic home".

She returned by the first train next morning. He apparently told them what had happened, but, I was later told, never wanted to speak of it again. I only asked him 30 years later.

His signal section was unable to get up to Dunkirk, so had burned the lorry & equipment, & set off, with the refugees, to Bordeaux. They finally arrived where they contacted some British forces, & were made part of the guard to protect the politicians evacuating there. Vic was therefore one of the last of the forces to be evacuated on one of the last ships. All he could tell us when he wrote was "left from B & arrived at D".

Marjorie was still away at the time, so had to learn by letter. This letter came from her mother, but Marjorie noted at the top of the letter that she had heard from Olive first.

Received Thurs 27<u>th</u> June 1940
Wed. from Olive – heard Vic safe
88 Alverstone Road
Milton
Southsea

Dear Meme

I daresay you are busy, but I have not had my letter from you this week yet, I hope you are quite O.K. & ready for home. I told you, I believe, in my last letter, Aunt Lily was here, well, she returned on Saturday. She had a wire from Victor to say he was home, she was delighted. I do not know how long he is home for. He has not had any news of anyone for nine weeks. Grandma is staying here this week, she has been poorly again, so is having a little change. Victor has had a pretty rough time, they have been a week tracking through France, & only 6 of them returned, & they had had very little to eat, so Aunt Lily says she must look after him. He thinks he is very lucky himself to get out of it. He had to Hitch-Hike 400-500 miles & come over in a Cruiser to D.

Monday night was the first night Gran was here, & about twenty past twelve we had to take cover, twenty past three we had all clear. Doesn't it make you feel tired next day & I shall be so glad to see you home again, what day will you come?

Joyce had a second inoculation for Dipi Tuesday, & Thursday she goes to Slough.

Well, is now nine o'clock & I want to hear the news, so Goodbye for a little while, come home soon as you can

I remain your loving
Mums

Gran in this letter means Emma Jane Tanner. D is probably Devonport Dockyard. Joyce is Joyce Holton, the adopted daughter of Minnie Holton (and Bob's great-niece) who was ten years old, and the 'Dipi' would be Diptheria.

Time to hear from the war hero, Sergeant Vic Tyler himself, in a letter sent to Olive on 23rd June 1940 – the day Hitler visited Paris.

The Moors
Sunday 23rd

Dear Olive,

Thanks very much for your letter and good wishes.

Glad to hear that you all at Milton are O.K. and bearing the great strain very well.

It certainly a puzzler to know how & when it will all finish up.

Please thank Marjorie for writing, but I am afraid that I did not receive anything for the last 9 weeks, as practically all communications were cut, even for official mail.

Glad to hear that she will be finished with her exams by this week-end and will be back home again. I certainly wish her the best of luck and hope that she can get fixed up with a job pretty soon.

Well, how have you been getting on all this long time. I expect pretty busy one way and another. Plenty of new orders to attend to but it is good to see an attempt at organisation, for there is nothing in France at all and it is just a mad rush for all, everyone for themselves when Jerry comes along. A pitiful sight to see and a rather nerve racking experience, for it was really of no avail and in the end they must go back to their homes, for there is nowhere else to go.

Was very lucky myself to get out of it, had to hitch-hike about 400-500 miles across France to Bordeaux, and eventually come over in a cruiser to D.

I see that there is plenty of French Navy in port. I only hope that they will stay here and help us to carry on.

Don't know what my next move will be for I am more or less an orphan, for I have no idea where my Head Quarter Unit is, and am just hanging on here for some instructions on where to go.

Shouldn't be surprised if they don't send some of the Army abroad to the Colonies.

Well, I know that Bert is still doing his stuff with the Air Balloons. Please give him my best wishes next time you meet.

Please also accept my thanks for the mittens, gloves, scarf, & pullover which you all sent and which came in very handy at the time. I had intended bringing you all home some real French silk stockings on my next leave, but I am afraid that I did not have time to stop and buy them.

The night we sailed out they dropped something like 120 bombs on the town, a town undefended and full up with refugees. Close on 3 million entered it in one day.

Well, I don't think that I can write of much else at present so will now close wishing you to remember me to all, and wishing you all, all the very best of good health, good luck, & good fortune.

> *So with best love*
> *Your loving cousin, Vic*

Less than a month later comes this letter to Marjorie.

> *2318395 Sgt W Hutty*
> *PO Box A100*
> *Harpenden*
> *Herts*

Dear Marjorie 15/7/40

Thank you ever so much for your gift which I received quite safely by first post today, & so I thought to show my appreciation you should have the first letter off the pad by return of post.

It certainly had a good trip round and has cost a few pennies in postage. C'est la Guerre!!

Yes, as you say things are beginning to brighten up a bit, we have been pretty fortunate here in only having a couple of alarms sounded but we get visited pretty surely every night, but no alarms sound to rouse us from our beds.

I have heard from various sources that Pompey is getting its share of fun.

Hope that your future job will take you well away from it.

Yes, I expect that it seems pretty queer to you that the seafront is def. I expect all the hotels etc are shut up now aren't they? Will break a lot of people up.

Is there plenty of troops stationed out that way now?

I expect that there is loads of barbed wire etc spread all over the place.

Well, I don't seem to have very much to write about for all the news seems to be war news and one gets pretty bored with that these days.

This place here is not too bad I suppose. It's well away from everywhere, of course, in the country which is pretty good around this district. There is plenty of space restrictions, guards for this & that – keeps the ball rolling.

Things generally, as far as the B.E.F. is concerned, seem to be gradually getting organised. Although there seems to be a lot of disappointment due to us as far as promotion is concerned.

It seems as though those who remained behind and joined up after we all had left have picked up all the plums.

So you won't be able to sing the Sergt Major's song to me now!!

The problem of leave is rather difficult, for officially it is all stopped, but they are allowing one or two to creep silently away. I have worked mine out and reckon that with the help of God, I should get mine in about 10 weeks time (5 days leave). I don't know what the chances of seeing you then will be.

Hope that Olive and all the family are getting on all right between air raids.

Can't you persuade Mother to go up to Aunt Lils to live. It was quite peaceful there whilst I was there & as safe as anywhere in England I should think.

Well, I don't think that I can bore you much longer this trip, but hope that you will drop me a line sometime and let me know how you are getting on & what the new job entails.

Here's wishing you all the best of good health and good luck.

> *Best love*
> *Vic*

This next letter also came from Vic, but clearly somewhen in 1941.

2318395 Sergt W V A Hutty
C/O Sgts Mess
Royal Signals
Prestatyn
N Wales
Sunday

Dear Marjorie

Thanks very much for both yours & the enclosed letter of Aunt Ethel's, to which I have been so long in replying. Thanks also for the good wishes & the little teases regarding the voluntary giving up of single bliss.

These things do happen, and I trust that I will only get the chance to pull your leg one of these days, for its rather nice to think that somebody is really interested in you, because you are you, kind of thing.

Bert certainly put a fast one over on me and caught me on the hop, but good luck to them both. Daphne seems to be a very nice girl, she wrote me a couple of letters just before they both got married.

Well, I am almost 29, so I have had a pretty good innings I suppose and really can't grumble in fact now I think I am one of the lucky ones.

I am sure that you will like Rita, and she is most definitely not a Welsh girl. I don't like the Welsh at all.

She is a Sundridge girl and I met her in the shop when I was on Sept. leave. Served her with two jelly Spitfires for her sister's little boy, quite a dear little kid.

You mention Nene in this hook-up business. What is she doing these days and is she married yet. I bet it's the R.A.F. their bounders, so beware!!

Well, I have heard thro' Rita & Mother that you have suffered another bad blitz and quite an amount of damage to No. 88. I am so sorry, but again so very glad to hear that you are all safe and sound.

I expect that you all must still be very busy with dirty pots & pans and sacks of spuds, "Schoolmarm!"

Still I suppose that we must all keep smiling, and make the best of it all, although sometimes it makes me wonder if it is really worthwhile and how it will all end. Pray God that it will be all over by this time next year. One seems to live from day to day, not knowing what tomorrow might bring, in fact there seems to be no future.

Rita will have to register for this first batch of conscription work. I don't know what will happen yet, but if she has to go she seems rather keen on entering one of the women's services as a clerk, but the pay is so poor and I don't like the idea much, for it is much different to home life.

Everything is upside down, isn't it?

Up here things have been fairly quiet but Liverpool & Birkenhead and district have suffered very badly and they say the damage is terrific, mostly civilian from landmines.

The old job still goes on the same with not much variation, except that the older they get the harder work it becomes.

How is Olive getting on and is she still at Chichester? About time she found herself a partner. I don't suppose that you get much time to run down to Pompey these days, but if you do, don't forget to give my best wishes to Joyce at Windsor now?

I am expecting my leave for 7 days from Good Friday 11th April, (provided that nothing unforeseen happens) so if any of you can get to Sundridge, I should be ever so pleased. We have got quite a lot of room in the barn.

Well, Marjorie, I don't think there is much else that I can say at present, so will pack up. When you have a minute to spare you might drop a line and let me know all the "doings".

So cheerio for now, please give my best wishes for good health & good luck to all, and hoping to see you all soon.

Love Vic

We have been having some real decent weather just lately although a little on the chilly side in the evenings, it cheers me up a bit though when the sun shines. Hope that you have been getting the same at Purbrook, must be nice there now, Cheerio, Vic.

As the letter suggests, there was more than one wartime marriage. Bert Holton married Daphne, and Vic Hutty, in 1941, married Rita Smith – then his brother Edward Hutty married Dorothy Martin in 1944. Meanwhile Maurice's first cousin Victor Tyler married Maureen Canning in 1943.

Marjorie left teacher training college ready to start working as a teacher. She received an offer dated 3rd April 1940 of an appointment on Hampshire's Permanent Supply Staff - subject to recognition by the Board of Education after what the letter described as the 'Certificate Examination'. So she had to pass that examination, and must have expected similar experiences to Olive years earlier.

I have found two references that Marjorie received during her course. One was supplied in the middle of her second year, dated Feb 24th 1940 from a D E Cockerill, Teacher of Needlework & Handwork, which read:

Miss Tanner has attended my classes while she had been at this college and had taken a short combined course which includes needlework as far as is required for Juniors, & some Senior work, and Handwork including Paper & Cardboard work, & simple Bookcraft & Weaving.

In addition Miss Tanner is taking the Advanced Course in embroidery, with subsidiary Cane Basketry. She is very much interested in this course and is doing good work in it.

Marjorie completed an 85-page *Embroidery Thesis,* with 35 picture cards or magazine cut-outs illustrating a history of embroidery beginning with the ancient empires of the Egyptians, Chinese, Assyrians, and Chaldeans and continuing up to the 20th century. I still own examples of her basketry.

The second reference came after being awarded her teacher certificate on 26th June 1940, saying that her course of training *had special reference to Senior schools or* classes and *included a story of the following subjects:- English, History, Advanced Handwork, Art, Music.* The actual reference read:

Miss Tanner is a pleasant and steady student whose college record has been satisfactory. Her work is careful, sensible, and accurate. She has taken much interest in the study of her advanced subject, Handwork, and has produced some very nice work, especially in embroidery.

As a teacher Miss Tanner is diligent and willing, with the ability to learn from her mistakes. She works hard, and has a pleasing helpful manner with her class. She tackles difficulties with a good spirit.

Miss Tanner is thoroughly conscientious and trustworthy. She has always shown herself ready to help in college affairs, and with further experience she should become a useful teacher.

Signed June 27 1940   D Dymond Principal

So Marjorie started looking for employment as a teacher, but before she could start tragedy nearly struck very close to home.

At the start of the Blitz the Tanners stayed in their house at Alverstone Road, as Marjorie remembers:

At Alverstone Road, the Hyslops & our Air Raid Shelters were only divided by the boundary wall between us, so we could talk across from the doorways. Mr Hyslop went out some nights as an Air Raid Warden. Then I went to sleep in her bedroom so that, should the sirens go, I could wake Mrs Hyslop in her bed across the room and get her down to the shelter. She was in the habit of taking an aspirin (or aspro) to help her to sleep.

One day, when we had to go down to the shelter we had a milk pudding in the oven. Naturally we turned it off. When there was a lull in the air, Olive & I rushed into the kitchen. Olive took it on a tray while I took plates & spoons. Mother doled out from the dish which was placed on the ground just by the door of the shelter. I think the pudding tasted especially good on that occasion.

But it was not at their home that a bomb first struck at Marjorie's family, as Marjorie describes:

Portsmouth did not like to take new students just out of college so I applied to Hampshire. They accepted me on the supply staff. However on Aug 24th Portsmouth was targeted by the bombers and a bomb slipped through the ventilating shaft to where the Dockyard workers were sheltering. Luckily Dad was not in the compartment where it exploded. Nevertheless he had concussion.

As he did not come home, Olive and I went to Eastney Police Station, very early next morning, where there was a list outside of people 'killed' or 'injured'. His name was not there.

Mr Hyslop said that he would go down and find out. Goldsmith Avenue was littered with fragments, mainly of the premises of Evans. By the Dockyard Gates there was a notice, and Mr Hyslop learnt that Dad was at the Royal Hospital. He went there and found Dad just becoming conscious.

I opened the door to a happy Mr Hyslop who told us that Dad was all right. Mum had not been able to sit and grieve because she was comforting Dad's mother. Grandpa was dead, and so was Mother's mother.

I have a distinct memory of my mother telling me that Mr Hyslop's exact words were "The governor's all right!"

This is also the second time that a close family member was missing and feared dead but turned up alive.

Olive went back to school and Mother and I went up to St Richard's Hospital where Dad had been transferred. Before we got back to the bus there was an alert, and Olive took us to a brick shelter, above ground.

St Richard's hospital was in Chichester, where Olive was working, so she knew where to go. Chichester was some distance from the prime bombing target of Portsmouth, but close to the prime bombing target of RAF Tangmere – now a museum but then a major airfield for fighter squadrons in the Battle of Britain.

I remember Olive talking about being in Chichester and taking cover while deafeningly low level dogfights were fought overhead. Fortunately Wally Tanner was not in hospital too long, as Marjorie continues.

Dad was there for a while, and suddenly arrived home in his slippers.

We had to laugh at one incident. When the alert sounded, we three shot under our solid wooden table, which would protect us from glass splinters should the window break. Dad hopped round wondering how to get his wounded leg under. He managed finally. When the all clear sounded, we left Dad wondering how to get out.

I heard from Hampshire. They wanted me to take up a position at a school just outside Southampton. This was while Dad was in hospital. I wrote back and told them what had happened and said I could not leave my mother and grandmother just then.

The Tanners were luckier than many. Thanks to William Richard Tanner the builder, they were able to move, as his widow Emma Jane proved by joining the exodus of people who were escaping the Blitz to accommodation over Portsdown Hill. Emma had bought a bungalow at Westbrook Grove in Purbrook, & had moved there after the North

End area in Portsmouth was bombed back in the summer. The family were able to take refuge there away from their threatened house in Milton where they had lived for so long, as Marjorie described:

We transferred from Alverstone Road to Westbrook Grove, Purbrook, where Dad's mother was now living in a bungalow. Dad was still a bit shaken when the sirens went, and this was outside of Portsmouth, and so felt safer. The first night there we, Dad, Mum, and I slept on the floor with a makeshift pillow. Mum was squashed between us. Olive was in Chichester where she lodged during the week. We got beds arranged next day, and Olive came there for the week-end.

Returning to Marjorie's beginning her teaching career.

They contacted me again in October and asked if I could manage now. I said 'yes' and I was sent to Emsworth. My first week's wage was £4 4s 4d.

One day we had a troubled night with alerts. In this case Dockyard workers were allowed to go in later, so Dad went off on the bus. I suppose it was late for me too, and so I borrowed my father's bike. Luckily he was not a tall man, so I coped. I got up to Waterlooville, and turned right to go through the Hulbert Road on my way to Emsworth. There was a rope across shutting the road off from traffic - UNEXPLODED BOMB. A man had arrived there also. We looked at each other. Then we ducked under the line and cycled through, hoping we could do it safely.

A couple of weeks after Christmas, school was closed, and we had to house and feed some bombed out people from Portsmouth. At night we took turns, two at a time, to sleep in an upper room so that we were there should there be an alert. The Head, Mr Viney, went round on his bicycle getting food, etc. His wife said '"you wouldn't do that before for me". One teacher looked after the mothers and babies section.

After 3 wks we were able to re-open school for a while. Then we were shut again for people from Hayling Island. After about two weeks we were able to open school again. You can imagine how difficult it was to restart lessons. Yet a third time we were forced to close. This time it was for our own people as some in Emsworth Harbour had lost their roofs. When they went we looked forward to our Easter Holiday week. Shock for me. I was to leave Emsworth and go to Funtley. Here they had already had their week's holiday, so I missed out.

It was for these emergencies that Marjorie was sent this letter from Havant Town Hall dated 21st May 1941.

Dear Madam

Rest Centres

I desire on behalf of the Council to express to you thanks for the valuable services you rendered in connection with the Rest centre at the Emsworth Council School, Washington Road, Emsworth, in April when the Rest Centre had to be opened to accommodate persons rendered homeless by enemy action.

The Council appreciate the spirit in which you kindly volunteered your services to administer to the wants of those unfortunately affected by enemy action.

> *Yours faithfully*
> *Albert Madgwick*
> *Clerk to the Council.*

The letter was addressed to Marjorie at Thurso, Westbrook Grove, Purbrook, but by the time it was sent she was no longer at Emsworth but at Funtley. Emsworth is just on the Hampshire/Sussex border on the way to Chichester, but Funtley was off to the west on the far side of Fareham.

At Emsworth, when the classes divided for handwork, I had to take the boys for Art - at which I had no skill - while another teacher took the girls for needlework. At Funtley I, who had trained to teach seniors, was given the class just above the youngest class which was taken by Miss Butler. As the school had taken in children evacuated from the towns, the brightest in Miss Butler's class were sent on up to me. When it came to a writing lesson, therefore, I had to have two blackboards - one with printing and one with writing. The youngest had pencils to be sharpened and the others had pens. These pens were the sort with nibs which had to be dipped into inkwells. Inkwells would get choked and ribs broken.

There were about 4 groups for reading as they were at different stages. Arithmetic was similarly staggered. At home I was forced to make out work by writing sums on pieces of cardboard. Children could progress from one to the next. There were not many printed school books.

Miss Tapper took the class above mine, and Miss Deall above that. One poor little boy, who was obviously fostered, went from my class with a teacher named Tanner to class with a teacher named Tapper; then he was transferred to Chichester and joined my sister's class there. I think he must have been bewildered to find out that his teacher was again 'Tanner'.

Miss Tapper, though she was a good teacher, was uncertificated. One day she met us most joyfully. She had been told that she would move up to Certificated Class, which meant a considerable rise in salary.

Mr Bennett was Head, and lived in a house next to the school.

At both schools we had sometimes to go into the air raid shelters. We had to occupy them with chanting their Arithmetic tables, or saying bits of poetry.

The family had been sleeping at Emma Tanner's home in Purbrook but returning to Portsmouth during the day, and it proved fortunate, because their old home in Alverstone Road suffered bomb damage in 1941, as Olive described:

In the Easter holidays we went down, as usual to our home at Milton, to the shock of finding that a bomb, or more likely a landmine, had exploded in the hospital fields opposite. The front door was blown in - windows blown in, roof damaged. Broken glass, splinters of glass, soot, over the furniture. A heavy case of books put across a window was blown across the room. It rained, & slates were sliding off the roof. At least the house was still standing. In time, squads of workmen were sent round to the damaged areas in the city, & the houses patched up & made habitable. Some neighbours, needing a bigger house, moved into ours.

We were burgled. Some precious emergency tins of food were pinched, with winter coats, the old gramophone, & various other small things taken. The brandy kept in the medicine cupboard was taken & the bottle refilled - with water!!

Like Emma Tanner, Wally and Ethel were able to move away from their bomb damaged home in the best way possible, by buying a house in Brecon Avenue on the southern slopes of Portsdown Hill, as Marjorie describes:

We bought a house in Brecon Avenue, in December 1941, for about one thousand pounds, from our former music teacher who had taught us both to play the piano. She and her sister were moving away from Portsmouth to live with their brother. Miss Skelton always amused us with her hat, which she never removed. She had a big veil over her face, reaching to her chin. However it was too loose, and she was always twiddling up the base under her chin to tighten it.

That was how Marjorie and her family came to live in Drayton, just ten minutes' walk from Maurice's address in East Cosham – and just six houses away from the church where they would eventually marry.

Marjorie with friends Kath Bone & Edna Shaw (tallest one) on a South Coast holiday trip days before World War 2 began.

Maurice with Arthur & Bertha Cook - he lodged with his Aunt Bertha in Waterlooville for a while during the Blitz

Victor Hutty weds Rita Smith - l to r: a friend of Rita, Edward Hutty, Vic & Rita, Rita's nephew David Banfield & Rita's sister Aileen

Vic Tyler marries Maureen Canning 1943 - back row l-r: Maurice Burwood, Alf Tyler Jnr, Ada Burwood, Edie McLees (nee Brown), unidentified woman, probably Tony Canning (brother of bride). Front row l to r: Alf Tyler Snr, Edie Tyler, Vic & Maureen, probably Maureen's parents Maurice & Ethel Canning & unidentified baby.

CHAPTER TWELVE

Hockey Lovers

On 2nd July 1942, Maurice was sent this letter:
To: M.R.Burwood Esq.,
  Lindorber Ave.,
  COSHAM.
From: - 127 A.A. 'Z' Bty. H.G.
 Subject: - Enrolment.

With reference to your letter of the 24th. Inst. this office is open during the week from 9.0.a.m. to 9.0.p.m. and if you will call here during that time I shall be pleased to give you an interview.
  C. Green Lt R.A. Adjt & Quartermaster
  127 A.A. Z BATTERY HOME GUARD
    Gladstone Hotel,
    Clarence Parade,
    SOUTHSEA.

Maurice already had a Home Guard Identity Card issued 3rd Jun 1942 by A.S.E. Unit, Surrey Home Guard, but he did not enrol until 16th December 1942. Though registered with Surrey Home Guard his registered address was still Cosham as work was moving him round the country. He recorded moving to Haslemere on 27th May 1941, being at Stroud, near Petersfield, in early February 1942, moving to *Mrs. Cooper, The Ivies, Station Road, W.Liss*, on 2nd March 1942, and on 29th June 1942 changing to the Haslemere Branch of Lloyds Bank.

Between December 1942 and May 1944 Maurice rented 10 Bellair Road in Havant from a Miss E S Dowdell for 32 shillings and sixpence per week – or possibly it was only rooms at 10 Bellair Road as 10 Bellair Road is also recorded on the rent books as Miss Dowdell's address. Interestingly Mr Burwood is named as tenant on the rent books for 1942 and 1943, but the rent book for 1944 names the tenant as Mrs Burwood. Complicating entries in his diary include references to a Mrs Holland *moving in* on 27th March 1941 being given notice on 2nd September 1944 and leaving on 20th September 1944 – which sounds as if he was sub-letting Lendorber Avenue to help pay for him and Ada renting elsewhere. Maybe I am misinterpreting that entry, but it seems a reasonable supposition that his delay in actual enrolment until December might be down to him not having a settled address.

His diary goes on to record *Home Guard stand down* on 9 December 1944, which is confirmed by a certificate he was given which went as follows:

In the years when our Country
was in mortal danger
MAURICE R BURWOOD
who served 16 December 1942 – 31 December 1944
gave generously of his time and
powers to make himself ready
for her defence by force of arms
and with his life if need be.
George R I
THE HOME GUARD

Joining the Home Guard did not mean abandoning his ARP duties, as on 15th January 1943 his diary records *ARP Lecture – 1st HG parade*. I do not know how he found time to do both and work full time on important war work. Bombing had not ceased, and his diary records *Bomb at Bellair Road* on 11th February 1943. There is nothing to indicate that their digs were damaged, but that must still have been too close for comfort, and family life was carrying on – for good and for bad.

Winnie Henson, née Sparshatt, gave birth to her first son John Michael on 23rd March 1941. Fred Mclees, husband of Ada's niece Edie Brown, died on 12th February 1943. On 2nd December 1943 Pearl Tyler went into hospital, missing the marriage on 11th December 1943 of her brother Vic to Maureen Canning. On 13th December Pearl had an operation for a tumour. Maurice visited Pearl, presumably in hospital in Brighton, on the 19th but tragically she died at 6pm on 24th December.

Pearl was buried on 30th December, for which event Maurice got leave. Pearl was only 40 when she died, so her death must have blighted that Christmas for the family, and not given Vic Tyler's marriage the happiest of starts.

On 12th March Maurice's Auntie Annie (Will's elder sister) also died. Happily Vic and Maureen acquired their daughter Jennifer on 30th June 1945.

There was also a near death. Eric's son Bill had come home from Canada, keen to play his part in the war, and on 28th June 1944 was at home at 21 Kenton Gardens in Harrow when a flying bomb landed four doors away. 9, 11, 13, & 15 Kenton Gardens were demolished, and 7 & 17 severely damaged. Shops and property within a quarter of a mile suffered blast damage.

According to his sister Marianne it was only because Bill had not drawn back his blackout curtains on his window that he was not seriously injured by flying glass. He was still blown backwards through his bedroom door and suffered a few minor cuts and severe bruising.

Maurice's diary records another death on 5th January 1946, but only names the deceased as Jim – probably meaning James Richard Hollingdale, Ada's eldest half-brother and son of Richard Hollingdale by his first marriage to an Elizabeth Foice. James was born in 1863.

Returning to Maurice - besides his full time job, looking after his mother, being an ARP Warden and joining the Home Guard, Maurice also somehow found time to get an MA. He obtained a certificate saying that *Maurice Richard Burwood of Jesus College in the University of Cambridge was at a full Congregation holden in the Senate House on 16 October 1942 admitted to the Degree of MASTER of ARTS.*

Heaven knows how he found the time. His job involved travelling where he was needed. On 20th April 1944 he went to Scapa Flow in the Orkneys, and acquired a mess bill for 3 shillings 11 pence at HMS Dunluce Castle – a warship saved from scrap in 1939 to become the main mail-sorting depot for the Fleet. He even found time to play the occasional game of hockey and visit to the cinema. I doubt that he would have time for much else, and he had not met Marjorie Tanner.

Marjorie was working at Funtley School - a long journey, as she remembers: *I had to go down the hill (I lived in Brecon Ave on Portsdown Hill by that time) take a bus to Cosham, then another bus to Fareham. At Fareham I met Miss Deall and Miss Tapper, and we walked up Trinity Street and then along Kiln Road to the school situated on a slope. Sometimes I would cycle - in reasonable weather.*

No doubt it was a trudge in winter, so Marjorie was seeking a permanent job. As a result she received a letter dated 29th November 1943 inviting her to an interview for the post of history teacher at Cowplain Senior School on 9th December. She went there supported by this reference from the headmaster of her school at Funtley.

Miss M. E. Tanner, who is a member of the County Permanent Supply Staff, has assisted in this school since April 1941.

I understand she was trained for Senior School work, but during the 2½ years she has been here she has gained Junior School experience.

I have found her a loyal & willing member of the staff & ready to assist in all school activities.

She is well qualified to teach Handwork & similar subjects.

She has a pleasant manner with the children & is liked by them.

I understand her reason for desiring a move is to be closer to home & also to obtain a permanent appointment. It is not possible for her to be appointed permanently here, as she is filling the place of a teacher on War Service.

A letter was sent to her dated 1st January 1944 from Hampshire Education Authority saying that she had been appointed as a Certificated Teacher at Cowplain C1 Senior Girls School, but that she should work out a month's notice at Funtley School, and a letter dated 3rd January stated that her salary would be £162 15s per annum.

After a few years, I applied to Hampshire for a permanent post at Cowplain Senior School. I was interviewed by several people sitting round a table. Strangely enough the chairman was a Mr Tanner.

I was accepted and started at Hart Plain Avenue. The boys had one half of the school with a Headmaster, and we had the other under Miss Maidment as Headmistress. Now I climbed up the hill to the George Inn and caught a bus.

I had my A level in French. Cowplain School started French lessons with the top class & I was offered the chance to take it. I was glad to do so.

When air raids might still occur we had 2 people to be there overnight. Accommodation was in the men's staff room as it was the largest. I took my turn with Miss Ash. One night we were rather worried. Some troops were allowed to hold some gathering? Celebration there. Some men – must have been French Canadians, went whooping down the corridors sounding like Indian cries. We felt them rattling the door. We did not dare to make a sound or show a light, & did not dare to sleep until they had left.

Before our troops returned to France to push the Germans back to their own land, there were troops camping in the forest not far from the school. We were forbidden to keep anybody from leaving immediately school ended. Some of the older girls looked like young ladies. Parents, & other adults, were waiting at the bus stops to escort them home.

One day Miss Ash brought along 2 kittens for me that her cat had had. At the end of the day I had to transport them home. One girl offered to hold one till she got out at the George Inn on top of the hill. While we waited for the bus, a continual, evenly spaced, line of motor cycles went past. We had to hold the kittens very firmly as they went by, as you can imagine. From the George I had to hold both, as well as my bag of marking, till I reached Brecon Avenue, luckily on the lower slopes of the hill. We kept one, & my father's mother took the other.

Marjorie was not only teaching at this time. In November 1943 she received a Fire Guard Training certificate saying that she had attended training courses at a Fire Guard Training School.

Marjorie was also about to take up another activity – and dramatically change her life. As the war was coming to a close her old school friend Kathleen Bone was to play a vital part in Marjorie's life – as Marjorie describes:

Kath Bone had got a teaching post at Hayling Island. One of the staff heard that, as we were almost entirely free from attack by then, the Civil Service were restarting their hockey games. She asked Kath if she would like to join. Kath phoned me & I said I would like to do so also. We managed to fix up some matches.

The men were unable to make full teams. However when men came on leave, or were working here, we ran mixed hockey teams on Sundays.

This was good fun, especially as some had not played hockey before, & would raise their sticks high above their shoulders – not allowed really. We also learnt to take harder strokes.

Some U.S. troops were accommodated in the next area to our playing field at the United Services Ground in Copnor Rd. One incident amused me. Behind my back, as I was playing, some of them were sitting on the bank watching. A ball came out & hit my instep. I gave a bit of a hop & said 'Oh!' but went on playing. I think I heard an amused sound from behind. Then another hard hit stroke went over the boundary & right beside a U.S. soldier. He lazily put out his hand to catch it, & then said "Oh, it is hard." Ha! Ha!

At the end of the winter hockey season several hockey teams met for a competition at Southampton. We had an A & B mixed hockey teams. One year we heard some teams sounding quite peeved because the final was played out between our A & B teams.

Maurice's diary records on 22nd April 1945: *Win mixed hockey 6-a-side Southampton.*

Kath Bone was not just another hockey player playing for the Civil Service team. As late as 1952 she would be a member of a team of Portsmouth women hockey players who would travel to France to play two matches in Le Havre then in a tournament in Paris, and the programme for the 1946/1947 year for the Hockey Section of the Portsmouth Civil Service Sports Association recorded Miss K Bone as a member of the Section Committee.

That same year the name of the Chairman of the Section Committee just happened to be Mr M Burwood.

Maurice's diary began to mention hockey again. On 4th March he mentions playing hockey versus Civil Service Ladies. I cannot tell if Marjorie was one of the ladies, but a newspaper article dated 1 May 1945 confirms that many hockey matches were being played. The article mentions that the Civil Service Hockey Section *won the six-a-side mixed hockey tournament at the Southampton Sports Centre recently and the shield, which they hold for a year, was presented by the Mayor of Southampton, had a most successful season, for the mixed team had played nineteen games of which sixteen have been won, two drawn, and one lost. The women's team have won eight matches, drawn two, and lost four.*

I found a list of players for Civil Service Hockey teams at a tournament – possibly that one. The lists of players include Burwood as 'kicking back' for the Gents 6-a-side, and Tanner on the team for the Ladies 6-a-side along with Bone. The mixed 6-a-side lists contain Burwood in the team for the 1st Game, and Tanner and Bone in the team for the 2nd Game. Finally there are two teams for an 11-a-side with Burwood and Tanner on one team and Bone on the other.

The Civil Service Hockey Section would continue its success next season, as this extract from a newspaper article in the *Portsmouth Evening News dated* 22nd May 1946 would explain:

The Portsmouth Civil Service Club has recently received the two shields won by the hockey section at the six-a-side tournaments held at Southampton, thus confirming the form suggested by match results. The men's side has been particularly successful, and "doubles" have been achieved against such opponents as Havant and Chichester.

The mixed side, though sometimes below full strength, won most of the scores and scored over a 100 goals for the second consecutive season. Fixtures for this side have been difficult to obtain, and the club would welcome engagements for next season. Of the women's side it may be recorded that it more than held its own and shows promise of developing into a strong side.

Peacetime was restoring normality including trials for a Portsmouth team. A newspaper article dated 13th March 1946 confirms the re-establishment of Ladies Hockey in Portsmouth with representatives of six clubs meeting for trial matches on the Canoe Lake ground in Southsea. The six players for the Civil Service team included M Tanner and K Bone, but only Bone was selected to play against the Wrens on 24th March.

I am sure Marjorie would have been glad for Kathleen even if disappointed for herself, but she had other pleasures in life – like going on holiday with her sister Olive to Longshaw House – a Holiday Fellowship Guest House in the Peak District. All I know about her holiday comes in the following letters to her parents.

Longshaw House
Via Sheffield 11
11.8.46

Dear Mum & Dad

I thought it would be a good idea if I wrote down what we do in chronological order & sent to you every other day. Please keep these letters so I can see all that we did, afterwards.

Saturday, as I told you, we travelled comfortably to Sheffield from where we caught the 2.5 train to Longshaw. In our carriage were 4 people obviously father, mother & 2 children, armed with luggage & rucksacks. After a short time they mentioned Longshaw & we realised that they were bound for the same destination – a cheery crowd they looked.

At Grindleford Station we found there were about 14 (total) waiting to be picked up by taxi. A girl chauffeur took us in 2 parties of 7 with luggage packed on behind. On arrival our names were ticked off & we were shown to our rooms. This contained 4 beds – the 4th was Ena Oke who arrived late after a terrible journey from Southampton. She & a friend of hers & husband seem the only other people from South of London here. She is another of our clan – a teacher! & fits in very nicely with us. After unpacking a bell rang for tea at 4.30.

(Marjorie here drew a small diagram showing a kitchen with dining room 2 beneath it and dining room 1 to one side and a common room with a movable screen dividing it from dining room 1.)

Tea is always held in Common Room and Dining Room 1 (see diagram) with dividing screen drawn back. We had cups of tea, bread & butter, scones & cake. The men had to bring the tea round while we sat comfortably & had tea on our laps. We sat on after tea in the Common Room (with screen back in place) & did knitting. It was raining outside.

Dinner was at 7.30. We went to D.R.2 & had Ham & brisket, salad (lettuce, peas & cubes of carrot etc.) biscuits & cheese, cake.

At 8.30 we went to the Common Room & D.R.1 & had games & dancing (various parlour games). Then we packed off to bed. We have 3 thin blankets & another blanket folded on top to pull up if necessary – so we are not cold.

Sunday breakfast is later, at 9.0 (rising bell 8.15). We rose & were washed before the bell went. Breakfast consisted of porridge, sausage & fried bread, toast, bread & butter & marmalade. For breakfast & supper (or late dinner) we have choice of tea or milk coffee. You know what I choose, of course. For midday dinner we had water.

<u>Monday evening</u>

After breakfast there was a choice of 2 voluntary excursions. We chose the shorter which was a tour of part of the estate – trees, bracken, winding paths, cows, a steep stony descent to the road by Burbage Brook. A longer slower climb back by grassland – a stone stile, a plank to cross a stream etc. – very pleasant indeed with view of moors with tors in distance all the time.

Sunday dinner was roast lamb, potatoes, cauliflower, rhubarb tart & custard.

After dinner we tried to sit in the garden, but it was cold & then started to rain. We sat in the Common Room knitting & reading till tea. Besides white bread & scones we had brown fruit bread & 2 kinds of cake, sandwich & slab. After tea we amused ourselves again till supper – meat pie & salad – then a kind of trifle of chocolate blancmange, jelly & raspberries – biscuits.

After Supper Olive went to the discussion in the Common Room, but Kathleen & I came upstairs, got out things ready for Monday, & I started this letter.

On Monday morning it was pouring so they decided to put off our walks till later. We played indoor games while some played whist & some bridge. At 11.30 we set out in the rain to walk mainly by main road through the moor to a place where drinks had previously been ordered & which we should have reached by a much more circuitous route if it had been fine. It was interesting to witness the mist on the moors more especially as on the return journey it had rolled away & we could see all that we had missed before. The drying room was well occupied on our return & still is with shoes & clothes being dried. We had had packed lunch (sandwiches) which the poor men had carried again for our meal with our hot drink before we returned. This afternoon we saw to our wet things etc. & then went out for a short walk in the sun, for of course it had dried up then. We had tea on our return & now I am finishing this letter so I can post it this evening ready to be collected at 8.30 a.m. the only collection each day. With all this wet weather I am nearly up to the armholes on my jumper.

We have games & dancing tonight after supper again.

Our money was collected for a week this morning – our ration books are to be seen this evening. I don't know whether they will keep them – it doesn't seem so.

Well, cheerio for the present – hope it will be fine for your trip tomorrow. – We hope it will be fine also for we are supposed to be climbing Mam Tor tomorrow & don't want it to be cancelled again.

By the way they book coaches here to extend our journeys a bit – they collect us & deposit us further afield on certain days.

Love,
Meme

Longshaw House
16.8.46

Dear Mum & Dad

Hope you have a nice day at the Island yesterday & will have a nice trip today.

The weather here has much improved though it was rather windy & chilly. Tuesday we went by coach to Hope & walked through a little valley over stone-stiles, stones, through tiny gaps (I don't know how fat people get on around here!) by a small river to the little town of Castleton at the edge of the High peak District. Here we looked into Peak Cavern – like Wookey on a vaster scale but not so pretty for there were comparatively few stalactites & stalagmites & little colour. Emerging, we had lunch & then a party set off up Winnats Pass along the High Ridge Walk & down Lose Hill back to Hope. We were lazy & climbed a little way up a road seeing lovely views of Win Hill, Lose Hill & various 'edges'; we returned, bought post cards & returned via main road to Hope whence we were collected by coach again. In the evening we had 2 short plays performed by various members of the party – amateurish but enjoyable.

On Wednesday we were free so we 3 & Ena set off to Sheffield. While waiting at the bus stop we were offered a lift by a worker going in from his home at Hathersage. As we were 4, we accepted. He was very decent & took us in by a longer route pointing out places on the way – the 'round house' at Ringington which is really octagonal, the western suburbs showing out on the slopes, the new secondary school, the Botanical Gardens, the University etc. - & then he dropped us right in the main shopping centre by John Lewis' shop. We went in there and had a good look round. I bought some wool & Kath a mackintosh. We wandered into a good many shops for Ena was looking for a costume. We had a nice dinner. Ena & I had chicken, really tender, & Olive & Kath had roast lamb for tea later in John Lewis' shop & caught the bus home for dinner at 7.30p.m. In the evening we had a kind of fair – competitive side-shows - & a treasure hunt.

On Thursday we set off walking, in a party, through the estate & on through woods, down stoney passes & over meadows via stone stiles, finally up a short steep climb & down a narrow steep path into Stoney Middleton where we looked inside the octagonal Church. Here 1 girl had to be left as she had slightly strained her ankle & a woman who had blisters stayed behind with her. Thence we walked on up 'Dirty Rake' which rather puffed everyone & into Wardlow for lunch. Afterwards we walked through the Dales – Cresswell Dale & Mousal Dale (very beautiful) to Great Longstone for tea. There was a concert with individual songs, piano-playing, variety turns, magic sight-seeing etc.

Today (Friday), as Olive's postcard shows, we went coach to M – through Lathhill Dale to Alport for lunch – Haddon Hill & on to Bakewell. Tonight is a social evening & many are, of course, packing to go off early tomorrow. Some nice new people will be arriving then.

Love Meme
Hope

20.8.46

Dear Mum & Dad,

We were at Hope <u>hoping</u> for the coach to arrive, & it came just as I wrote the address.

Well, Saturday morning we spent washing out handkerchiefs, socks etc & knitting. In the afternoon we walked into Hathersage along the main road, had tea there, & walked back.

The tea-place was in a garden by a 'babbling brook' & the sun came out gloriously. After tea we met the new arrivals & had games & dancing.

They are certainly a very different lot, 'either under 20 or over 50' said the secretary. One set came here by mistake – a child of 3½, grandma & grandpa & great-grandmother. The sec. has had to arrange a C party, besides the ordinary A & B, a C party which can bus & train to the lunch & tea places.

Sunday morning we went on the other alternative route to last Sundays – i.e. over Burbage Moors & climbing Higger Tor. It was well rewarded by a marvellous view. After dinner back at the house we strolled out & sat on the other side of the road in more of the National Trust grounds & did some knitting. We returned to tea, again served & washed up by the men to the delight of the ladies.

On Monday it was very misty & tried to rain several times ending with thunder. It was really too muggy to be pleasant walking. We went out over the moors (very poor visibility) for 3 hrs before dinner at the Clarion huts on the Sheffield road as last week. After dinner we went across the Burbage Moors, over Higger Tor seeing misty outlines unlike on Sunday, & on to Hathersage where we had tea. After tea we cut off by the R. Derwent & back through Paddley Woods to our own National Trust ground – amongst the rumblings of thunder & feeling very sticky. After dinner we gave in ration books, paid for the week, cleared up & got to bed.

Today (Tuesday) we went by coach to Earle. Olive went along the valley with Ena & her 2 friends while Kath & I climbed up to Lord's Seat, quite an easy climb & well worth it for the view. It is the 2nd highest pt – 1806 ft. Believe me there was nothing dangerous & we thoroughly enjoyed it. After lunch at Edale we joined B party to walk via fields & the old Roman Road just above Edale Valley & between Win Hill & Lose Hill into the Hope valley – to Hope for tea. Thence we have just returned by coach, washed & are hungrily awaiting dinner at 7.30 (45 mins yet).

Tomorrow, the off day, we are joining a voluntary excursion by coach to Dovedale only 4-5 mils down the valley & being picked up again at the other end.

Olive is sending a p.c. with times as far as we can tell for Saturday. I hope you have had a nice time although, according to report, weather hasn't been too good your way. By the way we have no wireless or newspapers here & Olive seems to exist quite well.

Love,
Meme.

Marjorie did not only write to her parents from that holiday. She also sent a postcard to Ada Burwood, and it follows the first entry in her 1946 diary to specifically mention anyone with the surname B. On Friday 9th August – the day before departing for Longshaw, her diary reads *Visited Mrs B.*

A week later she sent this:

Dear Mrs Burwood

We are spending a very enjoyable time here – it is a great change of scenery and the air induces a large appetite. I fear I should get much fatter if I stayed here long. Love Marjorie.

Referring back to Maurice's diary produces some interesting entries – beginning with 26th January 1946 which records *Longmoor hockey: M from Havant*. The diary does not specify who 'M' is, but Marjorie's diary records: *Municipal College (not playing) 2.30* home, but then adds *Longmoor* just below that apparently for 27th January. I think there was a Municipal College at Havant. Another entry in Maurice's diary on 23rd March 1946 records *Hamble: M from Hamble*. Marjorie's diary records the words *Hamble Away Won* for March 24th but only after she had written enough to fill the dates 22nd and 23rd.

My mother did tell me that my father gave her lifts back from hockey matches on the back of his motorbike. On 21st April he records *Ladies 6-a-side Soton*, while she records *Women's tournaments 1p.m. Cosham – by coach.* On 28th April Maurice records *6-a-side mixed hockey Soton, both teams in final* while Marjorie records *Mixed tournaments 1p.m. Won shield 2 teams in finals.*

Hockey is not the only sporting activity recorded in Marjorie's diary. March 26th and 28th and April 6th and 8th all mention *Netball* and Marjorie records evidence of her undertaking another physical activity – namely dancing - on 25th and 26th April, and 9th, 16th, and 17th of May before mentioning a Victory Dance on 8th June.

In June and July the entries get even more interesting. Maurice records Pirates *M&M&M* for 21st June, while Marjorie's diary just says *Pirates* while both mention *Mikado* earlier in the week, though on different days, and Marjorie also mentions *Yeomen of the Guard.* They shared a liking for Gilbert and Sullivan as well as hockey.

4th July provides *7th Beethoven (M),* 5th July provides *Mass in B Minor (M),* and both are mentioned in Marjorie's diary, though without the M, and 28th July provides *walk to Harting (M&O),* though Marjorie records it as *Hike from Westbourne.* M&M&M might mean Maurice and Mum and Marjorie, but M&O must mean Marjorie and Olive. Clearly Maurice and Marjorie were attending concerts together. October 6th and 7th bring *testing M's wireless set* and *repairing M's wireless set p.m.* Marjorie's diary just says *Wireless.* On 9th October comes *Visit to Britain can make it Exhibition – notable arm* - his first use of the word 'notable'.

Sunday 13th October added three separate entries, the first two being *Commandos at Drayton* and *Methodist Church,* but the really interesting one is the third one-word entry: *Proposed.*

Marjorie's diary for the same day has just the single word: *Proposal.*

Neither diary says engaged – maybe they decided against official engagement in favour of what Will Burwood called 'an understanding'. Possibly they wanted to do some planning first.

For the 15th October Maurice records: *walk to Portchester. Theatre.* Marjorie records *meat & walk – tea out Kings?* (Kings in Portsmouth means the Kings Theatre). Both diaries record 16th October: *Arundel.* On 17th October Marjorie simply records *London,* but Maurice records *London - Harrods & Gamages* - not likely that Maurice visited Harrods alone. 18th provides another 'notable' Maurice entry: *Hambledon notable occasion.* 27th provides *Church – walk,* while Marjorie just provides *church.* For the 28th Maurice provides *Pictures - Outlanders HI a notable occasion,* while Marjorie just provides *Pictures.*

The next most interesting entries are only in Maurice's diary. 19th November: *dancing practise,* followed on 21st November: *dancing practise with music.* Something had motivated Maurice to learn dancing.

The first letter between the two that I have found closely follows the dancing practice, and immediately precedes Marjorie's birthday:

John Burwood

My Dearest Marjorie

This letter is to wish you many happy returns of your birthday. I should like to have offered a really nice present but did not find anything I considered adequate in the time available. So please accept the enclosed articles as the nearest token of affection & esteem. They are offered in the hope that they may give some fun & pleasure in the opening & in the consumption of the more edible portions.

If they do, I am content. I hope that the inedible portions prove useful & last longer, and that by your industry (or influence) you may convert a portion (or have it converted) to something normally requiring the production of coupons. What a life, requiring the constant production of coupons. It is fortunate that love has nothing to do with goods & needs no coupons. Touching upon this subject, I want you to understand that you come first in my thoughts and can call upon me to the limit. As regards you & I, I feel we are groping our way together into new territory,, though many have passed this way before I have never travelled it, & if we falter & hesitate or travel rather slowly, put it down to this. It seems a delectable route. Perhaps it resembles part of Christian's way to the delectable mountains.

I have waited a long time to meet you, & when we are together, I feel a harmony of spirit which seems to go very deep & offers much hope for the future. One feels a sense at last of being complete & our complementary character to one another is more striking & beyond anything I have ever experienced. Descending a little from generalities, the effect upon me when you are gay, as you have been once or twice lately, has been remarkable, and even more when you show a flash of affection as you do, perhaps unconsciously at times, What will happen when you growl at me – I shudder to think. If you raise me to the heights can you plunge me to the depths. Life is full of uncertainties, isn't it. I am content that it should be so.

Returning to the subject of this letter, again I send greetings. In spite of handicaps outside your control, may you have a pleasant day full of pleasant thoughts & be assured that you remain constantly in mine. Be *assured also that I find myself perfectly happy & content in your presence & wait only for the next meeting, in each of which I hope & strive to improve on past efforts. So I close now with love, x's & ⊙'s.*

From Maurice

Maurice's diary then records for December: 11th *M's birthday Eric here.* 12th *M's birthday party.* 13th *Ballet,* and 14th *Eric left – dancing another milestone.* The 24th provides *walk on hill notable.* It also provides Marjorie's first letter to Maurice that I have found.

24.12.46

My dearest Maurice,

I enclose this letter to wish you a very merry Xmas this year and for many more. It is a difficult task to find a present but I was so intrigued by these tray figures when I saw them a few days ago that I could not resist them. Please accept this gift as a token of my affection until I can persuade you to assist me in purchasing something more suitable & far more useful.

Great courage was needed before I dared attempt a letter to you, due to the fact that I cannot hope to emulate or even approach your masterpiece of letter writing. Please believe that I have not thanked you for your letter or even mentioned it simply because the subject was too dear to me & I feared my powers of control. You will say it was cowardly; perhaps so, but I could not mention it although I meant to, several times, on that first dancing night after my birthday.

As a result my concentration was poor & my feet also failed to respond adequately. Still I do not feel that we need words between us; I feel & indeed hope that you sensed my appreciation, agreement & gratitude though it was not expressed in words.

The last few months have been the most happy & contented months that I have ever spent. I have often seen the contentment of others, but never realised what it could mean. I can only hope that I shall not give you cause to be 'lowered into the depths' as you call it. The only consolation I shall feel it & when you affect me thus will be that the lower I fall the giddier will be the heights afterward. Life is after all a certain adventure & we must be prepared to take the rough with the smooth.

Also I enclose a small diary which you actually said you wanted. I hope when you have filled the diary there will still be a small place for me in your affections. So once again the old words. A merry Xmas & a happy (or happier!) New Year.

Love Marjorie

Maurice's response was somewhat quicker.

26/12/46

My Dearest Marjorie

Thank you for your lovely letter, which was all the present you need have given me. I was charmed with the little chess set as my mother will testify. And there is no need to worry about the cost of a present. The cost has nothing to do with it. If it happens that the obvious present looks expensive, that is just too bad. I was very doubtful about getting you the necklace after hearing your views on it, but after all, your arguments were not sound. They were only based on money, which does not count either way in small cases.

So I fell back on my deeper instincts which I know by experience to be sound, and when I saw how charming you looked in it I knew I had done the right thing. (My little heart went pitter patter) I spent a lot of time Tuesday morning chasing after it and I am only sorry it had to be secondhand. There is one thing, even if my presents are secondhand, at least I am not, even if a bit the worse for wear at the moment.

And let us not worry about being so inarticulate about the things that matter. That's how we are, and I think, for us, better so. We shall find a way of bridging over the danger inherent in such a mutual tendency. Let us continue to grope our way, hand in hand, through the bushes & things that are strewn on our way. (At least, perhaps, we can manage to go round some of the bushes, or get a better supply of coupons) I am writing this letter in bed, where I think I shall have to stay today, until my cold is a little better. I hope I can shake it off sufficiently to avoid spoiling the last part of the holiday.

All my love
Maurice

30th *"Matter of Life and Death" - walk on front,* and 31st *"School for Secrets" - walk on hill.* Two movies and walks on two successive days followed on 1st Jan 1947 by *Visit to Ventnor & Wroxall with Marjorie* – and I have found Marjorie's 1947 diary which concurs with *Day spent at Ventnor,* then takes over the entries with 2nd January *Evening at Maurice's.*

Marjorie added extra entries that week. 3rd provided *Tea with Stephanie (Kath also).* 4th: *Tea with Kath.* The 5th got back to business: *walk in evening Maurice to tea.* The 7th: *Evening at Grandma's & Maurice's* – meaning Grandma Emma Tanner in Purbrook. The 9th *Evening dancing - Tea at Maurice's.* 10th *Kath to tea.* 11th *Dance at Southern Sec.* and the 12th *X-word evening Maurice to tea.*

Maurice's entries for the 9th and the 11th are slightly different. 9th: last *dance practice,* and 11th just says *dance.*

At this time a serious problem emerged in the form of a period of severe cold weather from late January to the middle of March. It was one of the worst winters of the century, causing shutdowns of power supplies, temporary closures of many businesses, and restrictions of domestic electricity supplies – and lots of colds – as this letter illustrates.

> *Lendorber Avenue*
> *Cosham*
> *Sun 9th Feb 47*

My Dearest Marjorie

This writing paper is far too small, isn't it? I believe you have gone sick so that I should have to write letters. Well, I find it very nice to write you a letter so you are partly forgiven. Only partly, because you are partly punished by me going sick in turn. If I've still got this cold in the morning I shall stop in bed. Horror of horrors, after all my promises, I did not catch it from you, but from someone else, probably at the dance. What! Did I go to the dance? Well, to be quite frank I did not. Did I give you a turn? As if I would go without you! Waste of time! I think I caught it from my mother. We did a crossword puzzle & got too close together I think. I have found that only close infection really gets me down. There have been lots of cold in the office this winter but I avoided too close contacts & dodged them. You've heard that one before, have you? Sorry!

Reverting to the subject of the letter, when am I going to see you again? I tried to think of some excuse for bursting into No 12 Saturday or Sunday but when I felt this cold coming on this afternoon I felt almost relieved because otherwise I should have to have forced a way in somehow without a proper excuse. Did you feel neglected? I hope so, or do you know me enough to appreciate that I must have met some wild horses or some atom bombs. Too many I's in this letter, we must have some you's & we's.

Your absence has not enabled me to get many jobs done because they are all outdoor or frigid indoor ones. Too cold or too dark to do them. And of course I was too worried about you to settle down to a job. Careful now, let us not exaggerate. It is so easy to write more than one means. I have hitherto been very careful not to do this. You can take it from me that any of my "serious" statements have been true.

The truth is that I am not worried about you & never have been. I cannot explain this. I have a most delightful feeling of security, is it? Inevitability? Or is it just happiness? Where you are concerned. I feel that our paths are marked out together & while I feel certain there may be boulders & things in the way, I don't feel unduly worried about them. Most peculiar because I am far from being a happy go lucky sort of person.

We have crept so surely and steadily into one another's lives that I think that we have already achieved something solid & enduring. Let us pray & hope so. We want to build on a rock if we can. Oh dear, here I go bursting into a sermon. It must be Sunday. Two days since Friday. You know you looked so languid & pretty in the big chair there, & me all that way. Not that I liked you to be languid, I prefer to see you active & pretty. Now don't be so modest, you do, when you smile at me just as if I am worth a smile. I can supply evidence on request. Now, how did I get on this subject! I must wind up this letter before it gets too late. If my cold goes off I will be round on Tuesday evening, if you don't arrive here first. If I don't arrive shed a tear because I shall still be in bed.

> All my love & kisses
> From Maurice

Friday was the 7th and Tuesday the 11th, and clearly Maurice did go round on Tuesday because his entries for the 7th, 11th, and 13th of February consisted of the single letter M, and next comes an exchange of Valentine poems not written by professional poets.

A Valentine poem from Maurice to Marjorie

A Valentine A Valentine whatever
is a Valentine
Why! don't you know my
darling Girl?
A quaint old-fashioned rare design
To indicate with quip or twirl
The depth of one's affection rare
(In spite of being short of hair.)
No longer is there need to hide
The beating of his manly heart
Because the writer don't confide
His name & number for a start
Nor gives to you the slightest clue
Of what or who he wants to do.
Well, never mind, don't sit & pine
But say you'll be his Valentine.

Marjorie's Valentine reply

A Valentine, can I be thine!
O sir! You put me in a flutter
(But is there anything to sign?
The maiden fair was heard to mutter)
Indeed 'tis true I think of you
But then – what else have I to do?
No longer need I sit & pine
And ponder on his manly shape
May e'en allow myself to dine
And joke & have a merry jape
Oh yes oh yes I will indeed
Be yours, I think you'll meet my need

So thus replied the maiden blushing
Instead of as is usual pushing.

But the cold continued. The 16th of February brought *Walk on Front* and the 20th *Short walk on hill – very cold*. The weather conditions which they were enduring might be summed up by the entry for 23rd February: *Thaw started. First sun for 3 weeks.*

The 25th of February brought a much more dramatic entry in Maurice's diary: *Date of wedding suggested.*

Then a likely consequence of the cold weather interrupted their interactions. Marjorie fell sick again, but it provided this exchange of letters.

12 Brecon Ave

My dearest Maurice

I'm sorry, but I shall not be going to school today so shall not be able to meet as arranged Sunday. My cold has come on rather heavily and I am staying in bed to nurse it up. Please keep away, at least till Thursday evening, because I am very infectious at the moment & don't want to spoil next week by having you in bed instead.

All my best
Marjorie

Lendorber Ave
Wed

Dearest

Make haste & get better. If you continue to lie there day after day thinking of me all the time you may find when you do get up that the reality isn't nearly so good. So I am worried. Besides, I want to talk to you. I so rarely have a chance for a nice quiet chat, don't I? Enclosed is a book, on loan, you may find interesting. It was sent me by my friend, the potty one, Frank, on loan, so I cannot give it to you. I have assumed you will not be well enough to go to the dance tomorrow. The Air Ministry forecast cold weather for several days so stop in & look after yourself. I will be a good boy & try to avoid catching a cold from everybody else except you. I don't suppose we will have any hockey this week end but if we do, can you play? Well, don't forget I waiting to kiss your hand, & I have forgotten how to do the reverse turn.

Considerable love
from Maurice

And Marjorie's reply:

12 Brecon Avenue,
Thurs

Dearest Maurice

N'ayly pas peur. The reality is far more substantial & attractive than the dream-world however pleasant the thoughts. You are far more likely to discover how attractive someone else is while you are impatiently waiting for me to get better!! If you find my hairs going grey with worry, you will know why now.

My three days were up today so I had to have the doctor in to provide me with a certificate. I hope he won't keep me out too long. I was up by 4 o'clock today, & am sitting by the fire writing this. Thanks very much for your letter & I'm sorry I did not have one ready to return – not of course that I really expect you wanted it. To tell you the truth my eyes burnt so much Tuesday I gave up even the attempt to look at a newspaper & nestled in forced inactivity. On Wednesday I got as far as attempting a X-word but my eye ached so much in the evening that, - awful confession – I was only just able to read your letter & did not look at the book. Today my eyes are definitely better & I have re-read your letter & read some of the book which seems very interesting & written in a very readable style. I will look after it & return it safely.

I'm sorry about the dance. I didn't even realise it was this week or that you seriously considered going as you had only mentioned it once. You forget that I am in the Uncivil Service & don't get details of dates of social events. Never mind, I expect there'll be another dance later we can go to instead.

If you continue to be a good boy & keep away as you were instructed, I shall ask mother to drop this in to you as she goes by tomorrow. If you call tonight I shall be forced to hand it to you, because it would be a pity to write it in vain.

Well, dearest, after all this rigmarole, be assured I am longing to see you, & in all my recent time for contemplation have found no room for regrets – except that I've had the misfortune to tie myself in with flu. Look after yourself & remember me to your mother. Tell her I hope she is enjoying her peaceful evenings to the full without me to worry her.

Love

Marjorie

P.S. I hope you no longer 'have a little list' of jobs to be done.

Marjorie's reference to the 'Uncivil Service' is because she worked for the Local Education Authority rather than the Government's Civil Service, so technically not a Civil Servant. Fortunately Civil Service Sports accepted 'Uncivil Servants' among their ranks.

The last line hints at how often Marjorie was spending her evenings at Maurice's house, and she seems to have recovered quickly enough to meet Maurice on Sunday 2nd March at Maurice's house which produced an entry in his diary of *ENGAGEMENT ANNOUNCED*.

On 5th March the Portsmouth Evening News printed this announcement:

BURWOOD-TANNER – The engagement is announced between Maurice R. Burwood, M.A., B.Sc., A.M.I.E.E., younger son of the late Mr W.J.Burwood and of Mrs. Burwood, Lendorber Avenue, Cosham, and Marjorie, younger daughter of Mr. and Mrs W.R.Tanner, Brecon Avenue, E. Cosham.

The entry in Maurice's diary for 6th March is interesting: *discussion re obey*, but there is no record of the conclusion of the discussion.

Preparations were clearly getting underway for the wedding. On 22 March Marjorie wrote off for parachute silk – it was common in the 1940s for wedding dresses to be made from parachute silk. On the 24th she wrote to Rita Hutty (Victor Hutty being abroad in Singapore serving as Regimental Quartermaster Sergeant of his Signals Regiment), and her Aunt Lil. On either the 1st or 2nd of April her diary records *rang Smith & Vosper's. Failed to get Food Permit – must go to*

Elm Grove. Rang Gauntletts. Smith and Vosper were a well-established Portsmouth bakery, the phrase 'Food Permit' reminds that 1947 was a time of severe rationing of food. Gauntlett's Dairy Café in Waterlooville would host the Wedding Breakfast.

Meanwhile Maurice was spending money to make his home ready for his bride. On 27th March he drew £85 from his Post Office bank. On 5th April he bought a kitchen cupboard and tallboy. On 8th April he bought a bed (double?) and linoleum. On 12th he bought wallpaper, and on 14th a wedding ring was purchased from Pursers in Southsea.

On 17th they visited Marjorie's grandmother Emma Tanner in Purbrook. The 18th saw a *Hockey general meeting*, with hockey matches on 20th, 27th, and 4th May.

Marjorie was also spending. On 22nd April Marjorie bought a sewing machine, and on 23rd and 24th sent off invitation cards. There were no doubt many more preparations not recorded in their diaries, but Maurice records stripping his bike gear on the 30th May – ready to take his bride off on honeymoon.

He was also very diligent at his work. He worked until 11 in the evening on Wednesday 4th of June to finish up his work before getting married on 5th of June and taking a month's leave on his honeymoon.

Maurice and Marjorie were married at the Church of the Resurrection in Drayton on 5th June 1947, and headed off to Ventnor on the Isle of Wight to begin their honeymoon – which was to take them, inevitably, to the Lake District.

So two families joined to become one family.

But that is another tale.

Ed Hutty marries Dorothy Martin 8th April 1944. Back row l to r: Marjorie, Ethel, & Walter Tanner, Albert Geary (Best Man), Annie & Frank Scott (aunt & uncle of the bride). Front row l to r: Rita Hutty carrying son Richard, Olive Tanner, Ed Hutty, Dorothy Martin, William & Lily Hutty, parents of the groom.

Bill Burwood Soldier

Maurice & Marjorie on honeymoon at the War
Memorial on the top of Scafell Pike - in the rain

APPENDIX

Family trees researched by Richard Burwood

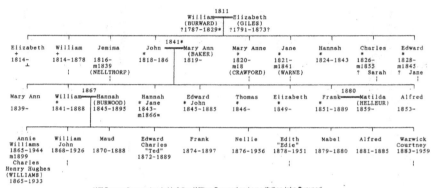

Will Burwood's ancestry via his father William Burwood and grandfather John Burwood

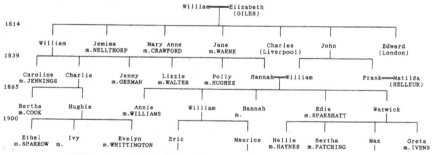

Will Burwood's ancestry via his mother Hannah Burwood and grandfather William Burwood

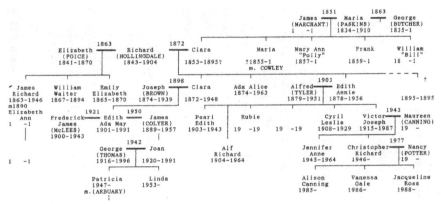

Ada's family

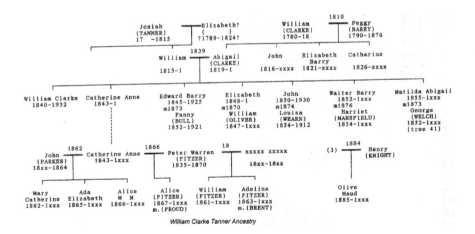

William Clarke Tanner Ancestry

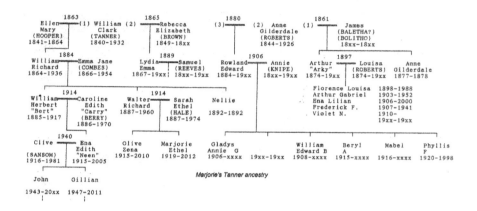

Marjorie's Tanner ancestry

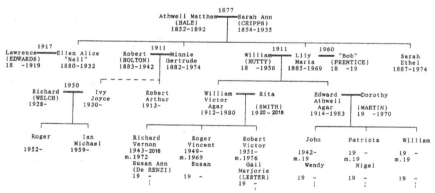

Relatives of Sarah Ethel Hale

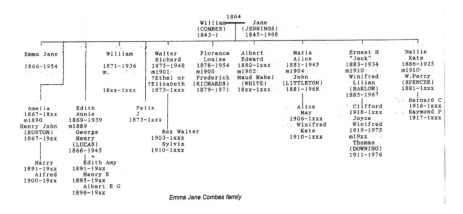

Emma Jane Combes family

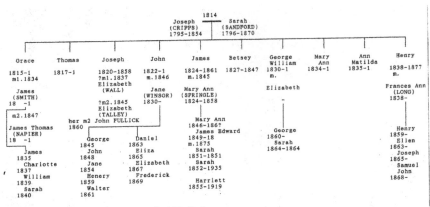

Sarah Cripps' family

367

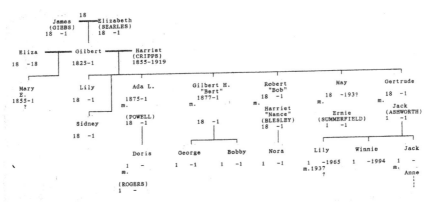

Gibbs, Cripps, and Ashworths

Lightning Source UK Ltd.
Milton Keynes UK
UKHW010151160221
378827UK00001B/8